OUR USELESS KIN

I0683787

Dunlop Otieno Ochieng,
FASS,
P. O. Box 23409,
Dar es Salaam.
dunotis@yahoo.com

ISBN 9789987982110

<<<*DEDICATION*>>>

For Luo traditional musicians, Swedish International Development
Cooperation Agency (SIDA) and German Academic Exchange
Service (DAAD)

<<<CHAPTER ONE>>>

If Sandra had known that the stench was from a different source, she would not have lost her tooth in that day's morning fight. She had accused her husband of polluting their shared blanket – and that eventually "earned her what she was looking for", as her husband said punitively. He was actually referring to his catastrophic punch to Sandra's mouth, after which his fist was escorted on its way back by an incisor and a flood of blood. Sandra, of course, overtly blamed her husband for overreacting but, deep down, she actually blamed herself for her forgetfulness.

Her 'husband' Cobra – a nickname he earned from his violent behavior – never entertained what he referred to as *nonsense*, especially after every tenth day of the month. By then, his beloved salary would have often commuted to some unknown destination – and accordingly, he would use every slightest opportunity to beat someone as a cheap way of venting his frustrations.

Sandra, who could not stand the rain of punches from Cobra that morning, tactically retreated to their plank kitchen behind their tin house – a base she chose to use for reorganizing her forces for a second round of the fight.

"I am down but not out," she said to herself as she figured out a befitting move to take after that miserable opening round.

After twenty minutes or so, she had managed to acquire a jug of boiling water for the ugly face of Cobra – and was ready to retaliate for the shattering blow that Cobra had earlier sent into her mouth. Nonetheless, Cobra had long since read danger into her quiet disappearance from the scene. His suspicion was based on the tooth-for a-tooth policy they adopted as soon as they had moved in together ten months ago. He and Sandra were fond of the policy since it had maintained their marriage longer than prophets of doom had previously predicted and always left each of them satisfied, irrespective of how fierce the exchanges between them had been. In this light, therefore, he knew very well that he still owed Sandra a tooth, but he was just not willing to give himself up without a struggle.

"That rascal is up to something," he concluded reasonably and on that premonition walked to the bedroom door and bolted it from inside.

Sandra, upon pushing the bedroom door found herself locked out and was now stranded with a jug of hot water in her hand. Maddened by this state of affairs, she intensified her slurs, whilst hitting the door as hard as if she was trying to smash it down – all in an attempt to flush Cobra out of the bedroom. All in vain though, Cobra unbelievably bore it all and no breakthrough was in sight.

But in a dramatic turn of events, Sandra overheard her neighbours grumbling about a horrendous stink in the air – and this both confused and distracted her from the deadly mission she had been pursuing. Accordingly, she dashed outside the house at the speed of a race car to find out at firsthand what the hell the neighbours were talking about. Upon crossing the threshold, she was amazed to discover that almost everybody in the slum was atop an elevated object or in a narrow alley just off the slum, trying to get fresher air than the polluted kind hovering all over the slum. Even so, there was no fresh air anywhere in the whole of Majengo slum.

That awful smell hence compelled the destitute residents of Majengo slum to endure it, either in silence or in noise. Many people chose noise. Most of the talkers, in small groups which were forming every ten meters or so, alleged that the stink was emanating from a neglected dump at the end of the slum. Even so, something did not add up, given the fact that the dump in question had been there for such a long time that it no longer wrinkled any nose of a Majengan: only that breed of travelers wishing to change everything in their destinations would lament over it for a while but they would soon return whence they had emerged, or rather would finally get used to it and shut up.

The brutal stench eventually necessitated the idlers of Majengo slum to meet at the market square to address the nuisance – an act which was quite unusual, considering that the spirit of working together for a good cause among the dwellers of the slum vanished as soon as their area was transformed overnight from a bunch of scattered villages to the fourth largest town in Kaya. Since then, everyone would tell you that Majengans only teamed up for committing a crime against humanity or shoplifting.

"It is like a witch is making a debut in our street today; and she is now having an orgasmic contentment with the havoc she is causing the children of women." One of the attendees of that casual meeting hypothesized the source of the smell, and sent those listening into raucous laughter at the strange opinion he gave.

"You are right; there was a witch who regularly did the same in our village," another attendee surprisingly supported him and even cemented his thought with an allegedly personal experience.

"This one in our village would eat the rotten innards of fish then go for two days without shitting or even farting – just to gather enough odours with which to torment the villagers," he said ill-manneredly.

"Eheehehe," his audience encouraged him in chorus.

"On the third day, he would then go to a hill on the windward side of the village and pose on the highest rock on the hill head down, feet up."

"Eheehehe," the audience encouraged him to speak further.

"He would next insert a two-meter pipe into his anus, and start fluting it with smelly gas from his rotten bowels. And indeed, he would blanket the whole village with his pungent smell for four good hours, I tell you," he said.

"Hahahahahahaha!" The crowd interrupted him with a thunderous laughter.

"Jerry," his colleague called his name sonorously, "today, I have believed, 'you are leading in telling lies and others follow'," he said amidst boisterous laughter.

"O-hoooo! You might think I am lying, but it is true. Ask Mwangi if you doubt me," suggested Jerry.

As if the crowd had believed Jerry, they dispatched three investigators to track the source of the stink on the windward side of the slum. They would report their findings back to the rest of traditionally staring bystanders. The investigators thus set off for the task, but were soon seen running back to the crowd as fast as their legs could carry them.

And in the light of previous experiences in the area, a concoction of panic and spirit of war now stalked the audience. Some thus started picking up stones sensing that the most hated police officers were as usual chasing their messengers for the wrong reasons; at the same time, cowards among them started taking to their feet to avoid an imagined police-induced disaster in their slum.

"Where are they?" One toothless freak, who was carrying a stone as big as his father's head, asked the first messenger to cross the finishing line.

"Who?" The slow-witted messenger asked the rascal by way of reply.

"The *ndatas*." The freak used an offensive tag of police officers in that area.

"Which *ndatas* are you talking about? Are you already tanked-up this morning?" The rascal scolded the freak.

As events transpired, it was soon discovered that the investigators were simply running on the double in order to share what they considered dramatic news with their itching audience. The crowd, which was already in panic mood, burst into jovial laughter, now realizing that the anticipated danger, was in fact illusory.

"People in this street are as anxious as antelopes in a park full of jackals," commented one of the rascals who had been poised for attack.

"The stench is from the Devil's Temple," the messenger divulged stinging news to the crowd, his breath coming in short gasps.

"Sure, it is from the Devil's Temple," his colleague reinforced the assertion.

Upon hearing this, the then lively crowd went quiet while digesting the crude information, which the hard-to-believe rascals had just pumped raw into their sensitive ears.

Actually, the Devil's Temple was as well known in that area as the return of Jesus Christ among the Christians. It was a modern house at the eastern end of the slum, belonging to an old man who a short time ago had emerged in Majengo slum from an unknown source as a destitute pauper but transformed himself overnight into the most revered black luminary of the town. Following this unnatural achievement of such an unpromising man, some residents claimed his success was because he had joined a secret cult – which he did not deny; others alleged he had joined a religion called Turmoilism, whose mission was to confuse everyone all the time. And as if to reinforce his mysterious image, the old man since then stopped shaving his goatee beard and switched from shaking hands in greeting to just clapping from a distance.

"What does this old man think he is now? How can he keep the whole street under the siege of his witchcraft? I think somebody should go and tell him that we only respect him; we are not afraid of him at all!" One of the rascals roared angrily, looking as if he was under the influence of something.

"Yes! Let us go and teach him a lesson that will remain in the books even after we have long thrown his corpse into a pangolin burrow: this is madness!" His colleague supported his proposal vociferously, yet nobody else responded

After a while, the crowd resumed its liveliness. The philosophers among them directed their efforts to hypothesizing over the possible source of the awful stench at the old man's compound. Five minutes later, they put two suppositions on the table for debating. The first supposition was that the old man was dead; the second supposition was that his gigantic black dog was dead. But after a lengthy deliberation, the meeting resolved overwhelmingly that it was the old man who had died, not his dog. One rascal even argued very logically that if the old man were alive, he would have taken care of his dog's carcass.

"Eeeee," his enthusiast supporters endorsed.

Another eyewitness confirmed the assertion that the old man would drive his expensive jeep to the market square every evening – and since they had not seen him doing that in the past four days, he was inarguably dead. Again, the owner of a restaurant at which he would eat and drink whenever he was in town also added that she had not seen him coming for his meal in her restaurant for at least four days – evidence that he was dead.

With all this screaming evidence, two courageous rascals or, rather, crazy ones, volunteered to find out what exactly it was that smelt so much at the compound. The alerted crowd thus held their breath in anticipation of doom looming at any moment for these 'suicide spies': the house to which they were tiptoeing had not earned its name of "the Devil's Temple" for no reason. It was popularly believed that four thugs whose corpses were once found rotten near the house had died of heart attacks after touching a perimeter wall of the house without its owner's consent. Contrary to expectations though, not only did the spies walk to the gate of the compound but also managed to peep through the keyholes of the house gate with all eyes, as the crowd keenly followed from a distance. The investigators eventually saw the old man's jeep, but not its owner. They also heard his dog, earlier on theorized dead, lamenting about a discomfort that the philosophers interpreted as a case where 'hunger was biting the dog.' And with all these pieces of information in hand, suspicion that the mysterious old man was dead was rife in Majengo slum.

The crowd thus unwillingly called the most hated police officers to come for one of their dirty jobs - wrapping up rotten and smelly corpses.

Traditionally, police officers would drag their feet for centuries for emergency calls emanating from that part of the town. Nevertheless, on this particular occasion, they stunned everyone by showing up at the scene just in forty-five minutes. As usual, they were in four jeeps mounted with deadly scatterguns and rocket launchers. What's more, they were, also as usual, shooting every street dog or cat they happened to spot - not so much trying to scare the unscarable rascals of Majengo, but rather making it very clear that they had enough ammunition - or rather that their guns did not jam due to poor maintenance, as had happened on numerous occasions in the past. They further reinforced their deadliness with inscriptions on their helmets reading, *Shoot to kill, and come for the medal.*

A large crowd of slum idlers now trailed the police officers to the house of the allegedly dead man, evidently motivated by a passion to figure out what exactly had transpired in the house of the most solitary and mysterious man in Majengo. Moreover, each of them wanted to witness how the evil spirits, alleged domesticated by the man, would mercilessly devour the most hated officers. They were eager to break out into enthusiastic laughter as the spirits were choking the officers to death.

Upon reaching the gate of the house, the officer in charge knocked on it in a tone he deemed fit for someone of his status, yet there was no expected response from the house's owner. Now, the officer boastfully bragged on behalf of his colleagues that they were the bona fide police of the Bewitched Republic of Kaya and demanded that the gate of the house be opened for them voluntarily; otherwise, they would resort to the use of force in the name of law. But even after this threat, nobody opened the gate. This assumed contempt, of course, maddened the state machineries - their reasoning being that the owner of the house should have known that their knock was actually the knock of the government. Eventually, they used the power bestowed on them by the state to break into the man's compound.

What was obvious now was that the stench was stronger inside the compound than it was outside. The repeated order of the police at the main door was again defied and the men in uniform were as agitated as wasps whose hive has been destroyed. Once more, they used the authority bestowed on them by the state to break into the man's house, and subsequently his bedroom.

To their amazement, the man they thirstily wanted to punish for naughtiness had been dead for at least seven days ago. The stinking and bulging body of *Eucalyptus, Satanic, King of the Suspects* was lying still on a wooden bed with a kitchen knife logged in a location adjacent to his heart. Small crows, sneaking in his bedroom through an open window, had already eaten half the contents of his bowels, giving rise to a concoction of blood and fat maggots all over the bed and floor. To add to the gravity of the situation, beside his decomposing body was a handwritten suicide note on a manila card, reading, *Don't waste your time looking for a killer; I died of a broken heart* – a message which was somewhat confusing.

Despite the stench from the decaying body, the surging crowd, consisting mainly of rascals, still shoved each other to get a glimpse of the man's body. Probably to shorten that nasty experience, the police officers inhumanly wrapped the disintegrating corpse in a polythene sheet and vanished with it to an unknown location.

The crowd was thus left stunned by the suspicious death of the mysterious man. Many hence departed his compound in a hurry, actually for fear of attack from his alleged evil spirits, save for the cold-hearted among them who remained purposely to test the existence of such spirits at the compound.

It was one suicide-researcher who launched the trial by plucking off a sight mirror from the deceased's jeep – and in fact got away with it as fellow rascals watched with a combination of fear and admiration. Twenty minutes or so later, the same person came back for the car's radio system, plucked it and disappeared again without the interception of any evil spirit claiming to guard the dead man's property.

Such heroic actions acted as a signal for the rest of his colleagues, who were slightly more careful with their lives, to embark on ransacking the compound. They did their work so well that after one hour of the exercise, everything movable had moved out of the compound and even the man's jeep was now lying on its stomach after its four wheels had been plucked away. His iron gate was, of course, the last thing to be smashed and sold to scrap metal dealers before the dispersal of the animated crowd, but even then the rascals still lamented that they had failed to strike some treasure, alleged to be hidden somewhere at that compound.

The death of the mysterious old man was therefore both a loss and a blessing in disguise to the idle rascals of Majengo slum. On the one hand, they had lost the man they considered their king but, on the other hand, they had inherited his wealth fairly and immediately. At around 3 p.m., many of these rascals reassembled at the market square allegedly, to celebrate the man's life. As usual, some were holding bottles of demon drink, whereas, others were smoking the forbidden cigarette or sniffing snuff. The burning topic all the while was the suspicious death of their mysterious king.

"The king was killed by bandits, who disguised their sinful deed by leaving a fake suicide note to mislead *ndata*," one rascal suggested, but his point was promptly rubbished.

"Noooo," the majority objected.

"That is trash meeen," one voice added. You and me are bandits, and we know very well that it is not possible to break into a compound with a new jeep like that without mutilating it, like it happened in this case." This was a reference to the state-of-the-art car, which belonged to the deceased.

"You are right meeeen," three quarters of the rascals replied together.

Then one of them sensationally asserted that he was quite sure that the King had died of his tumultuous love relationship with a new bartender in the white men's part of the town.

"He died of a broken heart, don't you guys get it?" He asked the crowd cunningly.

"You are right meeen," one rascal, who looked bogged down by drugs, said in a heavy, creaky voice.

"I know that bartender meeeen, she is so contemptuous to us, the *al-watans* of this town," he said while thumbing his chest.

Then another rascal asked him in a voice like that of a man being subdued by anesthesia:

"So, you mean the bitch you are talking about has come here to kill our King?"

"Of course, yes, the King told me about their affair face to face," the initiator replied very confidently, stirring murmurs among the unreasoning crowd.

"So, what are you waiting for meeen, let us go and f**k the bitch up the ass meeen," suggested one barefooted villain, who actually looked older than his grandfather.

"Oooooooooooooooooooo!" The crowd applauded.

But upon hearing this, one rascal who seemed like a new recruit to the gang differed from the rest.

"But that is not fair meeen, it is clear that the King bored his own chest with a kitchen knife meeen," he suggested.

"Noooooo!" The rest of the villains roared together.

"So, what are you waiting meeen, are you cowards? Let us go and f**k the bitch," One of them who had been all the while gulping forbidden-liquor reinforced.

"F**k the bitch, f**k the bitch, f**k the bitch," the gang chanted while surging like a torrent towards Aheko VIP Bar which was some three kilometers away in the western part of the town, where only the white men and stinking rich blacks lived.

Fortunately, the traitor among the gang became concerned for the well-being of the poor barmaid. He thus sneaked away and used his cell phone to tip her off about the woe looming towards her. Fortunately, the bartender knew how unreasonable those villains were, and thus took no chances: she quickly hired a cyclist and ordered the rider to take her away from that location at the speed of lightning.

Fifteen minutes later, the troop of rascals arrived on the scene, but the accused barmaid was nowhere to be seen at the bar. Armed with stones, bottles and screwdrivers, the rascals demanded that the bartender be delivered to them before they lost their temper, but all in vain. Some VIPs, who were cooling their throats at the bar with beer and wine, later poked their noses into the matter by asking the rascals to tell them what their problem was – and eventually realized that the rascals' arguments did not hold water. Nonetheless, their honest opinion earned them sufficient wounds to require their dressing for no less than three weeks.

The commotion of course continued as the scoundrels insisted the barmaid be delivered to them if the owners of that facility did not want to make an already bad situation worse. On the other hand, the manager of the bar, who could not find the bartender, persistently declared her absence at the facility, but the gang would only disperse after beating her up to their satisfaction, or if they were appeased with ten crates of beer plus a plate of chicken and rice each. The naive manager of the bar nonetheless rejected even the later proposal, which served as a trigger for the gang to start beating up employees of the bar, at the same time robbing them of their money and other valuables.

Seven minutes later, the villains had revolutionized the administration of the bar. They had broken the counter and storeroom of drinks, the evidence being that each looter was seen crowned with a crate of beer or two and was sipping it lazily under one of the tamed shades of trees at the bar – little did they know, or rather did not care, that the manager had informed the owner of the bar, who in response had called the police – who, as usual, were very quick to respond to calls emanating from that side of the town.

Consequently, in the blink of an eye, a battalion of riot police and their dogs arrived in full war combat in five jeeps with deadly guns and rocket launchers. The officers surrounded the bar and ordered every rascal inside to surrender by raising their hands, something that had never worked with such crooks before.

But before long, two rogues who had sneaked out of the bar's compound to gang rape a passing-by old white woman, learnt that the police officers had invaded their fellow gangsters at the facility. They instantly telephoned fellow rogues who were in the shanty street to support them in their abrupt battle with the police officers. On their own, they set ablaze four police jeeps that were parked a few meters from the scene.

Once the police officers realized their jeeps were on fire, they started spraying tear gas on the rascals, who reciprocally engaged them with bottles and stones. Another gang of rascals from Majengo, of course, joined the fighting rascals at the bar and together they overwhelmed the police, forcing them to use live bullets to clear their escape route. The war was so intense that after about the thirty minutes it lasted, six rascals were dead and ten seriously wounded. On the other hand, three police officers had been killed, three badly injured, all their five jeeps burnt to ashes, and their two dogs slain. The rest of the police officers had therefore no choice but run for their lives in front of their dogs.

As usual, dwellers of the streets carried away their dead, their injured and looted goods back to their street in songs and dances. Upon reaching their territory, they buried their dead hastily and took their injured colleagues to their health center that had not known any decent medical service for a decade. And after the multiple burials below the high voltage power line, the angry rogues consulted among themselves in their peculiar style and unanimously agreed on abducting a son and a daughter of their enemies at the international boarding school, 10 kilometers south of their town.

Upon reaching this location, the rascals bloodily slew the school's security guards, stole whatever they could get their hands on and abducted a daughter of the owner of the bar and a son of the zonal police chief (a white kid and a black one respectively).

That silent night, they slaughtered their abductees, scorched their bodies and set them in a love making-position, thereafter abandoning them at the roundabout at the western part of the town, along with a handwritten message on a manila card beside their charred corpses; *A special lunch for the white thieves and their black boot lickers.*

News about this horrible incident thus spread like wildfire across the Bewitched Republic of Kaya and caused the dwellers of the streets of Majengo to anticipate a repeat of the wrath of the furious government and angry investors that had befallen their area some ten years ago. Consequently, the obvious wisdom was for everyone to desert the slum at midnight. Luckily, they did not have many things to carry along with them, and their children were strong enough to march at a speed of 20 kilometers per hour without asking for food.

Accordingly, Majengo slum was absolutely a ghost street on the morning of 20th October 2014. The rogue rascals, poor prostitutes and mine laborers, who normally populated it to the brim, were nowhere to be seen. And as prophesied, even by sinners, the next morning saw the arrival of army tanks, shoulder-to-shoulder with bulldozers from the neighbouring Calodian Gold Mine. Uncountable military vehicles similarly spewed soldiers all over the place, each of them unblinkingly holding the trigger of a deadly gun and as hungry to shoot as a pirate.

Their immediate task was to sweep flat every standing object in the slum and to grind any solid objects they encountered in the same way. This unopposed operation took eight hours, after which the area was as flat as the buttock of an iron.

The next day, what used to be Majengo slum was completely fenced off and signboards hung every ten meters; *Property of Calodian Gold Mine. Access prohibited.* The soldiers and their partners were now quite satisfied by the operation they had carried out in Majengo slum: this was apparent in a speech by their spokesman who was heard saying on the radio, "we have at last managed to wipe out the habitat of the predators, which had been frequenting our poultry farm." Here the poultry farm denoted Calodian Gold Mine, and the predators referred to the rascals.

Following this development, an impatient man would think that Calodian Gold Mine and the soldiers had won the battle once and for all. But alas! Their temporary victory marked only the beginning of the bloodiest battle of supremacy between unethical rascals and reckless soldiers – a battle that was, unfortunately, instigated by a wolf in sheep's clothing: Mr. *Eucalyptus* Omollo, *the Baboon, Satanic, King of the Suspects, the Stone Crusher at the Quarry, the Busy Malan.*

<<<*CHAPTER TWO*>>>

That man who died as Mr. *Eucalyptus Omollo, Satanic, the King of the Suspects,* was born Mr. Omollo, *the Baboon* – a nickname suggesting that he was as mysterious as the baboon, a primate that always passes by hospitals with a deadly wound on its butt, but never seeks medical attention at the facilities.

Sixty-two years ago, Omollo, *the Baboon* was seen one morning marching cautiously towards a cow-dung bonfire at the middle of his father's extensive compound. That day, a land breeze was sweeping from east to west, keeping the land so chilly that a husband and a wife who owned a single jacket would inevitably quarrel over it at dawn. The Malans joked that on such mornings, the husband would want to put the jacket on for going to inspect safety of his cows in the kraal, whereas, the wife would equally want to put on the same jacket for going to milk the same cows before the arrival of the milk collector.

Omollo was walking so cautiously on that morning not for aesthetic reasons but to avoid stepping on the fresh cowpats scattered all over his father's compound. Fresh cow dung was not only cold, but also slippery, enough to cause an adult to fall on their face like an old cactus under the brutality of a July wind. On this particular day, he had just woken up from a mat in one of his brother's huts at their homestead. As usual, he did not wash his face, but just collected a maize cob from one of the sacks staring at him at the corner of the hut and immediately thereafter started marching to the cow-dung bonfire.

Beside the cattle shed at their extensive compound were his many mothers, busy with the milking of cows that morning. Upon spotting them, he inwardly prayed to his ancestors that none of them would spot him, for he was sure they would straightaway send him to drive cows out of the kraal, ready for milking outside the kraal. This task would inevitably force him to tread on fresh cow-dung in his bare feet; his mothers used to give him such work almost daily and he hated it so much he wished he could refuse to do it when ordered. The fact was, however, that he could not even attempt such an act of rebellion in a land where all adults were the major generals and children the recruits. In fact, it was unheard of for a child ever to refuse to be sent to do something by an adult; a popular wisdom of the land stated that a child who hated adults' orders had the freedom to go to the edge of the world and plunge into its dead end.

Omollo further wished he were in town, where he had gathered there were no cows, suggesting no cow-dung at peoples' homesteads, no tiresome work of looking after cows and no plowing the land at dawn with yoked oxen. To him, that was luxury at its best. Nevertheless, he still felt quite sorry for the town children, who apparently had no possibility of watching a bullfight and drinking *adila* – sour milk remaining after the oil had been removed, let alone roasting maize in hot cow-dung ash.

As these ideas rolled in his imbalanced brain case, he continued making silent steps towards the cow dung bonfire, which he had participated in making. On the previous day, he and other boys had collected dry cow-dung until it formed a big heap. Next, they lighted it up and it continued to burn even that morning: it would, of course, burn like that for two more days before they would repeat the exercise.

Bonfires had been the meeting place of the Kayan families from time immemorial. In a dry season such as that one, children would meet at it in the morning for warming their bodies from the fierce morning cold, like on that particular day. That morning, he was late at the bonfire; his fellow children had long trooped around the bonfire when he was still asleep. Each of those children had a maize cob in their hand and they were busy making popcorn. They would shell grains from the maize cobs, put them in hot cow-dung ash and turn them regularly with long sticks, thus causing the grain to explode into popcorn. The owners of the exploded popcorn would next pick up the pieces and hurry them into their oral cavities while hot. And even if they were unbearably hot, their collaborative tongues would toss them around the grinding hall, meanwhile spraying them with saliva until they were cool enough for their sensitive throats to swallow as quickly as a bitter capsule. It was, of course, a taboo to spit out popcorn for its being hot because popcorn from cow-dung ash was actually meant to be eaten hot.

That morning, Omollo's homestead was as noisy as a livestock auction market. As usual, cows were bellowing for their calves – still shut in pens; he-goats and rams made queer sounds of passion; cocks crowed unnecessarily and dogs barked even at hunger – all in all a prototypical state of the rich man's homestead in Malaland. The saying even went around in Malaland that every creature of the earth has something to chew at the rich man's homestead – and indeed this did apply at Omollo's homestead.

The kraal had always occupied the central part of Omollo's homestead. To the eastern and western side of it, six huts for his mothers stood akimbo facing the gate, each with a granary gazing before it. To the south of the kraal, ten square-shaped huts for his elder brothers formed a half-moon circle. To the northern part of their compound, a medicine hut-cum-clinic for his father was solidly standing still.

That morning, Omollo's father was attending his clients in this medicine hut. People queued outside, awaiting their turn to meet his father, one by one. Some of them were sick and therefore needed herbal medicines to cure their illnesses, whereas, others just needed charms to shield themselves from the missiles of witches. Women clients would need spells to reincarnate their disgusting co-wives into sacks of shit (so that their husbands would only spit and vomit at their sight), whereas, male clients required spells to reincarnate their aggressive lenders into smoke, so they would dissolve in the atmosphere, allowing the men to live in peace. Fortunately, Omollo's father had always dismissed such despicable requests, arguing that most of their wishes were beyond the realms of divine priesthood ethics that he was abiding by with all his might and soul.

Behind the medicine hut, stood a distinctive isolated hut for his grandmother, Adongo Nyowino, popularly referred to as *Dani*. As it was designed to serve as a rest house for nubile girls before they were married in distant lands, it was the biggest of all the roundhouses at their compound. Being so big, it doubled as a storeroom for totems that the senior elders of Rabar Village would use to perform rituals at the sacred rock – a gigantic pillar of rock, bending like a human being trying to enter a low dog's kennel, which was only a stone's throw away from the hut.

Elsewhere at the homestead, one could see dog kennels, goats and sheep's pens – all ringed with a shabby and thick euphorbia tirucalli edge, actually making it impossible for anyone in the compound to see anything outside.

As Omollo neared the bonfire that morning, a killing pain, whose nature and origin he could not instantly establish, was radiating from his back. He stretched his left arm to the painful area and discovered that it was completely colonized by bruises; this fully jogged his memories of the whole incident that had led to the bruises.

On the previous day, he had left with his father's cattle to Ramar Valley – the best pasturage in all the land on account of its evergreen pasture, ever-flowing fresh water, and seclusion from farms. At the valley, he met up with many other shepherds, including Obongo, the lads' leader. Obongo, as usual, proposed a sport of hooking fish, which they all endorsed and fished out their hooks from where they used to hide them near the bank of the river. Next, they started hooking fish by chanting their usual *Hook-Blessing Chant*, which they inherited from their elder brothers, who had also inherited it from their elder brothers. They genuinely believed in the magic powers of the chant in making their hooks sharp and effective. It went thus:

> *The hook, catcher, daughter of Opedo, I have a guest at home who does not eat vegetables. Do not let me down – I beg you.*

No sooner had they thrown their hooks in the water than Obongo, son of Opuk Mbuku, pulled out a middle-sized lungfish. As per their custom, he shouted out his praise names proudly and loudly for everybody around to appreciate.

I have caught you right here! I am Obongo, grandson of Othik Mbuku.

I am Obongo, *the Blind Man* – he who comes across a coin and envies the seeing men. He reasons, 'If I, the blind man, have come across a coin, the seeing men must have filled up sacks with the gathered money at this very moment.'

A little later, Dwardy pulled out a fat tilapia from the water; and shouted out his praise name as well.

Get the rod! I am Dwardy, *the Strongman* – he who steps on your mother's smoking pipe, and instead of fighting him, you take sides with him to blame your mother for carelessness. You say, 'But mother, you have to be careful with your pipe to see to it that it is not lying in the way to be trampled on.'

I am the Strongman who makes your mother his witness; and you have no balls to object your mother's inclusion in the case.

Tired of hooking fish, they made a fire and roasted their catch. Afterwards, they set out to hunt birds with stones, clubs and slings. They were targeting edible birds like *sileru, oluru, osogo, oswerere* and so forth. Inedible birds such as *atutu, otangle* and *oliktiga* were not targeted but would be warned if they played around. They managed to kill some birds but some lucky ones escaped with or without injuries. Since too much of anything is harmful, the boys put the slain birds in their pockets and switched to playing in the river.

Once in the water, some boys dug sausage sockets out of the river cliff and started competing in impregnating them, at the same time imitating the cries of passion of their phantom lovers. The biggest noise came from those playing the 'man and crocodile' game. Omollo specifically played the 'crocodile', while his fellow boys played the 'men.' The 'crocodile' would accordingly submerge underwater to catch the 'men', and the 'men' would avoid the 'crocodile' at all costs. As the mood was noisy, cheerful and so relaxing, no one kept an eye on the cows, which in turn used such rare freedom to sneak into Opungo's farm for a delicious meal of young maize for which they had been starving for a long time.

Opungo, a blood red-eyed little man, was bitter like the roots of the *ogaka* herb (no wonder the villagers secretly nicknamed him *Danger*). Actually, he was one of those people who can stab you in the stomach for a cup of tea and grin from ear to ear while you are twitching and dying on the ground. There was convincing evidence that he had so far hacked two people to death just for calling him names. A credible story went around that his first victim had called him *the Lizard on the Baobab*, and the second one *the Heavy Lifter* – the annoying nicknames derived from an imagination of how he might have looked when making love to his jumbo wife: considering that he himself looked as if he was a descendant of the mosquito. Despite everything, Opungo was still a force to be reckoned with in Rabar and its environs, especially due to his proven ability of making good on his promises to kill his enemies, if he happened to make some. It was said Opungo would stalk a victim even for two years if that was the sacrifice he had to make to extract revenge – often achieved by hacking an enemy into small pieces.

From his certified terror, he had single-handedly forbade all hoi polloi to utter the words *lizard*, *baobab*, and *heavy lifter* around his vicinity – as these expressions were the constituents of his derogative epithets.

Be that as it may, a story was told in Malaland that Opungo was not born with such bitterness that later on became his signature. Elders who had seen him in his youth claimed he only acquired such animosity towards two-footed creatures after they gravely wronged him. The story went that Opungo hated passionately the severe poverty into which he was born and was thus determined from childhood to overcome it through hard work and wisdom. Consonant with his mission, he started a sugarcane business with twenty shillings his visiting aunt from Mulongo gave him at the age of ten. According to the story, he would wake up at early dawn, walk seven kilometers to Nyamori Valley, and buy a bundle of sugarcane there at a wholesale price. Next, he would ferry the bundle on his bare head to the village market and sell it at the retail price. It was, of course, donkeywork, but it would always fetch twice the capital for every trip, and he would commute like this five times a week.

And to accumulate enough capital for the business he had in mind, he went to the main village shop and bought a *kibubu*, a wooden savings safe, with only a tiny outlet to slot coins through. The boy then worked for good seven years, secretly saving 90 percent of his profit in the safe, which was located in a bedroom he had deliberately darkened. From time to time, he checked his safe and ascertained it was constantly growing heavier like a pregnant goat. Eight years later, Opungo deemed it the right moment to break into his safe, count his savings, and open a wholesale shop in his village. For this purpose, he bought an axe and the work of breaking the safe started. To his astonishment, three-quarters of his safe was full of pieces of glasses instead of the coins he had been diligently slotting into it all this while.

Opungo now refused to accept this miracle. He was convinced someone had stolen his money and thus consulted a seer of his village to identify the evil thief. Unfortunately, the seer was as clueless as

Opungo himself, but did not wish to lose face by confessing to the public that he had no idea about who the culprit was. So, he duped Opungo that his coins would metamorphose into bits of glass because since birth he had never sacrificed to his ancestors. A furious Opungo rubbished this explanation, as he was still quite convinced that a human being had stolen his money; the only thing he did not know was who that thief was. And this is how he developed an enmity towards all upright moving bipeds.

That evening, the *Danger* chased the flock out of his farm like mad. As usual, he was quarreling alone, breathing fire and craving to devour someone.

"The shepherds of this flock will today know the reason I am called Opungo, the Dog – in full, the domestic animal which is never a legal tender for debts."

He now looked right, left, east, and west, yet he could not see any shepherd around the place. But when he revolved his ears slowly, he heard noises of full-stomached children swimming jubilantly in the river Ramar. Opungo's instincts correctly told him that the children were the group of idiots who had stepped on his tail.

"Right!" He shouted to himself.

"The fools are having fun while their cattle feed on my maize, Ehehhhe," he talked to himself in his trademark mumble as he hurriedly started off towards the river.

"Today I will teach these cockroaches a lesson they would grow to tell their grandchildren," he swore as he hurried towards the direction of the river – his legendary machete ready on his right hand for any emergency.

As he approached the river, he switched to tiptoeing as silently as a peeping Tom tiptoes to a brothel just to get to the bank of the river without detection of his arrival by the "silly boys". Indeed, he reached the bank of the river unnoticed and seized the clothes that the swimming boys had taken off and left at the bank. Next, he shouted thunderously:

"Are you the shepherds of those cattle there?"

Upon hearing the voice of a *Danger*, each of the shepherds bolted at the speed of light to a location close by the bushes, as none of them was willing to stop for "death". Opungo *Danger*, paradoxically, did not bother to pursue any of them.

"The game is not over yet!" He hurled a warning to the boys who had by then achieved a speed of thirty kilometers per hour into the surrounding bushes.

As he was expecting the boys back soon, he used their temporary leave to fine-tune his wilderness. That is, he cut a good number of *pou* sticks for the job he anticipated in the next few minutes, carried them to the bank of the river and laid them beside a big log by the riverside.

Next, he sat on the log, pulled out his dirty smoking pipe, filled it with raw marijuana, lighted it up and started smoking and coughing as dreadfully as a devout knight errant.

Ten minutes later, all the boys were back for peace talks with the *Danger*. They had now realized they had been running in their birthday suits like witches, having unfortunately left their clothes on the bank of the river with the *Danger*. They had realized they could not go back home naked, for their militant parents would promptly want to know where they had left their clothes, upon which they were sure they would harvest a communal beating from their elder brothers. With this in mind, the boys were now pleading with the *Danger* from a respectable distance to forgive their sin and return their clothes unconditionally. Opungo nonetheless played it tough and no solution was in sight.

But in a turn of events, a clever boy chanted Opungo's rare praise name of *Mr. Thin Iron Bar is Never a Thick Cypress Wood* and unexpectedly brought a solution to their problem. The utterance of the rare praise name threw a pang of excitement in Opungo's heart, such that he would now review his position. The fact is, he had been starving for this praise name for about two years and thus considered the boy who had addressed him so as the brightest of all the boys of his age in Rabar Village. For him therefore, he would give their clothes back at a small fee of three strokes on a back of each boy. It was of course not an impressive deal for any of the boys, yet the context dictated they accept it and move on.

Omollo thus received his bitter pill of whips on the back that evening, yet kept it to himself for fear of an additional punishment if the news leaked to his fierce father or his militant elder brothers. The pain from his back and the thought of the nasty experience of the previous day hence engaged his mind to the extent that he was neither seeing nor hearing anything around him and would likely have walked straight through the cow-dung bonfire, had it not been for his elder brother Ongilo, who had been watching him the whole way. Ongilo, who had long recognized that his younger brother was somehow preoccupied, thus chose to bring Omollo's back to reality by using mockery.

"Look at this crazy boy! What curse makes you talk with imaginary people like Nyandiri Nyobala? You are such a foolish boy that what you consider a job is only to wet your bed. Look at him, with a face like an old woman who is chewing Aloe vera roots."

He said and the other boys with him broke into uproarious laughter that fortunately revived Omollo's awareness.

"Were you yourself not funny in the head, wouldn't you ask Uncle Ongoro if a train also gives birth to twins?"

Omollo said and instigated fresh laughter.

"Eeh, you are fond of despising others, forgetting that
your buttocks are as flat as the base of an iron,"
Omollo added a joke to his brother and the boys now held their
stomachs with laughter – whereas, Ongilo, who now saw all the signals
of losing the verbal war to his younger brother, quickly responded:

"Go away with ..."
But even before his mockery was wholly delivered, a sharp woman's
wail radiated from an adjacent village and interrupted everyone in the
area whose ears were working properly.

"Uuuuuuuuwi! Uuuuuuwi!"
As a wail of that sort meant nothing short of a terrible event in
Rabar Village, many people were perplexed and thus rushed out of
their euphorbia tirucalli-fenced homesteads, to find out what the hell
was taking place in their village. As a rule, each tried to rotate their
ears to gather waves that could offer clues to what was happening.
In their assessments, more women had joined the one who initiated
the bewailment and men were equally reciting funeral dirges, blowing
horns or beating drums – an obvious sign that someone at Wiotel's
homestead was no more. The only remaining puzzle now was who it
was that passed on at the compound.

"Who was sick in Wiotel's home?" A starer asked a colleague
who, unfortunately, was as clueless as the questioner.

"It is definitely a sudden death," one man in his vicinity concluded.

<<<CHAPTER THREE>>>

A great man, from a well-to-do family had passed away. Nyambori Wiotel, a former colonial district clerk, was well known in Rabar and its environs for his wealth and knowledge. Given his greatness, his name was a default theme in most folk songs of Malaland. The most famous folk song about him was by none other than Aboka Nyobiga, the greatest singer of the land. Considering his fame, therefore, the news that he had passed away that morning clearly jogged Omollo's memory about the dead man's hottest folk song by Nyobiga. That morning, he recalled a verse and a refrain of the greatest song of all times – and even sang it aloud:

> *Whoooo was the first, with a bike in Mala?*
> *Whoooo was the first, with a gun in Mala?*
> *Whoooo was the first, with a car in Mala?*
> *Nobody, but Nyambori. Aiiii, ai, ai*
> *Nyambori was the first. Aiiiii, ai, ai*
> *Wiotel was the first. Aiiiii, ai, ai*
> *Apula was the first, Aiiiiiiiiiiiiii, AaaaHo!*

A whispered rumour about Wiotel went around that he was the first Rabarian to tickle the bellybutton of a white woman from inside for two consecutive years. His uncelebrated reputation was that he was the first man to have a serious motorcycle accident in the whole region north of Damasawa. With regard to this uncelebrated fame, the story went that Wiotel became irritated when every Tom, Dick and Harry of his village started buying Baatam bicycle brand, which had been his sole monopoly in the whole region north of Damasawa for *a quarter of a century*. It was claimed that for maintaining his nickname of Wiotel or "a pacesetter", the idea of sprinting to a motorcycle ownership before any other native now crossed his mind. Despite that, the availability of money was *by then an obstacle to buying a new motorcycle* (considering the fact that he was already a retired officer whose pension would not permit such luxury). Be that as it may, his inner voice assured him that an eye-catching used motorcycle could still do the same trick as a new one. And from what I gathered, he consented to his inner voice and declared an interest in buying a used motorcycle for himself.

As people put it, a vendor, who might have heard the news from an anonymous source, soon emerged out of the blue with an eye-satisfying motorcycle – exactly like the one Wiotel had in his mind. This same man – who they later learnt was a chronic con artist – camped at Wiotel's home for over seven days, allegedly, bargaining with him to buy his good-looking cycle. The story continues that the alien eventually surrendered his motorcycle to the old man in exchange for twenty bulls.

It is further attested that Wiotel's motorcycle did not disappoint. According to the story, the market women and the alcohol-drinking men of Rabar Village and its environs spent as much time talking about it as they did selling their wares and discussing politics. It is even claimed that the gadget inspired two more great songs about the might of its owner.

But in an unforeseen development, the brake system of the motorcycle suddenly broke down and unexpectedly turned completely deaf to both spanners and screwdrivers. This happened just five weeks after the motorcycle was bought. Allegedly, it could still start up and move on its own force at a constant speed but it never honored its rider's order to stop. And after injuring three of its riders, Wiotel's sons – who were initially very fond of it – came to dread it like the hind legs of the donkey. As a result, the machine slowly but surely started metamorphosing into a dummy of a motorcycle. Nonetheless, one of Wiotel's sons did not give up on this object, which he considered the priciest in the whole of Malaland, the *aturututu*. After some lengthy independent research, he discovered that the motorcycle would stop without a hitch when driven into a swamp. He found out that the mud in the swamp would slow the motorcycle down and a small spill of water into its engine would shut it off without fail. In other words, riders only had to know where the swamp at their destinations was, just as pilots have to know where airports are in their flight plan, and the problem was completely solved. Thereafter, the Wiotels started riding the motorcycle in black shorts and barefooted because they were then certainly heading to a swamp every time they were on the *aturututu*.

But after some months of riding the cycle in special gear, their same genius now discovered that putting petrol in the motorcycle tank that ran out exactly at the intended destination or a few meters from it gave better results than driving into swamps. From then on, the Wiotels started riding the motorcycle in suits and shoes, with a jerry can of petrol on its carrier.

From what I heard, they were initially very bad at estimating the petrol so that it would run out at their desired locations. Stories were told of cases where the riders, having reached their intended destination, had to ride back home without fulfilling the purpose of their journey because petrol would still be aplenty in the tank of the cycle, which was synonymous with 'it would not stop.' In opposite cases, the petrol would dry up in the tank far too early, forcing the riders to finish their remaining journey painfully by pushing the jumbo motorcycle along for far too long.

Most importantly, gossip had it that the last time Wiotel rode the motorcycle in person; he had gone to visit his daughter who was married in the tenth village from Rabar Village. The story continues that the renowned petrol estimator overestimated the amount of fuel on that particular day. Consequently, Wiotel reached his intended village, yet the petrol had not yet dried up in the cycle's tank, necessitating him to crisscross the village several times in anticipation that the motorcycle would eventually run out of petrol – but all in vain.

After about a half an hour of this, however, anxiety catapulted among the curious villagers who had abandoned their duties and lined up on each side of the roads to catch a glimpse of this thingamajig at close range. They started feeling disappointed and chastised the poor old man for his pride in not stopping the object, which they were actually seeing for the second time in their life, to allow them a closer viewing. Wiotel's daughter, grandsons and in-laws as well started getting angry with their kin, as the food that had been prepared for him was cooling down; meanwhile, their honorable guest appeared to be acting like a teenager with a new pair of sports shoes.

Narrators postulate that all these scenarios started taking a toll on the captive of the lunatic motorcycle, which Wiotel was. It was said he would have ridden back home as other riders of the motorcycle had done before but he knew very well that his in-laws would never forgive him for such a sin. He knew there was no way he could have let them slaughter a bull for him, show up on a motorcycle, then disappear without so much as tasting a piece of beef.

It is in this context that plan B of stopping the motorcycle crossed the mind of the old man. The official story had it that he started asking people, by gabbling where there was a swamp in that village but either the staring people did not hear him properly because of babbling motorcycle or rather that his mind had gone too blank to hear them properly. Whatever the reason, in an evident misdirection, he rode and plunged into the steep bank of a river instead of the swamp he was asking about. Things took even a worse turn as he fractured his pelvis in the accident and thereafter could only move in a wheelchair.

A concocted story, probably to preserve the old man's honor, nonetheless claims that he ran into a herd of cattle relaxing on a road and fell off his motorcycle in an unavoidable accident. All the same, his stumble never seemed to dim his popularity since he continued to be a respected and admired man to the very day he strangely passed on at Rabar Village.

In light of this reality, women wailed for him penetratingly and men recited their mourning songs for him at the full capacity of their voices. Drummers also beat their drums so hard that one's bowels would shudder upon nearing them. As time passed, more and more people joined in the lamentation of the great man, actually packing his compound so full that some people were overflowing outside the euphorbia tirucalli fence.

As usual, some men took along their herds of cows, while others took along spears, bows and arrows, bush knives, slings, clubs and shields to the compound in order to pay homage to the fallen hero. With all these ingredients in the bewailment exercise, the deceased was definitely receiving a decent send-off.

In the same vein, some men paraded in a long row for the funeral march dedicated to the fallen hero. These were holding spears and shields in their hands and looked as if they were going to fight the death that had stolen their loved one. These men would come forward from the row of the warriors and sprint ahead speedily and zigzaggedly with all his deadly arms in his grasp. Meanwhile, this man would be regularly banging his shield so hard with the haft of his spear, seemingly in an attempt to seek the attention of men and women around him. Then, as if confronting an invisible enemy, he would move his spear forth and back intermittently, while swinging his shield in all directions, as if obstructing enemy spears being thrown at him from all directions. All this time, warriors on the row would cheer for their advancing fellow, alongside chanting his praise names; that would constantly drive the advancing warrior crazier and crazier. Once the advancing warrior had shown all the fighting techniques in his repertoire, he would professionally retreat to the row of the rest of the warriors in order to make way for a fresh warrior to stage his own show.

Elsewhere, men with slings swung them in the air, as if they were going to sling out the rest of the mourners with stones, while, those with bows and arrows teased as if shooting whoever appeared in front of them. A little later, the most frightening band of mourners appeared out of the blue and began their show by running amok at the compound with feather hats and clothes made out of leopard or cheetah hide on their bodies. Probably to intensify their uniqueness, all wore ankle rattles, which rang systematically as they rambled in the compound like demons while others fastened their hide-wear with belts made of python slough. And probably to terrorize mourners for fun, they would toss their sparkling spears in the air scarily and catching them before they fell on the ground. All the while, they sang their funeral hymns in very coarse tones, some of which were appropriate to the bewailment process, although others were completely out of context.

The women accompanying the men were also not short on amusements. They carried with them cooking pots or wooden spoons – the traditional weapons of females in Malaland from the time of the dinosaurs, and equally sang satirical funeral songs and uttered incongruent wails:

"Uuuuuwi!" They intermittently moaned.

It was indeed noisy and wild at the compound, despite the fact that nothing new was happening in Rabar Village inasmuch as Malans had been mourning great dead men in such fashion since antiquity.

Omollo, as a kid, was however, experiencing what is known scientifically as Experience Deficiency Syndrome (EDS). Consequently, he hid himself under a granary; being uncomfortable with the armed mourners who carelessly roamed about the compound with all sorts of weapons in their hands. His inner voice had told him that some of them had smoked something and might at any time obey the commands of what they had smoked.

Equally, his mind deceived him into believing he was also hiding from the spirits oozing from the dead body. Since his childhood, he had heard elders saying that dead bodies were capable of doing whatever they liked to the living. He had specifically heard them saying that spirits of dead bodies have sharper eyes than living men and could visit living men at will for either peace or disaster. He had heard that in a peaceful visit they would play a role of clan instructors, irrespective of how hopeless they had been when alive. He had further heard that they would sometimes ask parents to give their own names to newly born babies; otherwise, the baby in question would never stop crying. In disastrous visits – mostly to evil doers – he had heard that they would inventively torment their victims at their own pleasure and without mercy. Regarding this, Omollo specifically remembered hearing of how the spirits of Ombare's first wife – whom Ombare had allegedly murdered in secrecy – tormented him. It was rumoured that the dead wife of the man would all of a sudden appear and sleep between Ombare and his new wife whenever Ombare's magic stick was boiling with passion for its conjugal right. As if to confirm this rumour, Ombare's new wife finally ran away without justifying her move. And that was just the tip of the iceberg about what dead men's spirits were capable of doing to living bodies.

Now the sun's arrows were unbearably strong and painful on the bodies of the mourners. As a result, they were profusely sweating, hungry, thirsty and tired. Most of them hence sought refuge under the eaves of huts or under trees at the compound to wait for drinks and food from the deceased's clan. As a rule, the ground was now left to widows to show their expertise in sobbing for their dead husband. They would jog around the whole compound, weeping and singing funeral songs in an array of styles. A few of the men, whose aim was to inherit them in the near future, would also run after one of their choice, hold her hands, and remind her that 'nature does not allow a vacuum,' or, 'Don't cry that much, my sister-in-law, even if my lovely brother has gone, I have remained and I care.'

But of all the moaning widows that noon, Apoda Nyodondo was a star in the mourning for their dead husband. Not only did she look pathetic, but also sung an irresistible and infectious funeral song than those sung by her counterparts.

Ohh! Apula my dear!
Who have you left me with Apula?
Where will I get bread, Wiotel?
Who will buy me pork, Wiotel?
Ohh! My clansmen!
Right from today,
I have abstained from pork.
I have abstained from bread,
From tilapia,
Apula my age-mate, you are gone forever.

Eventually, Omollo realized that the chaos in the compound had well and truly ceased. Accordingly, he emerged from his safe haven and joined the elders, who were lounging under a huge ng'ou tree at the western side of that compound (waiting for any hunger reliever that might come their way). As soon as he approached them, he saw an old log that had been used as a bench for curving hafts or clubs. Its face was therefore rough to sit on but it was the only available option for him, considering that children could only sit on chairs when adults were away, or were all seated.

As he was balancing his buttocks on that thorny log, the elders were engaged in conversation and, probably for that reason, did not even notice his presence in their vicinity. One old man was narrating something to his colleagues in a whispering voice. Omollo thus set his earlobes professionally to pick up what he was saying.

"These people are determined to turn Wiotel's homestead into a pumpkin garden," the old man said and paused to add more tobacco to his pipe.

"Only last year we saw Riwa son of Wiotel, collapsing like an old cactus tree before us. But even before we forgot the tragedy, we saw his beautiful younger sister, Apondo Nyopondo, turning into an all-season lunatic. How can a woman roam the whole village, barking like a mad dog? This ..." At this point a cough interrupted his speech, "koooh, khwaaaaah! Kooooh, khwaaaaah! Ahhaaaagh, pthuuuuh!" He emitted a dry cough and then a spit of interwoven black saliva, dispatched four meters away from where they were seated.

"This time, they have sent our bull down in the bizarrest fashion ever. How on earth can a mere housefly knock a fully grown up person down to death, if not by witchcraft?" He said and wrinkled his face, probably to emphasize his point, "I think they have now traded on our tails enough. We must this time tame this madness once and for all. And I swear by my mother Angira Nyoringo that this time they will not get away with it like that," he said and kept quiet to give chance to his colleagues to ponder his words. His quietness now gave Omwanda, *the*

Uncastrated Bull, a room to spew his venom, as was his custom.

"He whose blood a mosquito is sucking is he who bumps it," he said, referring to the community's wisdom, "what can we, the outsiders, do if you, his blood brothers, have left Waritu to mix you like the white man's playing cards?" He surveyed the group cunningly and it seemed he was contented to be receiving deserved attention. Then he continued with his speech: "You guys act as dumb as a box of rocks and it is common knowledge that even medical doctors do not have a prescription for imbecility," he said scoldingly, "as per your words, Waritu is slowly but surely turning your brother's homestead into a pumpkin garden," he added.

Upon hearing these prickly words, Maginga Obala, a stepbrother to the deceased, became possessed with a spirit of vengeance. Accordingly, he burst out into a queer wail that attracted the attention of every gazer at the compound. Next, he sprinted like a gazelle to a nearby grass-thatched hut, where tired mourners would always insert their spears, and there he pulled out a giant spear, and swore in a serious tone that attracted even the attention of the perplexed mourners.

"Waritu Nyagoli must die by this spear, to compensate for the death of my brother," he declared the motivation underneath his wild acts and with these words now threw the compound into total confusion. Men, in premonition of a tragedy, now formed a human shield between him and Waritu Nyagoli, who was then sitting leisurely with other elders under a grass-thatched tent some meters away. Someone quickly grabbed Maginga from behind and began struggling to snatch away the deadly spear he was holding in his right hand. Other men simultaneously whisked Waritu away from the compound for his own safety, but Waritu did not appreciate it. He hurled abuse back in protest at the man accusing him of bewitching the deceased and even wished that his two stray sons were there to confront his accuser and his family that day. But even after the chaos had well and truly ceased, mourners still debated hard about the event that had just flashed past their eyes at the compound.

One group sided with Maginga for wanting to discipline the witch tit for tat, while another group condemned the behavior.

"You don't need a priest of Handaki to tell you that witchcraft is countered by witchcraft in our land," they said.

Omollo, who had resorted back to his hideout, was chilled with fear owing to the fact that he had never witnessed adults engaging in a commotion like the one that had just transpired before his eyes. He would therefore have retreated back home, but remembered that he was of the same clan as the deceased, and that all members of his family were obliged to remain at that homestead for no less than a week.

Later, Omollo reluctantly reemerged from his hideout and this time approached a group in which his own mother and other women were sitting. To his amazement, they too were talking about how the deceased had passed on.

"It was yesterday evening that Obano's father was sitting by his bedside ..." a woman was narrating.

"Eeeeh," another woman encouraged her to speak.

"... that a speeding housefly emerged from nowhere, hit the tip of his nose and sent him down."

"Eeeeh,"

"And as the old man fell on his back, he did not stand up again before he died."

"Aiiii, did you say that a speeding housefly hit him in the nose and sent him down?" Another woman expressed her disbelief, "but how can that be?" She added.

"Don't joke with witchcraft, I tell you," a different woman warned before the chief narrator continued.

"Of course, nobody knows how it could have happened but the truth of the matter is that his stomach began trembling in the manner that maize grains tremble on the feeder of a milling machine; and that he started struggling with his body, but all in vain," said the chief narrator sadly.

"Eeeeh," another woman encouraged the speaker.

"He thus shouted for help and his people run to him,"

"Eeeheee," they encouraged her to speak further.

"They next rushed him to a wise man but ...," she said, only to be cut short by another witchy-looking woman before she could finish what she was saying.

"To whom did they take him?" She inquired dismissively.

"They, of course, took him to Wagasi – Ongola's father, who is well known for counteracting witches' missiles. I think you have heard of him, haven't you?" She sought confirmation from her audience.

But even before she received a reply, sharp loud cries of the male and the female mourners were heard from a distance. People now looked towards the direction whence the cries were coming in an effort to recognize whose they were. At last, sharp eyes uncovered that they were the deceased's sisters and their families from distant lands. The messenger sent to deliver the sad news was driving donkeys with their luggage behind them.

As per the tradition, many retired mourners got up hurriedly and ran to meet and support the newly arriving mourners to sob for the deceased. The turbulence and noise therefore revived in the compound again.

Omollo thus remained alone in the eaves of the house, as all the women he was sitting with had joined hands with the arriving mourners. As if day dreaming, he plunged into pondering about all he had heard and seen at the deceased's homestead. From the last woman's story, he could clearly see what his grandmother had been telling him about different types of witches and their activities.

He remembered that some witches were *nude night runners* and their pleasures were to frighten cowards at night. Such would run naked or ride hyenas at night with human arms and spit fire from their mouths to scare the hell out of you. Most of them would, of course, sacrifice their family members to their higher authorities as a rent for their acquired witchcraft. Some, like Waritu Nyagoli, were considered to be the sowers of *ndagla* – a juju hidden in a dead bat or rat to harm a victim who walks over it. It was alleged that *Ndagla* functioned like a guided missile – only affecting targeted victims out of the thousands of people who might have walked over it along the road in which it was planted. Then some witches were *jonawi*, or silent killers; these would often steal a part of their victim's clothing, underpants, or shoe. Or else they would pick soil from the footprints of their victims and would technologically use it to send them a disease of their choosing. Overall, the most feared witches of all were the keepers of snakes, crocodiles, leopards, or even thunder. Upon choosing their victims, they would order their familiar spirits to catch or kill their victims.

At this juncture, Omollo remembered how one witch had been caught at the market place a month ago with the head of an albino he had just slaughtered in his hand. It was a memory that often caused the hair on his body to stand upright.

"I hate witches," he eventually said to himself.

"If I became a diviner-priest, I will kill all of them in a fortnight," he continued talking to himself.

However, in his inner mind mingled an unanswered question about the witches. Ever since he was born, he had frequently seen the carcass of a cat, a dog, a rat or a cockroach and wondered whether the witches of their kind were responsible for their untimely deaths.

"Are there witches among cockroaches also?" He asked himself but did not get an answer, "and if not, how do these animals die without being bewitched?" He thought, smiled and kept quiet for thinking deeper.

"Probably, I am still too young to understand these things," He added, in allusion to what adults would always say to him whenever he asked them a difficult question, or rather a question they did not like to be asked. Then he kept quiet for a long time.

<<<CHAPTER FOUR>>>

Four days had elapsed since the glorious burial of Nyambori Wiotel and the event was gradually ageing. Evidence was that the old mourners no longer showed enthusiasm in the bewailment of the deceased and even the newly arriving ones only bewailed the dead man with less vigor than their predecessors. The widows, of course, still mourned for their husband elaborately, even though a close examination would reveal they did so just to meet the prerequisite of Malan culture, which required a widow to mourn for her husband non-stop, wear black clothes, shave bald, appear puffy-eyed, and look like her life had been shattered by the death of her husband. Without all this, people would have implicated her in the death. Accordingly, the widows kept on accompanying the arriving mourners and kept the routine of mourning for their dead husband from dawn to around 8:00 am, as was expected of them.

In so doing, they marked their homestead as a funeral scene; otherwise, a stranger might have confused it for a wedding scene, considering that the two ceremonies did not differ radically in Malaland. In fact, the land recognized three major ceremonies in man's life: birth, marriage, and death – the biggest of all being the death ceremony.

As Nyambori Apula was undoubtedly a giant in Malaland, his death ceremony attracted relatives and friends from as far as thirty-five villages away. For more than a week, they would remain at his compound to celebrate his esteemed life.

Incidentally, bulls, goats and chicken were aplenty at his funeral ceremony, causing mourners to be very busy with the consumption of their meat – actually, a food that Rabarians loved with all their hearts and minds. A story was told in Malaland of how Elder Jabuori – one of the Rabarian ancestors – planted a private part of a goat in his garden, watered it and supplied it with manure as diligently as a party strategist, expecting to harvest big tasty pieces of goat after a certain time. Briefly, he ultimately discovered that the planted piece of goat was bearing maggots. From there on though, his closest kin could not get rid of the cruel jokes inspired by that bad piece of research by their grandfather.

Once an animal had been slaughtered, Omollo and his posse, as the shepherds of the livestock, would be given animal testicles. His elder brothers would be given chest, to energize them and give them courage to carry out tough duties in their community. Humps of cattle would be given to the newly married men, in expectation of giving them vigor to make new members of their clan. Old men would be given the tongue and the loin, considered soft enough for those whose teeth had fled. Women would get the pancreases, considered to be as tender as the women themselves. And for the fallen ancestors, a little blood would be poured on the ground as a sign of communion between the living and the dead Rabarians. It was generally a taboo for the wrong group to eat the wrong part of an animal, and whoever did so would be mocked in folk songs or become subjects of ridicule in the tribal sayings and songs. But apart from such special organs dedicated to specific groups, the rest of the flesh would be eaten by anyone.

Away from the meat and drinks, musicians applied themselves to performing at the death ceremony of Wiotel – actually, a big digression from how they would be invited at funeral ceremonies in Malaland. This is to say, the death ceremony of Wiotel – the pacemaker – was replete with fun and joy, as of course, was to be expected of the funeral of a man of his caliber in Malaland.

<<<*CHAPTER FIVE*>>>

Days were passing so quickly to Omollo – considering that he liked the activities at the deceased's homestead very much. He even wished that the clocks were limping or rather that the Malan customs pronounced a stay of one year at the deceased's homestead. These were nonetheless pipedreams. The reality was that *teng'o* – the last celebration for the dead man – was looming on the horizon, after which everybody would be required to migrate from the deceased's homestead to their own homesteads. This meant that Omollo would miss the hot company of his posse, miss the games, music, activities, stories and unique experiences that all tasted better in that big company at that compound than elsewhere.

The thought of dispersing from the deceased homestead was, of course, so disturbing in his mind that afternoon that he almost injured himself with a machete with which he was curving a club. The day before, they had played *hide and seek*, and it seemed as orgasmic as watching an old woman beating a police officer. They further played the *father and mother game* and Omollo himself was lucky enough to win the competitive role of father; the beautiful Achieng played mother; other children played other families members and the unlucky ones played cats, dogs, or hyenas.

Amidst these thoughts, there appeared Dwardy – who was really meant to be Edward, had the Rabarians been a little more proficient in pronouncing names of Laurasian origin. Omollo and his colleagues considered Dwardy as their king – of his toughness and influence among his peers.

"Hey! How are things going on *the Baboon?*" Dwardy addressed Omollo by his nickname.

"Fine, what's up Strongman?" Omollo responded.

"Fine," he answered and paused a moment before continuing.

"Go and tell the other boys that we are getting late for Rabar Hill," he ordered Omollo who responded immediately by stopping what he was doing and galloping like a wild horse to gather his colleagues. After ten minutes or so, a band of 30 boys armed with slings, a catapults, clubs or bird traps was now rushing towards Rabar Hill like the wind.

On their way, stones or clubs were thrown from time to time at flying or perching birds just to announce that the strong Rabar men were passing by. Soon, they crossed Sirub Valley – a natural boundary between residential area and Rabar Hill.

A few steps thereafter, they met a group of boys from a neighbouring village, who were themselves hunting birds while at the same time looking after their heads of cattle. But as soon as Dwardy saw them, his heart jumped with an ecstatic joy.

Ever since he was born, Dwardy was actually a shell of two different demons: the first, a demon of dung, which would cause him, upon seeing a thick thicket, to perceive an urge to defecate; the second, a demon of fight, which upon seeing warring factions, would strike him with an urge to watch the encounter. With regard to the latter demon, Dwardy would go any length to ensure that things fight, be they dogs, bulls, sheep, children or goats. Accordingly, his second demon - the bad one - descended and rested upon him that evening to incite a boy from his group against a boy from the group they had just met by the valley. Consonant with this desire, he instantly came up with a dispute he was sure would spark a fight between the boys he had inwardly earmarked.

"Andila," he called the name of one of the boys from his group audibly enough to raise the attention of everybody around and only continued once he was sure everybody was listening, "that boy in a brown shirt bragged to me yesterday that he is strong enough to command you, your father, your elder brother and your uncle to sweep their compound with your tongues in the presence of all women in the village. Is it true?" As he addressed Andila, he simultaneously pointed to a short fat boy called Odongo, who was sitting on an anthill by the path they were following.

As expected, his venomous words raised the eyebrows of every boy in both groups. To Andila in particular, the slur from Odongo was reckless and deserved to be counteracted with equal force.

"Can that pig fight a leopard? Tell him to come now if he is on heat and is dying to be mounted by a real Malan." Andila reacted narcissistically to Odongo's slur and, indeed, his retaliatory slur hit the ears of Odongo like a hot nail in the nose.

"Aaaaaaaaa!" Andila's group booed Odongo's group upon hearing such a strong reaction from their man.

"Superb, Andila!" A voice of a boy from his group lauded his reaction, "did he consider himself uninsultable when he was conveying you insults?" He wittily added a rhetorical question in support of Andila's reaction.

Odongo, of course, knew clearly that Dwardy had cooked up the lie to incite them to fight, yet the unwise reactions by his age-mate pierced his heart like a jet to the clouds. He was not going to allow anyone to refer to him as a pig - and worse still, to mount him. Possessed by the spirit of anger, he hurried towards Andila alongside his group.

Within a minute, the two angry boys had moved so close to each other that their noses were within inches of touching. Everyone thus thought they would instantly fight but instead they remained as they were, asking each other "What?", "What?" Actually, for much longer than anyone would have expected - an indication that the two boys were afraid of each other, just like a policeman and a gangster.

From experience, Dwardy now learnt the need to add some fuel to the fire, if he was at all interested in watching a fight that evening. In response to his intuition, he now put his foot between Odongo and Andila, then declared:

"Odongo, if you are indeed such a strong man as you brag to be, here is my foot: step on it," he said, and kept quiet to wait for Odongo's response.

Being born in Malaland, Odongo knew that inherent in that act was a non-verbal insult. All the same, he could not stand being seen as a coward by his posse. In this light, he reluctantly stepped on Dwardy's foot and waited for Dwardy to decipher the slur encoded in the act. Dwardy now feigned shock at the ferocity of the slur implicit in the sort of the stepping Odongo had just made on him. The crowd simultaneously went quiet and attentively awaited decipherment of the slur, which was strictly done by the person whose feet had been stepped on.

"Yeah! Yeah! Yeah! Yeah!" A skillful Dwardy pretended to have been hurt by the slur himself before reporting it to Andila.

"Inherent in the sort of the stepping Odongo has made on my foot is that your mother's buttocks click-clack like the keys of the school typewriter when she is walking," he said confidently and waited to see the consequences his bombshell would evoke.

As expected, Odongo's group jeered up the revelation jubilantly – as if to say that their colleague was more ferocious than Andila. Conversely, Andila's group became quite pissed off by the way these other guys reacted to Odongo's response. They thus demanded that Odongo retaliate.

"Ahh! Aahh! Andila, how can your fellow boy throw such a terrible insult at you and you are just watching him like a movie. You step on Dwardy's foot too to pay him back, my friend," one of his mates 'advised' him.

Upon hearing these words, angry Andila also hurriedly stepped on Dwardy's foot and poised himself for hearing the decipherer's feedback on the insult intrinsic in the stepping he had made.

Then, Dwardy, the professional fight-inciter, took some minutes pretending that he was overwhelmed by the weight of the abuse intrinsic to the non-verbal action Andila had made.

"Should I decipher it or not," he hypocritically quizzed his audience on the obvious.

"Decipher iiiiiiiiiit," the enthusiastic audience answered together.

"Inherent in the sort of the stepping Andila has made on my foot is that he is your boyfriend," he said and appeared to be very disturbed.

As expected, Dwardy's latest revelation sent supporters of Andila into jubilation and laughter; on the other hand, Odongo's group was sent into a renewed grief.

Now Mikera, knowing that the fire awaited only a single blow to burst into flames, skillfully blew it.

"Andila, if you are really his boyfriend, as you claim to be, embrace your girlfriend now. What are you waiting for?" He asked in wonder, "prove your relationship to us now," he insisted and fortunately, his words ticked the right box.

Andila, who had lost the last vestige of his temper, took the advice for an order. He now sheepishly opened his arms to embrace Odongo, and got what he was looking for – a punch on his chest that almost blocked his esophagus. Andila now retaliated by quickly grabbing his fellow boy as tightly as possible, meanwhile repeatedly head butting him in the chest.

Odongo, who was almost fainting, fortunately realized the need to change his fighting style in order to free himself from the strong hands of Andila, who was now coiling him like a python does a dog. He hence gave Andila a crocodile bite on the arm, which not only caused Andila to free him as quickly as a hot potato on one's palm but also to emit a loud cry to the pleasure of an enthusiastic crowd. Odongo now took advantage of the confusion to pass his arm around Andila's neck and started to strangle him like a python – and, in fact, he strangled him so hard that the crowd feared for the worse. Fortunately, Dwardy, in the capacity of a commander-in-chief of the boys, now halted the fight and freed Andila from the strong arms of his opponent.

"No boxing, kicking, scratching or biting," he laid out specific rules of the fight in a tone suggesting authority, "only wrestling is allowed," he clarified the order.

Next, he ordered Andila and Odongo to proceed with the fight to a second round, which is what happened. Odongo launched the second round by embracing Andila tightly around his loins. He then planted his left leg before Andila's legs, where it became an obstacle. Next, he jerked Andila across it with all his might and caused him to take off in the air like a plane. The boys, of course, held their heads and closed their eyes for they thought that Andila would fall on his nose on that gravel soil – and that would be quite scary.

But alas, Andila rolled himself in the air like a cat and rested on the ground with only small bruises on his knees and hands. That attack nonetheless charged him threefold for the next rumble with Odongo. Slowly, he gathered himself up from the ground and looked as if he had been knocked out.

"If I am your wife as you said, why are your eyes welling up with tears then?" Odongo thundered, "retell the audience about our marital relationship now if you are really the man you claim to be," he yelled again, his eyes surveying the group, perhaps to elicit their appreciation on his latest performance.

But all of a sudden, Andila bent down and forced his head between Odongo's thighs. He thereafter swiftly lifted him up in the air like a crane to a shipping container. Odongo, now appeared helpless and could only peep at where he would be thrown. Everybody else closed their eyes to avoid witnessing an anticipated felony. But as if Andila had paused with him in the air for far too long, Odongo stretched his right arm down Andila's body and clung to the collar of his pullover without his knowledge. So, upon throwing Odongo down, Andila found himself falling together with him.

Yet no sooner had Andila and Odongo got up for another round of the fight than they noticed an adult encroaching on their crime scene. This confused everybody, because they knew very well the gravity of the offense they were committing. Each therefore asked his feet:

"My feet; have I eaten anything without giving you?"

Their feet as usual answered them: "No, you have always given me whatever you eat." As a result, their feet carried them away from the scene before one could say 'knife'.

After a considerable run, Dwardy sat down alone on a nearby rock, gulping air as rapidly as a fish out of water, and too exhausted to move an inch further. Now the bad demon left him and started questioning his action, yet he could not regather spilt milk.

After a while, Dwardy regained his energy and instantly launched a campaign of re-collecting his lost boys by whistling at them in a special way. Shortly afterwards, the boys started emerging from the bush one by one and eventually twenty three out of thirty boys had reassembled. Noise now resumed as each of the boys competed to narrate the run he had just made. Of course, nobody knew the whereabouts of the rest, including Andila, yet no one was worried about them: they were sure that these cowards had returned to the village. Next, the group advanced to the hill in an exited small talk – actually so noisy that none of them felt the steepness of Rabar Hill. Soon they were at the summit and the whole world was now below them.

As a rule of thumb, they would observe silence at the summit for twenty minutes, either spying or praying. Boys who chose to spy during this period would look for people who were relieving themselves or Adams and Eves who were stealing God's fruit in one of the bushes down the hill. Upon identifying such people, they would scare them by shouting their formulaic scaring expression, going like:

'Aaaaaauuu! You man in a black pullover, I seeeeeeee you!' – Upon which, the evil person would flee at the speed of a spotted thief, sometimes in his birthday suit. The boys on the hill would then roll with laughter at the excitement of scaring the hell out of a devilish man.

On the other hand, those who chose to pray would normally ask the gods to overturn a lorry loaded with soda at their village so that they could have a free drinking spree, as had indeed happened a long time before they were born. Alternatively, they would pray to gods to send a whirlwind to their school so that they could have a disaster-induced school break. Fortunately, gods had always laughed off their wish list on that hallowed hill – concrete evidence being that nothing of the sort happened very often in Rabar Village. That evening, Omollo went straightaway to the top of a big flat rock on the far eastern part of the hill. It was the highest point on that hill, from where he could see as far as Lwaland, Waland and Moland, whose people spoke the same tongue as the Malans. On the other side, he could see Ifugondiland, Barokiland and Magitaland whose people spoke a language other than Malan.

That evening, all these lands looked green and bushy. He could also see dams, ponds, streams and rivers that formed white spots on the green surface. In the northwest, he could see the arm of Lake Nyaki, the most enormous of all the water bodies one could spot from that point.

Thick forests, valleys, and mountain ranges dominated the edges of every village he could see from that height. For a long time, such places had been homes to spirits and wild animals. In the far western part of his village, a chain of iron-thatched houses was visible amidst a sisal plantation. It was a residence of white men, who were then the supreme rulers of the Republic of Kaya. No villager, however, knew much about their lives for they did not mix with the villagers in social life: they would only draw near to the village for a military show, or crisscross the village for collecting head tax, or for driving adult villagers to go and work in their plantations for free.

Down the hill, Omollo could see a web of homes fenced with either *ojuok* or sisal edges. Herds of cattle scattered all over the village adorned the land with their beautiful colors. A few corrugated iron-thatched houses seen from that point were the dispensary, the school, the court, the warehouse, and the church. They had all been built a long time ago and it was very difficult to identify their traditional paint.

That evening, such scenery reminded Omollo of his uncle Ongoro, a seaman who claimed to have travelled to many countries and collected many stories on the voyages. Whenever he returned to Omollo's village after a lengthy absence, his age-mates would congregate around him and children like Omollo would complete the circle to listen to a chain of fabricated escapades from different cities and countries. On those occasions, no one else from Rabar Village would contribute anything other than interjecting the man's talk with questions. On such visits, Uncle Ongoro would take Omollo along with him to that rock, where the two would sit down for the one-sided stories that Omollo had in fact discovered were made-up, but still liked listening to them on account of their novelty and creativity. That evening, he burst out into an audible laughter upon recalling a story his uncle had once told him, at the same location, about a country called the People's Republic of Zhang.

'The People's Republic of Zhang has so many people that they cannot find original names for newly born babies.' Omollo remembered what he was once told by his uncle. 'When a baby is born in the People's Republic of Zhang, an iron wheel is banged down and the sound it produces becomes the name of the baby in question. That explains why its citizens are called *Wang Tung, Li Jing, Wang Ping, Zhang Yong* or *Teeng Puung.*' Omollo laughed even more as he recalled what his uncle claimed to be the origin of the onomatopoeic names of the Zhangians.

"I miss you my uncle," Omollo later said and his eyes now started welling up with tears.

It was then five years since his beloved uncle had been brutally murdered for allegedly annoying his assailant. It happened that his uncle had impregnated somebody's daughter in the village and, instead of apologizing and paying damage for the offense, he started calling himself *the Digger of the Dug*. The story adds that the father of the girl warned him several times to drop the name but Uncle Ongoro turned a deaf ear, thinking that he was smarter and more well travelled than the father. But at the end of the day, he was found hanging on a tamarind tree and people said it was the father of the girl who had taught him an eternal lesson. That evening, Omollo wondered where such unique lands that his uncle would talk about so animatedly could possibly be, as he thought he could, from that elevation, see a point where the sky was joining with the earth, at the Ramatula Mountains.

"What did my uncle exactly mean by 'world has no end?'" He mused to himself, but could not find a convincing answer.

"Mmmm!" He sighed deeply and said audibly to himself, "I wish I could go to such lands by myself and prove the extent to which that man was lying."

"I swear by the God of Thunder that when I grow up, I will go wherever my uncle went," he added, "I will go and board a bus at the village bus stop and travel to distant places. Why not?"

He now looked down to the highway, which would take him to the lands of his dreams: it was meandering across the villages in that region like a snake on a lawn. His uncle said vehicles on that highway were commuting between a town in the west and another one in the east. Omollo at that juncture imagined the funniness of a place called *town* and grinned. According to his late uncle.

'A town is a beautiful place where human dung is revered more than a village chief.' He recalled how his uncle had once defined a town for him.

'Town dwellers build a house for human dung, plaster it, and fit it with an artificial waterfall for the dung to glide-swim down the valley like a swan on a stream.' He remembered the clarification of the term *town* by his uncle, and was amazed at how the man could have been so good in telling lies.

"Mhmmh, my uncle was a talented liar," he wondered aloud upon that memory.

"Since when is a house built for human feces," he thought and a broad grin spread across his face.

"Even Professor Girado himself has a town-like house, yet he has not such a side house for dung," he reasoned.

"He, like any other villagers, relieves himself in the bush when here in the village," he mused and smiled long again.

That evening, a few vehicles were passing on the highway – most likely to and from the towns at its opposite ends. Some of his mates sitting on the lower rocks had their eyes fixed on the highway too. Unlike Omollo, however, they were contemplating neither about their past nor future escapades; rather, they were paying attention to possessing such vehicles as were emerging from either side of the highway.

As soon as a vehicle came into view, they would quickly notice it and compete to shout: 'That is mine' and as per their rule, the first to shout the expression was the bona fide owner of the vehicle in question. Then the rest would wait patiently for their turns to come – if another vehicle appeared at all. Omollo, however, pitied the boys for how unrealistic their dreams were, considering that no Rabarian, apart from Professor Girado, had possessed a motorcar since the creation of the planet Earth. In fact, a joke was going around that a stone lion in front of Gagamoya Palace would roar whenever a Malan bought a car; again, he grinned at the image of the stone lion roaring.

Tired of thinking 'non-sense', he got up, climbed down the rock and walked at a snail's pace towards his colleagues eating *ochuoga* some meters away. There were so many of such fruits on the trees and they ate to their fill, even packing some in their shorts pockets for their sisters at home.

Obongo, grandson of Othik Mbuku, one of their ringleaders, next proposed the sport of taking aim with stones. All the boys applauded his idea and lined up in a row. Obongo then walked about seventy meters away and fixed a pole on the ground as a target. The boys would then take aim at the target in turns. Everybody had ten chances to throw. Accordingly, some missed all their throws and were booed and laughed at with great enthusiasm. Omollo, however, was good at the game and only missed a few chances. Others hit the target so hard it blew away, necessitating Obongo from time to time to run and re-fix it.

But at some point, they grew tired of taking aim and hence replaced the activity with the sport of setting up bird traps. For twenty minutes or so, each of them was busy setting up his bird trap in the form of ground trap, gum trap, thread trap, elastic trap or *odheru* trap.

Soon the boys realized that the darkness was encroaching upon the earth. Consequently, they hurried to the Rocks of Happy Ghosts for the last sport on the hill as their own rule required. At the Rocks of Happy Ghosts, one would shout something and the rocks would shout it back to the villagers loudly and clearly. Everybody believed that joke-loving ghosts lived amongst that pack of giant rocks – everybody except Uncle Ongoro, who idiosyncratically claimed the rocks were *echoing*.

That evening, the boys on the hill joked about boys in their village who would sleep in their mothers' huts, steal food from their mothers' cooking pots, wet their beds at night or stay with their mothers in the kitchen. The mode of the joke was that they would shout the jokes to the ghosts and the ghosts would amplify them to the boys back in the village. The advantage was that the poor boys in the lowlands had no amplifier through which to retaliate to slurs from their fellows on the hill. Eventually, everybody had had enough fun on the hill and thus hurried home, meanwhile looking forward to returning to the same location on the following day for more fun.

<<<*CHAPTER SIX*>>>

It was the eve of *teng'o* – the last celebration to honour the deceased. It would be conducted a day before the dispersal from the deceased's homestead. As per the custom of the Malans, the clan had invited the best musician in the land to immortalize the event. That was, of course, none other than Abur Obala, *the Owner of the Dog*, his name suggesting that he was as creative as the owner of a dog – they who normally speaks Linglish language even if they had never walked through the door of a classroom. It was claimed that even a monolingual speaker of Malan who owned a dog would still command the dog in Linglish-like sentences such as, 'Come on, Poppy, we are livu now.'

Abur Obala, the man they had invited for the very day, played his music so well that even goats, the restless, would stop to listen to him playing. Given his fame, the dinner was, on the this day, not only prepared in a hurry but also taken on time to ensure that the music could start as soon as possible. And to brighten that pure dark night, two pressure lamps were lit and hung on two sisal poles at the compound.

The Owner of the Dog, who had been sitting in the middle of the compound, next burst out into one of his best songs of all time, by which, he was deliberately affirming to listeners that he was the real *Owner of the Dog* and not a counterfeit Obala, for other musicians would often impersonate him for the sake of pulling a crowd.

No sooner had he ended the first song than the youths from Rabar and its environs began flooding into the deceased's compound. These were in small groups of either boys or girls. As usual, they were carrying with them *sjamboks*, clubs, partly because they always moved in the darkness to and from their homes, and thus they were likely to encounter dangerous animals on their way. Most importantly though, they armed themselves because fights would always ensue among the youths in the funeral music for the simple reason that not showing violence during such music was tantamount to imbecility. The youths from one clan would plot chaos in the funeral music organized by a different clan, either for fun or for making a statement that they were stronger than the latter. Indeed, the funeral music in a clan of weak youths would not cross the night without disruption. Nonetheless, disruption of the music was out of expectations on that particular night, considering that the event was taking a place in Orina's clan, which by chance was also the clan of Okelo Chunja, a man whose name was synonymous with strength and aggression in Rabar and its environs. The rampant rumour was that he once hurled a club at a gazelle: the weapon missed its target but bore through the wall of a nearby hut and broke the jaw of a man drinking porridge on a three-legged stool inside the hut. Soon, the number of prospective dancers was many enough for the funeral music to start. The eager youths were gathering around the band and just waiting for *the referee* – the man in charge of all dancing activities at the dance arena – to be revealed. As per the custom, that *referee* had to be the strongest of all the attendees of the funeral music on that particular night in order for him to be able successfully to maintain discipline at the arena.

After a long wait, the referee popped up before the audience with the confidence of a military tank on a rampage. As expected, he was Okello Chunja, a.k.a. *Subduer* or *All of You Combined* – a nickname derived from his stock phrase of 'I can beat you, your father and your mother combined'. Following his appearance, many attendees welcomed him with thunderous applause, yet some mumbled words of disapproval of him as a referee, which Okello heard and did not take lightly.

As confident as a wooden spoon descending into a boiling pot, Okello swaggered from one corner of the arena to another with his deadly *sjambok* in his right hand.

"Who is that cowardly cockroach craving for a *sjambok?*" He tried to catch at least one of the youths who had murmured words of dissatisfaction of him, albeit without any success, but the crowd went quiet as no one wished to experience humiliation from this certified tyrant. Now, contented with the amount of threat he had oozed, he burst into a proclamation in a tone he deemed befitting the most powerful young man in the whole of Malaland.

"Ok! Young men, we are soon starting our music. All those who have come here to dance will dance until morning. Nevertheless, I know that among you are some rotten 'mangoes.' I take this opportunity to warn any 'cockroach' who plots chaos tonight to kill his plan with immediate effect. I swear by my mother Agonda Nyonjare that I won't let such a person go back home with a complete set of teeth in his mouth," he swore, while simulating the self-cutting of his throat with a pointing finger.

His words, as usual, stirred the crowd again, as some applauded his pronouncements, whereas, others murmured about him being too arrogant. Okello nonetheless paused and waited for them to finish their temporary disobedience. The he resumed his bluster.

"Keep on making noise, but be rest assured that I will break your jaw like a clay pot the moment I catch you," he bragged more and some youths again protested against what he had just said, which signaled him to intensify his terror.

"Let me hear mumbles again and I will now not bother to distinguish who has mumbled from who has not. I will just whip everybody in the direction that mumbles have come from. Do you hear me, cowards?"

His threat worked wonders. No more mumbles were heard (mumblers might have feared being reported to the certified monster by their coward colleagues). Okello now continued with his proclamation in the quiet atmosphere he had long wished for.

"All the girls who have come here have definitely come to dance. Now, if you are a girl, don't wait for someone to look for you in the darkness and drag you here," he said, "all other rules of the funeral music remain unaltered. I now ask girls to begin trickling here to the center," he concluded.

Next, he blew a whistle ordering the band to start playing, which it did. Shortly afterwards, a few girls were seen walking with their heads covered, out of shyness, to the center. Others let themselves be gently pushed to the center – lest somebody think they were easy girls. All the groups of the girls squatted down collectively near the band, most of them showing their ease by singing along with the musicians, but a fraction of them acting as if they were forced to be there, going by their gloomy faces. No one cared how they looked though, based on the fact that the girls of Malaland were well known for saying "No" when they meant "Yes."

The referee now pushed the crowd backwards until the arena was open enough for the dancing activity to start. His work this day was nonetheless amazingly easy, as the audience allowed themselves to be shoved (elsewhere, they would have resisted such pushing and a fight might have ensued but here they behaved themselves, well aware that they were between the sharp fangs of *Subduer*).

As the ground remained open, the referee gave the youths in shorts an opportunity to dance with the girls for five minutes without payment – which was, of course, a convention in the funeral music. Accordingly, the boys in shorts seized the girls and danced with them as thirstily as possible. No sooner had four minutes elapsed than the referee blew his whistle to declare that their free time was over. Procedurally, the same offer was next given to youths in trousers. Likewise, their free time soon elapsed and the dancing with the girls remained the monopoly of those few young men who could afford it – those who could pay to dance with the girls or let themselves be heard.

With cash, a man could now make people sit down for him, clap for him or stop dancing for him in the funeral music. And no sooner had the cash session started than Apuka Awiyo called the referee, paid twenty shillings and ordered that all men vacate the arena and leave him to dance with all the girls alone. The referee, as usual, announced the order and Apuka was the only man in the arena, who was now dancing with all the girls as vigorously as a healthy goat kid that has just fed on its mother's milk. He indeed danced for a while but, upon feeling enough pride, he stopped the music in order to chant his praise names.

"The musician!" He burst out into a loud, rough voice.

"Eee Baba, what do you say?" Replied Obala in a polite tone.

"Before you is Apuka Awiyo. I am *the Central Bank* – that which has never run bankrupt from time immemorial.

I am also the Government – that which can whisk your mother away and you do not have the balls to stop it.

I am also the Bees – they that chase away soldiers with loaded AK-47s in their hands.

I am also the Madman – he whose erection at the well sends women fleeing at the speed of a whirlwind."

He then paid 30 shillings and left the arena, leaving the enthusiastic audience laughing like a pack of feasting hyenas because of the entertainment he had just given them. No sooner had he left the ground than another youth by the nickname of Thousands and Thousands stepped in. This one dug his palm into his pockets and fished out a fat, black wallet, which was actually older than he himself. He opened it, took out a 100/= note and handed it to the referee for buying his time to brag.

"*The Owner of the Dog*," he addressed the chief musician by his praise name.

"Eee baba," replied Obala in his normal soft and soothing tone.

"I am declaring to you, for sure, that no one is greater in this land than I, Abola, Thousands and Thousands.

I am *the Bridegroom of the Ugly Bride* – he who takes his ugly bride to his uncle's place and his uncle inwardly disapproves of his choice of a wife but externally deludes him with sweet talk, saying, 'Oh, my dear nephew, is this a wife whom God has blessed you with?' His nephew out of ignorance answers, 'Yes, uncle, this is the one whom God has blessed me with.' His uncle next gives him a long, but bogus piece of wisdom: 'Right my son. I pray that you guys everlastingly stay together in peace and harmony. A human being is not food, to say that one would eat it. We all know that a good wife is she who is capable of bearing someone babies – and after all, who has ever predicted the mother of a king just from her looks?"

Leaving the crowd in raucous laughter, he ordered the deduction of 30 shillings from his note to suspend the order of not dancing with girls, which Apuka had earlier on imposed. But upon hearing that his order had been revoked, Apuka immediately paid twenty shillings and recaptured the arena. He next paid 30 shillings more to restore his order. Abola in retaliation paid forty shillings to suspend the order that Apuka had instituted but Apuka paid fifty to restore it.

Followed by Abola sixty, Apuka seventy, Abola eighty. In the end, Abola carried the day and now the men resumed dancing with the girls after a long pause.

All these activities pleased Omollo so much that from time to time he found himself grinning from ear to ear. He wished he were grown up and had money on him to take part in such shows. That day, he would have got up and told the crowd his praise name that he was sure would have also thrown them into shrieks of laughter. He would have proclaimed:

"I am Omollo, *the Ewe* – a name deriving from the fact that I am as difficult to understand as milking the ewe – that which it takes ten strong people to milk. That is, four people holding its four limbs apart to make it stay put for the milker to milk. Plus the fifth person milking it. Plus the sixth person tightening its mouth so that it cannot bite the milker. Plus the seventh person blocking its anus so that it cannot drop dung in the milking pot. Plus the eighth person picking out fur from the milking pot for the milk to remain pure. Plus the ninth person covering its eyes so that it cannot see a dog, struggle and pour the milk away. Plus the tenth person wiping its runny nose so that it does not wet the milker with its nasal discharge."

All the same, the boys of his age never spoke in the funeral music. The only thing for him to do was eat a lot and grow big to qualify for participation in that sort of music. Understanding his limitations, Omollo remained just admiring the show.

Then it reached 12:00 midnight, which was synonymous with the most interesting session of the funeral music – *the girls' auction time*. During this session, the best male dancer would dance with each girl competing for a female dance trophy that had to be awarded each time the funeral music was conducted. To be the best male dance and have the privilege, one had to win the male dance contest on that particular night.

No sooner had the referee announced the session than fifteen young men invaded the arena to compete for the male vacancy – to dance solo with each girl in the show. As per the custom, the band played them one of their danceable hits for them to show what they had in their dance stores.

The contest of the young men, of course, appeared tough from its onset. All staged incredible performances that caused the referee and the audience to be at a loss over whom to pick as a winner in that first round. But as long as pruning participants in such contests was as unavoidable as a death of an old man, four youths eventually got the green light to take it to a second round in one of the most controversial decisions in Malaland to date.

The ground was thus left free for the four best of the best on the given night. The band again played them another danceable song so that they could play their cards better, lest they raise any excuse of a bad tune. Wow! It was an incredible dance, such that judges were again at a loss over who had actually won in that session. Nevertheless, a winner had to be declared and the lucky two were the famous male dancers in the villages: Odanga Nyambeu and Ochila Mudho.

The crowd now applauded the judgment as wise and just – actually, because everybody longed to see these two competing again since they had previously competed for the title twice: Ochila won the first contest, whereas, in the second contest the crown went to Odanga. In this light, it was thrilling like a dinner in the sky to see who would take that title that night.

Immediately, the referee blew his whistle to order that the contest proceed and the band began playing another good danceable song of the time. Odanga Nyambeu was the first to get the chance to compete. He was assigned a beautiful girl to accompany him to the arena – to inspire him to perform to the best of his capacity. Odanga launched his winning campaign by dancing like a drunkard, whereby, he occasionally teased as if he had stumbled on something and appeared as if he was about to fall down every time, but did not fall at all. The style was quite amusing, yet this was just an introduction of his dance. As his dance progressed, he bent his legs until his buttocks were as low as the height of a dog and then started swaying his waist back and forth and sideways – all according to the beats of the music. He danced like this for about four minutes – the crowd now wildly cheered for him for his incredible performance, actually considering that to be his best style. Contrary to their expectations, Odanga soon folded his hands in the manner of a kung-fu fighter and started quivering every organ of his body, simultaneously moving forward slowly but as gracefully as a chameleon on a lawn. And as the song ended, a colossal noise engulfed the arena – as no one believed Ochila could have something to show to that already predisposed audience to convince them he was better than Odanga.

Ochila, who all the while had been watching Odanga, indeed appreciated his performance. Notwithstanding, he was still most determined to prove the predisposed audience wrong in their bias that

Odanga had already won the title even before they had witnessed the amount of resistance he would exert. First, he closed his eyes and drew inspiration from his inner voice. Next, he reminded himself that he was not ready to see a second defeat from Odanga in less than two months.

"By hook and crook, you must win this title today," his inner voice scolded him and he heard it.

"You must prove to these people that you are the coach and that Odanga is a trainee," the voice added and the words pierced his heart like a rocket to the sky.

According to the procedure, the referee now blew his whistle to mark the beginning of Ochila's round. Accordingly, Ochila stepped in the arena with all eyes on him – obviously to pity him for losing the competition by a knockout. Determined to turn the tables though, Ochila began his victory campaign with a funny old dancing style called *rigirigi* – which honestly split the lips of every attendee in the form of laughter or giggle. While the audience was still admiring his nostalgic style, he suddenly plunged on the ground and started jerking his hands and feet up as intermittently as the rhythm of the then playing music. After a while, he stood up and launched a dancing style I can refer to as the *kill mosquito style*, whereby, he would slap here and there on his body with his palms, just like someone attacking biting mosquitoes. Wonderfully, his slap jigsaw fitted the beat of the playing song and the audience was bewildered. In the twinkling of an eye, he kept the rest of his body static, except for the area between the belly button and the knees – a.k.a the naughty area – which he kept on swinging back and forth rhythmically like a belly dancer. What's more, he appeared to be shrinking in height like a lorry on a muddy road and, all of a sudden, he was on the ground. As people widened their eyes to get a clear picture of the proceedings, Ochila was crawling on his stomach like a python – again, amazingly, according to the beat of the playing music. And as people continued to gaze at Ochila's miracles, he somersaulted up and rested with his head down and his legs up, yet continued dancing as if he was in a normal posture. As the music stopped, the crowd now shouted unanimously and intermittently: "Ochila!" "Ochila!" "Ochila!"

Ochila's victory concluded the males' dance contest. He was declared the best male dancer and was accordingly rewarded with dancing with every competing girl at that night's girls' dancing contest.

It was then the ladies' turn to compete for the coveted dance trophy of that night, this time one by one. The girl who won the trophy would enjoy popularity throughout Rabar Village and its environs and hence would drive young men crazy in her own village and beyond. Every young man who mattered would want to be in a relationship with such a girl – and in that way, she would be a queen with all instruments

of power in her hands. Besides, the winner would become a topic at
the bathing gatherings by the riversides.

In this light, every girl wished to win such a dance trophy and
would thus always work hard overtly or covertly to win it. Unlike in
men's contest bouts (where a decision was by applause), the victorious
girl would be decided by the amount of money she fetched in what was
known as the "girls' auction mart." In such an auction, men competed
in buying the dancing girls and the highest priced girl would be the
overall winner of the contest. In other words, the girls' dance contest
was also the girls' auction session. As per the tradition, the referee
surveyed the group of girls and chose Anyango Toti to pioneer the
contest. He led her to the arena and signaled the musicians to stop
playing so that he could introduce her to potential buyers. He now
burst out in proclamations:

"Dear young men. I am hereby presenting to you a black
beauty. Here is Anyango Toti, a girl whose skin has never
been touched by a pimple." He paused shortly as the group
cheered for her jubilantly before suddenly continuing.

"Oh Yes! 'Bon twenty,'" he announced the initial price.

"Thirty!" An unknown bidder upped the price.

The referee next called: "Thirty for the first time ..."
Then, after a pause, "thirty for the second time ..."

"Forty!" Another bidder shouted. Then it became quiet
again.

The referee now blew the whistle signaling the band to resume playing
and at his command, they did. Anyango thus began her winning
campaign by girding her *khanga* tightly around her hornet's waist
– actually so tightly that an astronaut could have seen her *kibo* and
mawenzi from outer space. Thereafter, she began dancing shyly and
lazily in such a way that many people gave up watching her, thinking
that she was not motivated enough to win the dance trophy that night.
On the contrary, she kept on accelerating her moves as the music
continued playing and by the fifth minute, everyone was up on their
feet, struggling to get a glimpse of Anyango's live miracles. At the
climax, Anyango and her male professional dancer were performing
a bumping style, in which a man and a woman knock each other's
butt, fists, cheeks or chests, then dance separately for a while and
bump again. From their expertise in that area, each move they made
persistently bewildered the spectators, who generously rewarded them
with cheers at the top of their voices.

The referee, who knew very well the right time to tap money
from the youths, now blew the whistle in the midst of this beautiful
performance by Anyango and her associate, thus obliging the music
to pause. The whole crowd, of course, shouted their disapproval,

despite the fact they knew very well that funeral music was supposed to be conducted in that manner. The referee surveyed the crowd, then continued with his auction:

"Bon, forty!" He shouted.

"Bon, fifty!" The first bidder bade.

"Sixty!" The second bidder scaled up the price.

"Seventy!" Another shouted.

"Eighty!" Another bidder yelled. Then the crowd felt silent again.

<<<*CHAPTER SEVEN*>>>

Two months after Nyambori's burial, the village was quiet again. People carried on with their daily duties and the sun, as usual, kept rising in the east and setting in the west. The graceful moon equally carried on with its full cycle, while the wind blew as it had been doing from pre-colonial times. Cattle, goats, dogs continued mating, while beans germinated and grew, just as they had been doing since the beginning of the world. It was therefore crystal clear that the death of Nyambori Wiotel did not bring any of the changes envisaged by prophets of dooms to Malaland.

It was further clear that even those who pledged to die with Nyambori, like Nyorondo, were simply garnering the attention of mourners, or to put it kindly, were professional actors of the village. Nyorondo in particular had earlier suggested through her funeral song that her life was empty without Nyambori and, of course, went as far as begging death to descend and scoop her so she could be with Nyambori, *Father of Mercy* in Paradise. And as if death immensely felt sorry for Nyorondo, for missing Nyambori too much, death did indeed approach her at the end of that week.

On the day that a benevolent death came for Nyorondo, she and other young women were swimming at River Ramar. As usual, all were naked and did not know that naughty boys from the opposite ridge had agitated wild bees in a nearby tree. The revelation only came when a swarm of bees swooped on them like a hawk on a chick. Ooh, Gash! The villagers were then treated to a nerve-wracking drama after it was discovered that Elder Nyorondo on that day outran all the young women and children with whom she was swimming at River Ramar – all in order to remain alive and continue eating. Believe me, she became the first escapee to the village, exceptionally in her birthday suit and without the walking stick, which everybody had earlier on supposed she could not walk without. Philosophers of Rabar Village later joked that her reaction stunned death itself.

In summary, life in Rabar Village was quite normal even without Nyambori Wiotel – evidence being that Omollo and his kin were that evening killing time, as usual, by telling each other folktales and fables at the bonfire.

"Story, story." One of Omollo's younger sisters opened the storytelling session.

"Story come, entertainment abound," her listeners replied together.

"Long time ago a rat and a snake were living in a thick forest," the young girl continued.

"Ehee," her listeners encouraged her to speak.

"Now it happened that the rat who was trotting around stepped on the snake who was sleeping leisurely in the tall grass.

"As bad tempered as he was, the snake now hissed *disgustedly* and thereafter asked the rat angrily: 'Why are you stepping on me young man?' 'I am very sorry, bro. I did not do it on purpose,' the rat apologized. But the snake rejected the apology: 'Nyo nyo nyo, you are so ancient-minded: no wonder you have grown beards all over your body at the age of seven,' he reacted and now drove the rat to respond to his insult: 'And you are so childish, no wonder you are still crawling at the age of seventy.' The rat joked and its joke angered the snake everlastingly – evidence being that, the snake is chasing the rat for revenge to this day." The young girl now finished her story and left her audience rolling with laughter. Thereafter, Omollo took his turn to tell the audience his longer and more interesting story.

"Story, story," Omollo said in his usual sonorous voice.

"Story come, entertainment abound," his listeners replied together, as was required of them.

"Long, long time ago, the goats played bao, the monkeys played drums, and the pigs conducted weddings." He paused as a ripple of laughter radiated from the bonfire at the center of their father's compound.

"In those days, the lion was the King of all animals in the land for his strength and wisdom.

Lion, the King, lived peacefully and happily with his family and his citizens. Ceremonies were, however, part and parcel of the King's life. It was rumoured that he would have ceremonies at least once monthly for whatever reason. Interestingly, there was no clear cut between a small and a big event to Lion, the King.

Accordingly, it occurred that the King had his father's memorial ceremony on that day. As per his custom, he set to immortalize the day through memorable things to the attendees of the event. First, he prepared a lot of food and plenty of drinks. Next, he invited all sorts of animals to come and see his pride.

For Lion's honour, most game abandoned their daily duties for the King's feast. Every animal put on the best they possessed. And as clothes make the man, even the ugly warthog was effortlessly handsome in his black suit on that particular day. Overall, everyone was sure to eat, drink and dance to their capacity. Of course, they ate and drank as much as their tummies allowed them – even Mr. Hyena, who had been bragging to everyone that his stomach was elastic, could not finish the King's food.

With regard to music, the event was graced by Mr. Ong'eche – a musician who was better to his fans known as 'the magician'. As he and his band started playing their first hit, every game guided their partner to their allocated dancing arena – big animals on the one side and small ones on the other. Wow! Every minute that elapsed accelerated and intensified the dance, with every dancer showing their best in the dancing arena. A long-necked giraffe was for instance dangling his long, springy neck back and forth until it looked as if it was going to disintegrate. Mr. Snake, his neighbour, was standing up on his tail, meanwhile twisting his body up, down, and sideways just in the same way old men dance with their heads.

Ooh, Gash! Even the always-shy sheep was jumping up and down rhythmically to the beats of the music, swinging her fatty tail sideways like the windscreen wiper of a car: this actually causing her to attract more applause than all the rest of the dancers at the arena.

Mr. Ong'eche, the Monkey, was, of course, well known in Malaland for his 'Confusion Song' – such a good song that a demon would descend and rest upon dancers whenever it was played. In particular, the song would inexplicably confuse a son to dance with his mother-in-law or a daughter to dance with his father-in-law and so forth.

Even so, no attendee of Ong'eche's music would be satisfied without listening to the 'Confusion Song' – no matter how it breached animal culture. In this light, the applause was almost causing an earthquake when Mr. Ong'eche eventually announced he was going to play the Confusion Song.

As soon as Mr. Ong'eche started the song in a clear and sharp voice, all the animals got up and invaded the arena together. Once there, each danced wildly as if competing with its neighbour. As a result, it became as chaotic as a site where a bomb has just gone off. That is, hooved animals blew a thick dust, which blurred the whole environment, and the odor of the dancers made the air even thicker than blood.

It thus reached a point where the boundary between the provision for jumbo and minute dancers was blurred by the ongoing chaos. Consequently, big game mixed with small in the arena and they did not even perceive the danger involved in the act.

To make matters worse, Mr. Ong'eche's band, intensified every note of guitars, stretched concertinas to the fullest, rang bells to maximum effect with time. The dance was therefore hot like fire.

(Tundi x 2, tundi x 2)^4, (tndelele x 1, tndelele x2)^6

(Tundi x 2, tundi x 2)^4, (tndelele x 1, tndelele x2)^6– it went.

But amidst this excitement, there came a cry of agony that shocked everyone around.

"Wallahi! Toba, you have killed me!"

The dancers, who had been accelerating, now found themselves knocking each other's heads like rams as they tried suddenly to stop their gliding bodies to make sense of what was happening. But even after coming to a halt, they still could not locate the source of the cry of agony they were hearing, due to rising dust all over the place. As a substitute, they used their ears to recognize the voice of the victim.

At last, it was established what had happened. Mr. Tortoise, the Coat's Owner, had been trampled on by Mr. Elephant, the Giant. In consequence, the whole group of animals congregated around him to assess the extent of damage caused on his body and to try to give him first aid. Upon scrutiny, it became apparent his shell was fractured, his nose bleeding and his hearing gone. And when he tried to cough, only fire came out of his mouth and flew straightaway to the king's grass-thatched huts.

The huts thus caught fire and it was obvious that the entire palace would burn down. To make a bad situation worse, the wooden fence enclosing the homestead would soon catch fire and the life of every participant at the compound would be in danger. In the face of this eminent threat, what followed in short order was a stampede hitherto unseen in the history of the land, as everyone tried to flee the compound as fast as their feet could carry them. But luckily enough, Lion, the King, was famous both on Earth and in Heaven. Therefore, as Mr. Rain saw his palace burning, he immediately rained heavily to quench the fire before it caused any serious harm to the king's buildings.

'Splendid!' Every animal heaped praises on Mr. Rain for his heroic act of quenching the awful fire, except Mrs. Crow whose eggs he rained on. Mrs. Crow had that morning observed the sky and concluded that there would be no rain – hence left her eggs uncovered on the nest.

As she expected, upon arriving back home, she found her eggs literally floating on a sea of rainwater in her nest. This made her so angry that she vowed to take Mr. Rain to the King's court the next day, allegedly, for malice against his fellow citizen.

Nonetheless, Mr. Sun, who had been watching Mrs. Crow the whole way, sympathized with her greatly and chose to shine to help her dry her wet eggs.

Mrs. Crow thus praised Mr. Sun very much and cooperated by spreading her eggs on a nearby rock to dry. But to share this sad news, she flew away to her sweetheart, who was then on a hunting mission some kilometers away.

But no sooner had she left her eggs to dry, than Mr. Adhagaria, the Monitor, came across them spread on the ground. As the Monitor, had been going hungry for two days, he supposed these were abandoned eggs and thus thanked his fair god for that rare gift as he gulped Mrs. Crow's eggs greedily. So, in the twinkling of an eye, the rock's surface was left with nothing resembling eggs. Mr. Adhagaria who was now full, then walked away quite satisfied and happy.

Soon, Mrs. Crow was back to return her eggs to the nest. But to her surprise, there was not even so much as a shell where she had spread her eggs to dry. She and her posse, of course, searched everywhere for the eggs but did not find any in the wider area. The Crows thereafter reported the sad event to Lion, the King, who became quite offended and thus vowed to cut the head of the culprit in public if caught. To show commitment to his words, he ordered his state prosecutors to do their job and soon the terrorist in question was apprehended. To the amazement of everybody, the terrorist was none other than Mr. Adhagaria, the Monitor, which surprised everybody. For a long time, his colleagues had noticed his unsocial and unfriendly behaviors, yet tolerated them in the belief that he was harmless. Now that the evidence was screaming that he was a wolf in sheep's clothing, they altogether approved that he be executed.

At last, the day of the execution of the terrorist of the land came. Accordingly, the King called on all animals to come and see how justice was implemented in his Kingdom. Following his words, they turned up for the event in such numbers that one could not find even a place to throw saliva. Sitting on his throne, the King ordered his guards to bring out Mr. Adhagaria before the spectators. As he was being led to the witness box, everyone shouted enthusiastically that his head swiftly be cut. Even so, the angry but wise King, who had his eyes fixed on Mr. Adhagaria the whole way, saw something unexplainable in the face of the accused. That is, he appeared to the King too innocent to have committed the crime he was charged with. Due to this supposition, the King spontaneously wanted to know what might have motivated that innocent-looking creature to commit the offense. What followed is, of course, a legend still told today in Malaland:

The King: Adhagaria, the Monitor

Mr. Adhagaria: Naam; his Royal Highness.
Adhagaria your servant is loyal to you and your Kingdom eternally.

The King: Why did you gulp the Crows eggs?

Mr. Adhagaria: His Highness, for I found the eggs scattered on a rock, near no one's habitat and thus I supposed they were abandoned.

Upon hearing this response, the King was moved even more and now ordered that Mrs. Crow be brought before him to explain why she had scattered her eggs on the rock. After Mrs. Crow was brought, the king carried on with his interrogation.

The King: Mrs. Crow, is it true that you scattered your eggs on the rock?

Mrs. Crow: Yes, His Highness. I did that because they were rained on.

The King: And who rained on them?

Mrs. Crow: It was Mr. Rain, His Highness.

The king then ordered that Mr. Rain be immediately brought and, by command, he was soon standing before the court. The King then went on with the interrogation.

The King: Rain! Why did you rain on and wet Mrs. Crow's eggs?

Mr. Rain: I did not mean it His Highness. I just rained to quench the fire that was burning your palace.

On hearing this, the king immediately released Mr. Rain and ordered that Mr. Fire be brought out – and, by command, he was in the dock in a few minutes. The King continued with his interrogation.

The King: Fire! Why did you choose to burn my home and cause all these troubles?

Mr. Fire: It is not my fault His Highness. It is the fault of Mr. Tortoise who coughed me out.

Visibly angry, the king next ordered that Mr. Tortoise be brought in the dock and he interrogated him.

The King: Tortoise! Why did you cough out fire and cause all this hell of troubles?

Mr. Tortoise: It is not me, His Highness; it is Mr. Elephant who injured me to the extent that I could only cough out fire.

Next, the King summoned Mr. Elephant – and proceeded with his case.

The King: Elephant! Why did you trample on Tortoise's back, caused him to spit fire and cause all these troubles in my kingdom?

Mr. Elephant: It was not my fault, His Highness. It was the fault of Mr. Ong'eche who played 'the Confusion Song', which got all animals confused. It was also the fault of your servants who gave us so much beer that we could no longer reason.

After hearing this, Lion, the King, bowed his head down and thought deeply. He came to realize that the case was intertwined like a cobweb and that the newest thread was aiming towards him. He would have dismissed the case right away but he knew very well that his people would then *smell a rat in his* proceedings. He thus raised his head and ordered that Mr. Ong'eche and his servants be brought before the court. Then, went on.

The King: Ong'eche! And why did you play too good music, which confused all the animals and brought all these troubles in my kingdom?

Mr. Ong'eche: Did not I do as you ordered me, Ooo His Highness? Blame your servants who made them drunk with beer, Oooh!

The King, hurt by Mr. Ong'eche's reply, next turned to his servants and asked them sternly:

The King: And you servants, why did you serve

animals with much beer and hence caused
all these troubles in my kingdom?

The Servants (*in chorus*): Didn't we do as you told
us, His Highness?

They replied and broke the King's heart – for their
evidence was now leading to him as the only perpetrator of
the offense. He thus once more bowed his head to ponder
the issue deeply. At last, he raised his head and faced the
audience.

The King: Abathimassss, (*He addressed the people with
their special name*)

The Crowd (*thunderously*): "Ooooh!"

The King: "Abathimassss"

The Crowd: "Ooooh!"

The King: "Your king, the King of....

Pooo! Poooooooooooooooooooooooooo! Poooooooooo! The silent
night was now interrupted by the sharp familiar sound of a bull's horn
from atop Rabar Hill. Everyone, of course, knew it was Adika's horn
and thus kept quiet to avoid a fine for talking when the horn was being
blown – normally a fat ram or a he-goat

Adika was a village crier charged with the making of all
proclamations from Rabar Village Chieftainship. His clear, far-reaching
voice, oratory strength and wit qualified him as crier for life of Rabar
Village – and indeed, everyone at that moment wished he would open
his mouth and say something. Interestingly, Adika was only paid in
kind for his noble service to Rabarians: a permanent seat in every
feast in the village and the left forelimb of every slain beast slain in
a hunting event he had proclaimed. That evening, all who guessed
he would proclaim a hunting event lost miserably. Instead, he had a
message he had never delivered in his entire career. Accordingly, that
day he blew his horn idiosyncratically and longer than usual. When
he was sure the whole village was listening, he appended his tin-made
speaker to his mouth and burst out into a proclamation.

"Ooooooooooooooooooooh shyap! X 2

"Malans, the grandchildren of Ramogi, we are lucky
over other people. We have a good land, and our land is
willing to gift every talented son or daughter. Those who
can do things which none has ever done, or those who
can do things which have been done but in new ways they
have never been done before. Our sons and daughters are
talented and our offspring are enjoying life.

However! The Devil has planted thorns among us. You
all remember Nyambori Wiotel, he was a bull of bulls, but
wicked people deprived us of him in untimely fashion.

The village has in consequence invited a magician who is going to separate tears from the wheat. So, tomorrow! I say tomorrow morning! Every adult shall gather at Wiotel's home for the exercise. Whoever is absent is our professional witch and we will right away excommunicate them together with their families for good. Peace and love blossom in your lives forever the grandchildren of Rapemo."

Then quietness dominated the whole village for almost three minutes. Later on, everyone was discussing the pronouncement and their perception of it in their own way. Nevertheless, it was late and soon each of them had to go to bed.

<<<*CHAPTER EIGHT*>>>

Following the previous night's proclamation, Omollo was experiencing a blend of child-like excitement and fear about what would transpire on that memorable day as he walked towards the homestead of the late person. For a long time, he had heard people saying that Ghati could reincarnate herself into a bird or a goat. More recently, the story was told of how Ghati had caught the thief of a cockerel at a nearby village. It was said, shortly after receiving an invitation from the cockerel's owner, she put her talisman at the crime scene and left for an unknown destination. According to the story, no sooner had she left than the cockerel started crowing in the thief's stomach. Moreover, Omollo had heard that she could fly from one corner of the earth to another on a mere winnowing basket. To Omollo, therefore, it was an indescribable experience that such a legend was in the same village as him to perform what she had been gifted with by the compassionate gods of Gondwana. In this light, he now wanted to appreciate the performance of the diviner priestess, whose praises were as rampant as poverty in the slums.

When he arrived at Wiotel's home, the crowd was already congregating around Ghati, the Magician. In other words, he had to push and shove others for no less than fifteen minutes to catch a glimpse of Ghati in action (the woman he longed to see with all his emotions).

When he first saw her, she had a long knife stabbed in her stomach and blood was gushing down her lower body from an unknown location like a spring. Elsewhere, a big python was coiling around her body from foot to head. And as if that was not enough, she held in her hands the head of Otilla Mberu, whom she had just slaughtered. As usual, people who knew Ghati better were smiling in the knowledge that she was capable of killing and resurrecting, whereas, those who did not know her better, like Omollo, were mourning for the brutal murder of Otilla. What was not adding up to Omollo though was the fact that people were still gathering around her, just gazing at the tragedy she had caused. Omollo, who was quite afraid of blood, now wished he were not there in the first place. But as if Ghati had read his mind, she unexpectedly brought things back to normality – first, by fixing Otilla's head back to his torso and, secondly, by waking him up as healthy as if his head had never been severed. Thirdly, she ordered her giant snake to untie itself from her body and get back into its special case, which it did. Lastly, she pulled out the knife from her stomach and she was now a normal woman with whom someone would fall in love at the village well. Thereafter, the crowd dispersed in all directions with everyone saying something about the power of the woman. Now, everybody who was expected to come had arrived and the place was so full of people one could not find any room even to throw saliva. Old Odongo Nyambula, who was presiding over that day's event, now marched before the crowd and gave the final announcement in a more sober tone than usual.

"Dear clansmen, the time we have been waiting for has come. Let us all march quietly to the cemetery. Our magician is already there and it is there we are going to carry out today's special ritual," he said and started leading the way to the clans' cemetery. The bemused crowd followed him quietly and sheepishly.

Upon reaching the cemetery, all the people were quiet except Ghati, who was continuously chanting words to her gods in a language indecipherable to anyone in the crowd. Next, she called on all adult members of the Orina clan to form a queue before the grave of the deceased and ordered non-members of the Orina clan to stay away from the grave – if they did not want to die a humiliating death. Everybody obeyed without the slightest protest: it was only members of Orina who would go through this test, based on the fact that witches had no power over members of different clans, which explains why they could not harm the colonial masters who had tortured and humiliated them for years. The killer of Nyambori was thus plausibly a member of the same clan as the victim himself. The first member of the Orina clan to undergo the test was a woman called Nyachera. She had red eyes and was considered a witch in the village. Many people looked forward to seeing her capture. The diviner-priestess handled a gourd of liquid medicine to her and asked her to swallow it in one go. Nyachera obeyed and handed the gourd back to the priestess. Next, the magician asked her to sit on a big, black pot, placed upside down in the center of the victim's grave. As she sat there, the magician picked up one of the horns with magic ash in it, poured it on her palm and scattered some on the woman's body, while praying in a language of the gods. Next, she guided the woman around the grave of the victim seven times, meanwhile, holding the deceased's underpants and chanting the words:

"Nyambori, grandson of Opondo, if I am the one who killed you, let it be known to this congregation."

Everybody was quiet and following the procedure keenly. But all of a sudden, the third wife of the deceased broke down and started crying like a baby stung by a wasp. Almost everybody supposed the sight of the grave had reminded her of her dependable husband. But alas, people who led her away from the graveyard came back laughing the hell out of themselves (after learning from her that the underpants of the deceased, being used in the ritual process, reminded her of what used to be inside them).

Once the temporary turmoil caused by the third widow had

calmed down, Nyachera continued with the procedures and nothing happened to her at the end of the process, implying that she was as clean as cotton regarding the death of Nyambori. The next person also underwent all the procedures but nothing happened to him. The third in line was, of course, Waritu Nyagoli and his advancement towards the grave stirred the crowd for good reasons – he looked prototypically witchy and was the main suspect in the bewitchment of the deceased.

Every eye thus followed him keenly as he was undergoing one process after another. Unexpectedly, he was as sober as he had always been after the last procedure. This implied his hand was equally clean with regard to the death of Wiotel. Nonetheless, people did not agree with this verdict. Here and there, murmurs about the inability of Ghati to catch witches now ensued; some people now lost interest in the proceedings and started dispersing one after another to avoid the scorching sun which, in their own words, was burning them for no good reason, if even the likes of Waritu Nyagoli could not be caught by the priestess.

Omollo and his friend Obongo also retreated to the cool shade of an *otho* tree to avoid the sharp arrows the sun was shooting on them that morning. Like many other people, they too were talking in low, timid voices about the poor performance of Ghati in front of the crowd.

"I don't think this woman is capable of catching any witch as it is believed," Obongo doubted.

"Why would you doubt her power?" Omollo asked him in wonder, "were you not here before?" He added in amazement.

"I was here, of course, and I saw her first magic, but why hasn't she caught even one person to show she is capable?" Commented Obongo.

"Her fetish has not found a witch yet," said Omollo confidently.

"Aha ha, ha, ha, ha, ha," laughed Obongo joyously and asked: "Are you insinuating that even Nyagoli is an angel Gabriel today? I can't ..."

But even before he finished what he was saying, a crowd was seen rushing back to the cemetery at the speed of a modern jet fighter, owing to the fact that the first witch had been caught. To the amazement of everyone, that person was Omiesa, the church consultant. He was now jumping, hanging on the branches of trees like a bat and talking profusely – actually, as if to clear all the doubts that he was not a witch. He sometimes danced in a manner people said a sober person could not dance. When Omollo neared Omiesa, he was narrating how his group had killed Sigangu, Onjure, Ritwa and Nyambori. He further told how they made Apondo Nyopondo, the sister to the deceased, breath with his tongue out like a dog. His words certainly agitated the bereaved, who would have lynched him, had Ghati, the Magician, not been there in his defence against the crowd baying for his blood.

<<<CHAPTER NINE>>>

Years had elapsed since those days Omollo would hunt wild birds with his posse. He was now a teenager who resembled his father, even in his sneezing. Like his father, he was tall for his age and was blessed with big bones, projecting him as a tough and fearless man. And like his grandmother, he had a military-type personality – dark sparkling skin, red eyes and a strong deep voice, which scared even soldiers in uniform. To reinforce his identicalness to his father, he began to strut and speak in a tone he deemed befitting the strong Malan man, which he strongly felt himself to be. Inwardly though, Omollo had too much of his mother rather than his father or grandmother in him. That is, his appearance and character thus only gave as false an image as the elevation of breasts in a bra. In reality, he was a docile man who made jokes and took part in small talk whenever there was a window of opportunity for such.

In contrast, his father, Elder Orwa Nyamngwegre, was an everlastingly fierce and bad-tempered man and had always relied on his fists rather than his tongue to solve his manly challenges. On account of his militancy, Rabarians would always gossip to strangers that for Elder Orwa, beating others was as natural as walking. According to them, he would use the slightest opportunity to beat someone – and indeed people dreaded him like the hind legs of the donkey precisely because of that habit. Some people even claimed that by the time of his death he had beaten up the equivalent of a truck full of people. Ironically, it was said that Elder Orwa would rather face the hangman than admit that he was a tormentor of his kinfolks.

'People are so dear to me,' it was said he would launch his defence, whenever anyone who mattered accused him of tyranny. 'It is for this reason that I always beat stupidity out of them,' he would allegedly defend himself.

All the same, the fury of Elder Orwa was inexpressible. People would thus rather describe it by incidents than in words. A story was told of an episode where he and his third son were, on one occasion, eating lunch: when the old man broke wind relatively audibly for both of them to perceive with their ears. According to the story, no sooner had the old man done this than his son, for the sake of peace-maintenance, promptly took his father's sin on himself by shouting:

"It is me, Father, not you, who did it, forgive me, please." And from what I heard, Elder Orwa angrily gazed at that boy for longer than necessary and next yelled at him like mad:

"I forgive you for that stupidity today, but try it again when I am eating with you and I will have the justification to grind your balls into flour with my palms!"

Another episode illustrating the ferociousness of the man had since evolved into a well-known Malan satire, which went: "No problem, I will buy another one."

The news went around that Elder Orwa had an axe that he so loved much he would only keep it in his private hut, and would not allow even his elder sons to touch it. One day, however, his second wife stole the axe for simplifying her task of cutting wood at the bank of the River Ramar. The plan was to clean and return it to its rightful place after the work, without the awareness of the unreasonable old man. But as the elders say, 'All trees slide when it is the predetermined day for the monkey to die.' As the woman was cutting a tree with the axe, she missed her target, causing the axe to fly and plunge into the flowing river. Now the woman did not know how to face her 'lion' regarding the loss of his beloved axe.

But as fate would have it, that night Elder Orwa visited her hut to enjoy his prepaid meat muffin at the junction of her two hind limbs. The story adds that the woman cunningly chose to use that opportunity to relieve herself of a burden she had been carrying on her shoulders the whole day long. According to the story, she received the old man and warmed him up for the exercise more than she had ever done before. And when the old man was now warm enough and was about to take off, it was said she suddenly intervened:

"But father of Omollo, before you take off, would you listen if I tell you something, my 'rhino'?" She enticed him.

"Hurry up!" The old man screamed to her.

"I lost your beloved axe," the woman said.

"No problem, I will buy another one," the old man responded summarily and embarked on the exercise with immediate effect.

It was said that Omollo's second mother was thrilled to bits at how amicably the fiasco ended. She vowed, however, to keep the story to herself. Yet in spite of everything, it was claimed things reached a point she could no longer conceal the story without getting sick. But no sooner had she vented the story to her close confidant than its key sentence – "No problem, I will buy another one" – automatically become an element of Malan humor – allegedly, because there was nothing more thrilling to Rabarians than to learn how Elder Orwa's signature militancy lost terribly to mere sexual impulses.

One more famous manifestation of the man's fury was, of course, his act of maiming and divorcing his concubine just for gossiping to her fellow women at the village pool that, if his present behaviour were anything to go by, her husband would have made a better security dog than a human being.

But as long as Omollo anatomically mirrored his father, the old man naively believed he was the right son to take up his mantle when he was gone. With this view in mind, he started grooming Omollo in the traditions of his land from those days when he genuinely believed that the name of his genitals was a *pistol*. Omollo too loved his father and would always dance to his tunes. Evidence of the strong bond was that Omollo was the only child of Orwa who could trace his lineage up to God without dragging in the names of such white men as Jacob, Abraham, Abel and Adam in the chain.

The heirship plan of his father's homestead went well, until the forces of darkness intervened and demolished the trust and expectations of the old man in his most beloved son, Omollo son of Orwa, a.k.a *the Baboon*.

When Omollo was thirteen, his country of Kaya was celebrating its second anniversary of independence from the colonialists. *The Government of the People, by the People, for the People* was then certain that it had successfully chased away the colonial masters and opted to print its victory in the souls and minds of its citizens through actions. In that year's anniversary, the new people's president purported that the nation of his dreams could only be realized if the people scattered all over the land regrouped together in specified villages in order to reduce the cost to the government of serving them fried chicken and chips.

The next day after this statement, all organs of state now started moving people militarily from their traditional residences to the designated socialist villages. Omollo's family was nonetheless lucky that the location of their home was by chance the designated village where everybody had to move to, which spared his family the agony of abrupt movement that families living elsewhere incurred.

In the newly created villages, the government seduced villagers, or rather coerced them, to work together in communal farms, meanwhile singing loudly about the goodness of the new *Government of the People, by the People, for the People* – of course, with the prospect of receiving the promised saliva-oozing meals from the government in return. The sad thing, however, is that the promised meals did not arrive on time, prompting some men and women, who had long sold their chickens to buy porcelain dishes, to ask for an explanation for the delay of the government's meals. As usual, they were answered that the government was still setting the table for the banquet, and that their patience would soon pay off.

And in the spirit of setting the table for the citizens, the government early that year introduced a democratic election, which they defined as 'giving every citizen a say in the leadership of their own country'. In the same spirit, the Malans got their first opportunity ever to elect the president of the republic.

In that election, the Father of the Nation was contesting for president against *Nobody*. On the one hand, citizens who wanted the Father of the Nation to rule them would queue in front of his big picture in a frame hang on a trunk of a tree in every polling station. On the other hand, citizens who wanted *Nobody* to rule them would queue in front of a big stone on a sling tied to the branches of the same trees (a representative of *Nobody* in every polling station). In the end the freedom fighter garnered 55% of the votes, whereas *Nobody* received only 45% in an election marred with uncountable irregularities and rigging.

The victory of the Father of the Nation against *Nobody* now energized him to dedicate his service to his loving people unreservedly. Soon, he used a presidential decree bestowed on him by the constitution of his country to oust the remainder of the colonialists who still owned big farms, banks and factories in Kaya. Thereafter, he made the goods confiscated in this exercise public property. Bizarrely, he now told every hopeful citizen that those reminders of the colonialists were the ones who were delaying his government in putting smiles back on their faces. The way it was masterminded, the move tickled many citizens who, in turn, heaped all sorts of praises on their president – allegedly, for chasing away the demons of underdevelopment from their country. What's more, some of his diehard supporters even yelled from the rooftops of their huts that their president was such a selfless man he would soon declare his wife a public property.

Practically though, some unpopular policies of the outgoing government, like charging the unpopular *head tax* to every adult citizen, remained intact under the new regime. The tactful president now re-named it a *development tax* – and said it would enable the new nation to kick poverty out of its boundaries. And probably to disguise it from the colonial head tax, he instructed his tax collectors, in his monthly address to the nation, to collect the *development tax* only during the day and to arrest those who could not pay the tax only in the day time and in a friendly manner. Further, he said that even in the case where somebody's property had to be confiscated, the owner should be made to release his property with all their thirty-two teeth still on display.

All the same, the collection of the *development tax* still did not differ from the collection of the *head tax* during the colonial regime. Collectors of the *development tax* in the new government continued confiscating tax evaders' belongings in every crudest way they knew of. Further, they would still beat them up and drag them to the same cells that the outgoing administration had used.

In light of this reality, some people did not abandon their useful pre-colonial tax-evasion techniques in the new independent Kaya Republic. One such man was Olimo, *the Living Bicycle*, whose name implied he could outrun a cheetah in a fair contest. Indeed, he had thrice outrun hunting dogs behind antelopes to catch the fleeing antelopes with his bare hands. With this asset in his basket, Olimo had never paid a cent in tax to the outgoing government. Every time tax was being collected, he would spot the tax collectors and outrun them to his safe haven in Radieya Hill. In fact, no militiaman had an appetite for pursuing the man whenever he galloped. An added advantage was that Olimo did not have any material items at his home for such aggressive militiamen to confiscate as a fine for tax evasion.

One day, however, Olimo got on the nerves of the tax collectors of the new regime. On day in question, he was a captive of alcohol at the place of Ambalo Nyatiga, the revered brewer of Rabar Village. Under the auspices of the demon drink, he unveiled to the public his new praise name of *The Impossible to the Old and to the New Government* – a nickname implying that the old government had not been able to make him to pay the head tax and neither would the new government.

This nickname logically infuriated the militiamen of Rabar Village like no other. Subsequently, they also declared publicly that they would soon catch Olimo, beat him up and take him to prison, to serve as a lesson to anybody out there who dreamt of looking down on the *new Government of the People, by the People, for the People*. All the same, it was still unclear to even the militiamen how they could arrest a man who would often outrun a fleeing bank robber in a fair competition. In other words, it was an open secret that it would not be possible for the militiamen to arrest him on the spot if he happened to hear them during their noisy tax collection exercise. Of course, they would invade him at night when he was asleep – save that their new government had strictly outlawed arresting people at night in the independent Kaya Republic.

This minor conflict, which had started like a joke at Ambalo Nyatiga's drinking place, caused a sensation not only in Rabar Village but also in its neighbourhood. Some people now took a bet that the militiamen would never catch Olimo, whereas, others took a bet that they would catch him as easily as a spider catches a fly and throw his pride to the dogs. Overall, all members of the opposite blocs waited to see who would triumph in that long awaited contest.

Eventually, the day of the contest found Olimo plucking grass for the thatching of his newly built hut in an open space. On this day, four able mercenary militiamen had been brought from other villages for the sole objective of arresting Olimo alive. The operation began with these militiamen crawling in the tall grass in the direction where Olimo was busy with his work. Every alert villager was now attracted by the unfolding developments and stood at the edge of the village, looking at the open space where Olimo was continuing with plucking grass, completely unaware that the mercenaries were encroaching on his territory. His fans, of course, shouted and fluted to alert him but the wind was blowing in the opposite direction and thus Olimo did not hear their warning alarm. This, of course, saddened his fans for it seemed the militiamen were going catch Olimo as easily as a child would a kitten, thus depriving them of their anticipated entertainment.

Luckily, Olimo was a man with a mongoose's sixth sense of danger. In the course of events, he heard the rustling of grass behind him as the militiamen crept through it. Supposing that a python was hunting him for breakfast that morning, he stood upright and looked around, but could neither see nor hear any source of the movements he had perceived, as the militiamen, who had their eyes permanently fixed on him, ceased all their movements upon noticing that their prey was trying to locate them. The disappearance of the rustling of grass naturally scared the hell out of Olimo, as he now mused that only a lion or a leopard would play dead when the prey they are stalking is looking in their direction.

To clear his suspicion, Olimo now pretended to have resumed working, yet he set all his ears to the direction from which the rustling had come. As he had envisaged, he soon heard the resumption of pushing through the grass, and strongly sensed that the danger was approaching him. To ascertain his conviction, he suddenly turned around towards where the crackling was emanating and, fortunately, came eye-to-eye with four men crawling towards him in the grass. Now sure of the danger, he sprinted like a deer for his dear life; concurrently, the four hired guns stood up from the thick grass, at the same time throwing their clubs in the direction of Olimo with all their strength. By chance, none of the clubs hit the moving target.

Applause now erupted from staring enthusiasts at the edge of the village, as the ground was now level for any party to win the contest. The fans cheered even louder as the run between Olimo and the militiamen set for Radieya Hill – a point where Olimo would run and hide in one of the caves he had long discovered for this very purpose.

At the beginning, it appeared as if the militiamen would catch Olimo, considering that they were really good athletes and determined too. Nevertheless, it soon became obvious that Olimo had initially been making fun of them, especially after tripling the gap between himself and the hired guns in only the tenth minute of the race. After twenty minutes or so, he was already about four kilometers away from the militiamen and by then was just walking comfortably towards his usual hideout, whereas, the militiamen were just jogging towards his direction, if only to reduce the amount of shame and embarrassment he had inflicted on them in the eyes of the hundreds of fans.

Upon reaching one dark cave, Olimo, as usual, crawled into it like a python but unexpectedly spent no more than thirty seconds there. As soon as he got into the cave, he stepped on something spongy, which he supposed to be a gigantic snake. Now he composed his body for an instant bite, which, however, did not come. Instead, he heard a deafening roar of a lion, the king.

Instantly, he realized that a lioness and her cubs had taken refuge in the cave he considered his own and thus ejected himself at the speed of a galloping horse, lying to himself that he would escape scot-free. Unfortunately, the offended lioness would not forgive a fool for intruding into her privacy, worse still, for treading on her cubs. In brief, it was now the turn of the lioness to teach Olimo an unforgettable lesson.

The race thus reversed back to the village, through the same route Olimo had come. That day Olimo ran in a way even he himself did not understand until his dying day, as he would rather die at the hands of militiamen than in the fangs of the mindless beast behind him. As he emerged from the forest with a life-threatening beast, the militiamen were, of course, stunned but happy that they would now find a chance to reduce humiliation the Olimo had just inflicted on them. They did see something running behind him but considered it a big dog that they were not going to allow to scare soldiers. One of them even shouted aloud in excitement:

"So, he comes to us with a dog, thinking that we are scared of the dog? Let us teach this fool a lesson he and his dog will never forget in their pathetic lives."

As he approached the militiamen, fans back in the village were stirred by the rare spectacle 'of "the witches" getting a taste of their own medicine.'

The militiamen now raised their clubs to attack the fool and his beast as soon as they came within range. But as Olimo came nearer, one militiaman, who was actually an experienced hunter, realized that the beast was a lion – the king and thus promptly alerted his colleagues. The clubs now fell out of their hands and one of them even fell down and started crapping in his trousers, as others took to their heels: the crapper was lucky that the beast considered him respectful and thus spared him. The other three militiamen however bolted higgledy-piggledy to avoid the tragedy that was then looming around the corner, giving the villagers a sweet thing to laugh at.

Of the three running militiamen, Olimo followed the one who had earlier on thrown at him nastier slurs than the rest. Inwardly, Olimo was now so pleased that such a fool was on the receiving end and had to pay for his contempt of others. Soon, the militiaman was pleading with him to take another route with the life-threatening lioness: he even pledged three bulls in three days if Olimo averted the beast from him. But Olimo wanted cash, allegedly, because he could not trust such a devilish person. He thus kept on trailing him determinedly with the beast, despite all the fuss he was making. Within a few minutes, the three mammals were seen running in the same direction: Olimo at the front, the militiaman in the middle and the giant lioness at the militiaman's heels. It was obvious that all three were running for a purpose, though the purpose was different in each case.

So, the first victim of the lioness on that eventful day was the poor militiaman, whom Olimo had been trailing with the beast on purpose. The lioness broke his neck and plucked away his hand for having obstructed her run towards the man of her target. All over the Rabar Village therefore, it was indisputable that in fact Olimo had crudely killed that man.

Thereafter, the run continued towards the village, as villagers intensified their cheers and whistles to welcome Olimo as the hero of the hoi polloi of Rabar Village. But when Olimo was 500 meters away, a man with sharp eyes noted that behind Olimo was actually a lion, the king, not a dog, as everybody had supposed. Accordingly, he alerted everybody, by shouting about the approach of the lion – the alarm that the sighted confirmed and heeded by sprinting for their dear lives.

Even so, there was this blind man in Rabar Village who would fight his personal stigma singlehandedly and with all his might. And to be specific, Amara, would do everything that the sighted did – just to show that he was equally as capable as everybody else was in the village. Accordingly, he was doing what the others were doing on that particular hour – cheering for Olimo for his legendary race against the militia. Amara thus also heard the warning about the approach of the "lion", but rather understood the word to mean that Olimo was the lion who was now nearing the finishing line, victorious. Supposing this to be the meaning of "the lion, the lion," that everybody was shouting; Amara too intensified his honest cheers for Olimo and even ran like the others, but unfortunately in the direction from which the lion was coming.

To sum up, the lioness met him at the edge of the village while he was shouting, blissfully ignorant that the beast was encroaching on him for a deadly swipe. Indeed, it devoured him for unnecessary noise and obstruction to the man of her target. In light of this episode, many people blamed Olimo for the murder of Amara. One exception was a man known as Mangube, who constantly blamed the horrific death of Amara on Amara himself.

'Pretense is a very bad thing,' Mangube, one day, started defending his idiosyncratic point of view on the cause of Amara's death.

'There was a man in Ratiya Village called George.' He started by drawing on a parallel incident to illustrate his position on the cause of Amara's death. 'This man would plait his hair and dress like a woman, in spite of all the warnings from the elders of his village. Notwithstanding, he one day learnt the hard way," he said and now pressed his right nostril with his right pointing finger before jetting snot from his left nostril to a nearby lawn.

'One day George went to the well to look for a medicinal waterweed. Unfortunately, an alien madman had also gone there to waylay women, whom he was certain would always go to the well to draw water for their domestic uses,' he said happily.

"Fortunately, the madman netted George, supposing she was a woman,' he said and Ajulo, who had anticipated the end of the story, grinned from ear to ear of excitement.

'George then started making fuss, "oooho, I am not a woman, Ooooh, I am your fellow man,"' he continued. 'The good thing is that the madman did not entertain his nonsense,' he said, and Ajulo's lips now broke into a grin.

'And when he removed his skirt and saw a pistol in the supposed location of an axe wound, the horny madman was pretty mad at George,' Mangube said and Ajulo lips cracked with laughter.

'The fiery madman eventually hit and broke George's jaw for playing tricks on him,' Mangube added, and Ajulo now stopped his laughter to disagree with Mangube:

'But your example is far-fetched, Mangube,' he said laughingly. 'These cases are as different as night and day,' he added.

Apart from the debatable cause of Amara's death, the death of the third man, the village chairman to be specific, was indisputably caused by Olimo. According to the story, Olimo hated that man with both his heart and soul. As a consequence, he deliberately ran into him with the beast that day to avenge the contempt, which the man had been showing him over the years. As I heard, the lioness chewed the man's head and afterwards killed seven more people for loitering in between it and Olimo. Although Olimo's incident had happened five years ago, and not many people still talked about it, the sight of an animated militiaman in uniform would always rekindle Omollo's memory of the incident. It was such militiamen of the Government of the People, by the People, for the People who visited his father in his private hut one evening and argued with him for several hours. Omollo later learnt that the militiamen were on a mission to order his father that Omollo and his siblings should enroll in the village school since the new government of Kaya wanted all children to go to school and any parent who would not allow their child to go to school would face the wrath of law. The militiamen argued convincingly that they had only come to talk peacefully with Omollo's father over the issue because he was one of the respected elders of Rabar Village; – otherwise, they would just storm their compound one morning and whisk him away to a court of law to face the music of the new government.

As a result, Omollo's father called him on the third night after that hard talk with the militia to break to him the saddest news ever between father and son; that Omollo had to join the village primary school to appease the beloved *Government of the People, by the People, for the People.*

Omollo's father, of course, disliked white men's education and religion like the death that killed his grandmother. Recurrently, he purported that the white men's education only taught black men to be unconfident, dependent, self-destructive, self-despising, and submissive. Detailedly, he posited that an educated black man would only turn against himself or his own people – for their true mind would have been intoxicated by the white men's education. Elder Orwa long parked similar thoughts in the mind of his heir from childhood and was therefore just reminding him of what to do at school:

"Hear things at school and forget them once you cross the school boundary on your way back home," he said sternly.

"The teachings of the white men are for the white men, and we are the black men, remember," he stated as he closely assessed the attention of his son.

"Black teachers in the so called modern education system insist that you learn the white men's things simply because they are already the captives of their white masters. My son, never listen to those good-for-nothing fellows," said his father in a more fatherly voice than Omollo was used to hearing.

And as Omollo was as loyal to his father as a dog to its owner, he guaranteed his father that he would just go to school to please the new government, which was obsessed with seeing every child at school. Plan B would be to drop out of school after a while under whatever pretext.

As agreed, Omollo went to school not only to please the government but also to defend the ways of his land against the influence of the white men. And with this attitude at the back of his mind, he would from time to time clash with his teachers and Christians whenever they said something he considered inadmissible in his traditional doctrine. For his stand, he was soon nicknamed Nyadhi by his colleagues – an indomitable Malaland worrier who fought enemies of his land for ten consecutive years without losing a single war.

One remarkable man-to-woman face-off between Omollo and a spoiler of his traditions, Madam Bertha Mkami, happened when Omollo was in standard four. On that particular day, Madam Mkami had come to teach the causes of stomachache to her class – actually, a relevant lesson to the Rabarian children.

Madam Bertha Mkami was a tall, black, middle-aged, buoyant teacher. At the time, she had only been at Omollo's school for five weeks, yet was well known throughout Rabar Village and its neighbourhood, especially for her short, tight clothes that exposed all the hotspots on her body – her head teacher joked that her seamster would always run out of materials whenever he was making a dress or a skirt for her.

During her fourth week at the school, she was marking exercise books at a desk, in front of standard two pupils. From what I heard, she was so obsessed with the exercise that her hind limbs were asunder, yet she did not realize it. Worse still, the acidic liquid from the cradle of agony had long burnt the front part of her pants so that her bulgy adult's entertainment was open enough for all the pupils sitting in front of her to frequent with their own eyes. The story continues that one of her cultured pupils at that juncture pitied her, and thus approached her and murmured in her ear:

'Madam Mkami, your lower mouth is wide open, and the naughty boys are now busy drawing it.'

'Which mouth are you talking about, young girl?' The teacher allegedly asked the girl back.

'The bearded and the toothless one in the rift valley,' she elaborated to her teacher and now the latter understood what the little girl was talking about.

'AAAAH!' She uttered and thereafter gave the strangest response ever.

'I was not aware of it, but, after all, is it not enjoying fresher air than what is found in the pants?" She then added after a after a short pause: "Don't bother, young girl. Let the boys exercise their fine art."

Eyewitnesses claimed she continued with her work in the same posture until she was done with it. Pupils later leaked news of the incident to the villagers, who henceforth would always want someone to point Madam Bertha Mkami out to them – often without her knowledge. The incident also helped the villagers to find her a befitting nickname – teacher *Let the Boys Exercise their Fine Art* or, in short, *Lety*.

It was *Lety* who one day was teaching class four, in which Omollo was a pupil, the causes of stomachache. The story went that the topic was so relevant and practical in their area that the rarely interested class was on that day quite attentive and that even Omollo, son of Nyamngwegre, was following the lesson more keenly than expected of him.

At the end of the day, Madam Mkami wound up her lesson without mentioning *camera-witchcraft* as one of the causes of stomachache in their village. This stunned Omollo who, more than once, had seen people with severe stomachache going to his father for treatment against *camera-witchcraft*. Rumour had it that camera-witches were mostly red-eyed women who could bewitch food by gazing at the eater in a mystical way; the food would thereafter turn poisonous in the stomach of the victim. Actually, Omollo's father was the best healer of *camera-witchcraft* in the whole of Rabar Village. If a patient with such a problem attended his medicine hut early, he would give them liquid medicine to drink. Next, he would slightly cut the upper part of such patient's stomach with a razor blade; and from the cut, he would suck out the poisoned food from the patient's stomach. Having extracted the rotten food remains from the patient's stomach, he would spit them out and everybody would see them. He would at that point give the patient another liquid medicine to drink. Most patients of the kind would eventually walk home cured and as grateful to his father as a boozer who has been given access to a brewery.

With all this soliloquy going on his head, Omollo on this occasion found himself breaking his own rule of not contributing a single point to discussions in his class.

"Please Madam Mkami." Today, to the surprise of everyone, he called for his teacher's attention:

"You have probably forgotten to mention *camera-witchcraft* as one of the major causes of stomach ache."

He had offered his contribution sincerely; nonetheless, upon hearing what he had just said, teacher *Lety* burst out into a derisive laughter that in turn shook Omollo and, of course, shook all the other pupils too, since they could not establish what was amusing in Omollo's contribution. They had rather expected their teacher to thank Omollo for jogging her memory of an important point, now on the contrary, they were shocked at what she was doing. All the same, they remained silent, and eagerly waited to find out what Madam Let the Boys Exercise was laughing about. Teacher *Lety* eventually managed to bring her mocking laughter to a halt, and then made a comment that infuriated her pupils immensely.

"Hallo! It is ridiculous that you guys still hold these barbaric beliefs up to now. Nothing like camera-witchcraft actually exists." She giggled like a teenage girl, and struggled greatly to continue her speech.

"What you guys call *camera-witchcraft* is actually constipation that greedy people get because of eating mixed food, especially at funerals. If you really use your common sense, how can someone poison food that someone else is taking from a distance?"

This question made her class tumultuous: pupils grunted, stood up, and began to act up. Thereafter, a pupil called Auma, *the Hare is Small, but Gives Birth to Twins*, fired a question that Madam *Lety* could not answer.

"Teacher!" She called her scoldingly and paused a bit to ensure that everybody was listening, "with your common sense, if a person can't poison someone else's food from a distance, could you explain how the magician who performed here last week, turned stones into eggs?"

Her classmates showed their approval for such a well-thought-out question.

Despite being clueless, the teacher kept on grinning sheepishly in front of her class without answering the question, actually giving the pupils more room to heckle and boo her than was necessary.

In a nutshell, what had started as a vigorous debate degenerated into an exchange of abuse between the teacher and the pupils, with Omollo eventually calling his teacher the liar of the century, a shadow of white men and a professional pretender – actually, the worst insults a standard four pupil could hurl at his teacher.

For this transgression, Omollo was assigned twelve strokes on his buttocks, alongside uprooting the stump of a tree behind their classroom. Omollo, however, refused the punishments and was consequently suspended for a month – after which he would only be allowed to go back to the school upon showing up with both his parents – which was basically a daydream as far as Omollo's father was concerned.

Having learnt what had happened at school, Omollo's father was so proud of his son that he rewarded him with four bulls for what he referred to as a heroic action. Subsequently, Omollo stayed at home even after his one-month suspension had expired. Later on, concerned teachers of his school would persuade him to go back to school but he would never heed their advice.

In fact Omollo did eventually resume his studies but only when Professor Girado visited the village and intervened in his issue. For over twenty years, whatever the professor said had been law to Rabarians and their neighbours, based on the man's enormous wealth and assumed encyclopedic knowledge. In terms of wealth, only Professor Girado owned a modern house, a cinema, a tractor, a car, a solar panel, a camera and a white wife in the whole region north of Damasawa. Furthermore, it was only behind his house where a lucky kid could pick up balloons – which, Omollo later learnt, were used condoms. In terms of brightness, his nickname of Mr. Tell Them said it all. With regard to the origin of the nickname, his white secondary school biology teacher would ask a question whose answer she did not know even herself. Next, she would ask her students the same question row by row, but would always get the same monotonous answer.

"I don't know, Madam," the first one would say.

"Next!" She would roar and the answer would again be:

"I don't know, Madam."

"Next!"

"I don't know, Madam."

"Next!"

"I don't know, Madam."

Rumour had it that she would continue with the drill until three-quarters of the class had been asked the same question and all had answered: 'I don't know, Madam.' She would at this point raise her eyes to meet Girado's eyes, just to order him in a very seductive voice: "George of Giradooo, tell them the answer."

Rumourmongers even put it that whatever George of Girado would say would always turn out to be the exact answer for the unanswerable question of Madam Perth, as she was called. The story adds that, given this background, his classmates later on nicknamed him *Mr. Tell Them* out of jealousy.

The rumour adds that Professor Girado continued studying until he came across a poster written in bold letters, **No Class Ahead**. Another tale, which only true believers could buy, has it that Professor Girado was so clever he could inject patients on the tongue, whereas, common physicians could only inject such patients in their butt. It was further believed he could answer every question on Earth – and, indeed, he would behave like Halibati Heiniskeni whenever he was on his holidays at Rabar Village, – answering all villagers' questions from astronomy to cookery, lest somebody doubt his professorial expertise. And during this process, to convince everyone that his responses were drawn from a wealth of experience and profound knowledge, he would, before answering any trick question, zoom his gaze out across the horizon in a unique way – after which everybody would automatically believe his answers in their entirety.

Most of these words of praise were, of course, debatable; nonetheless, it was an open secret in Rabar Village that George's mother and father had long since divorced over a strong dispute concerning from whose side of the family his brightness originated. In this light, Omollo, like any other villager, appreciated the greatness of the man. He had frequently visited his home to watch films and the professor would occasionally visit their home and prove his brightness by leaving every member of their family with a banknote or two. On a personal level, Omollo would regularly introduce himself to attractive girls from another village as a younger brother of Professor Girado, a revelation that would always make such girls behave like dogs before pythons.

For his honour, therefore, Professor Girado was elected uncontested chairman of the village school committee. In the wisdom of the majority, he deserved the position, in as much as he was an embodiment of knowledge and a role model in all issues pertaining to modern education. In his absence though, his deputy chairman would act on his behalf to handle certain matters or he would write to him to suggest solutions for problems that were beyond the ability of members of the school board.

On the 150th evening since Omollo had left school in the name of defending his fatherland, it occurred that this famous professor was by chance on holiday in their village. As usual, teachers of his school showed up and stuck around him – basically, to get the handouts he would always dish out, though under the pretext of 'giving the chairman the school's progress report'.

Among all the gossips, or rather the reports, that the teachers gave him on that particular day, the story of how Omollo, son of Orwa, had dropped out from the school, appealed to the professor's headquarters of sympathy more than anything else.

In the professor's unique perspective, abidance to primitive culture and prodigious stupidity stood in the way of progress to his people – and he had to do something about it. In accordance with this view, he now reflected on the rigidity of Omollo's father to the adoption of the new ways of life and felt so sorry for the little boy, whom he genuinely considered a victim of a problem whose source he could not know. In this light, he asked Omollo's teachers to leave the matter with him and promised that he would amicably solve it before returning to Arwing City.

On the 160th evening since Omollo had left school, he was driving cattle back home after a daylong graze at Ramar Valley. All of a sudden, he saw a car moving towards their home and that shook him to the bones – for vehicles digressing from the highway would always be either bringing home the remains of brothers and sisters from foreign lands or carrying police officers ready to beat up villagers and take them away to jail.

"Probably one of my brothers in a distant land has passed away and the vehicle I am seeing is storming towards my home with his remains for burial," he thought, drawing on his bad experience with digressing vehicles.

"Or is it that one of the 'witches' of this village has betrayed my father with the police for possessing a demon drink?" This alternative thought occurred to him as he reflected that his father would always keep with him a pot of outlawed liquor in front of his bed, preferring to call it 'tears of lion' or 'a weapon of mass destruction.'

Police officers had always scared Omollo and he wished they were not the ones moving towards his home that evening. Whenever he set his eyes on them, he would always remember how they had helplessly slapped old Onjago in front of his wives and children: upon that memory, every hair on his body would stand on end. Given this premonition, he could not even now blink for fear of losing sight of the car that evening. With this thought dominating his mind, he now wished he were a falcon so he could fly ahead of the car and warn his father of the encroaching danger. They reality was, however, that he was not a falcon and could thus only leave fate to take its course. All he now did – was to move carefully towards his home.

After a few meters later, Omollo found himself grinning from ear to ear after discovering that the car in question belonged to Professor Girado. All the same, he still wondered what might have brought the professor to his home unannounced like that. In a normal visit, word would have been sent in advance and the whole home would have been prepared to receive him. Another oddity was that the professor went directly to his father's medicine hut – yet Omollo had often heard people saying that educated people did not have faith in traditional healing.

"Then what?" He said to himself aloud and even wished he had tiptoed to the hut to grasp at least a skeleton of what the learned man was talking about with his father in the hut. Even so, he restrained himself from doing so – as that would be the worst behavior a child in Malaland could show to his parents.

The crux of the professor's visit to Omollo's homestead was to take him along with him to the city to expose him to a bigger picture of the world. For this mission, the Prof had arranged things in such a way so as to play his game before Omollo's father, whom he inwardly considered primitive and conservative. He would especially use the issue of the gun to achieve his inner motive of changing the worldview of his poor son on education.

Orwa, who was a distant father to Professor Girado, welcomed the famous son in fatherly manner. As per the custom, he offered him a calabash of cold porridge from a pot he would always keep beside his bed. Further, he ordered that a cockerel be slaughtered for this famous guest under his roof. Professor Girado for his part willingly received the calabash and drank the porridge, in the same way as any other villagers would drink it. In reciprocation of this kindness, he fished out a few bottles of white men's drinks from his handbag and handed them to the old man, who, upon seeing the white man's spirit teasing him in the bottle, broke his vow of not smiling that year. Now the small talk continued as the two men waited for the cockerel meal to be served. As Professor Girado had hoped, the topic of a gun he had brought the old man a long time ago popped up in their conversation: Elder Orwa was, as usual, lamenting over how his gun had run out of bullets so he could no longer go hunting with it in the bush. As he had planned, Professor Girado immediately offered to supply him with four dozen bullets on condition that he be accompanied by one of Orwa's dependable sons to the city in order to collect the ammunition (it was illegal for a citizen to possess such an amount of bullets in the independent Kaya Republic and the Professor argued that he wanted someone who could keep the secret). He further promised he would put such a son on a direct bus from Arwing City to the Rabar Village Bus Stop; amazingly, all the offers were free of charge. As anticipated, the candid son of Orwa who deserved such a mission was none other than Omollo.

By the time the professor was leaving Omollo's father's compound, the deal had been sealed that, the following week, Omollo would travel with the Professor to the city. To strengthen the deal, Professor Girado bribed Omollo's father with two one hundred bank notes on his departure, which made the rarely smiling Orwa to grin, chant blessings and crack jokes.

"This is the only son of the land whom the white men's education has not completely castrated," he said to the audience who were waving goodbye to the disappearing man of means, "He is quite different from those low-learned Rabarians that only break out into broken Linglish language whenever they are tanked up or upon seeing beautiful women in their vicinity," he joked heartily and puzzled the crowd even more – for he was behaving as if he were in someone else's body that day.

A few minutes after the professor's departure, a curious Omollo wanted to find out if the professor had also sought indigenous cures from his father. In line with this urge, he stormed into his father's medicine hut and cunningly touched on some topics that could have induced his father to talk about the professor's mission to his medicine hut. Nonetheless, he got nothing short of what, at first, he considered a "joke", to wit, that he would go with Professor Girado to the city to fetch him something.

"I, Omollo Orwa! Go with Professor Girado to Arwing City?" Omollo thought to himself as he was leaving his father's hut, "is my father making fun of me?" He mused to himself, unable to understand the situation.

He would consider what his father told him as a joke. Nonetheless, as far as he could remember, he had never heard his father joking with a child or a woman. With this thought intensifying in his mind, he developed a feeling of happiness and concern at the same time: happy because he could get to know the lands his uncle Ongoro would talk about; and worried because it was not making sense that the professor would want to go with him to Arwing City.

"How will I come back to Rabar alone?" He mused to himself, without an answer. He now felt like going back to his father for answers, yet remembered that the old man had always hated persistent questions from children. Considering this impediment, he now relaxed and decided to give the issue time to see how it would end.

Even so, his relaxation did not last long. While grazing cattle at Ramar Valley on the following day, he shared the news about his journey with his fellow shepherd, Obongo, grandson of Othik Mbuku, who, amicably and confidentially, warned him to be careful about a looming disaster. Obongo claimed to have heard some news over the radio that scientists of Arwing City were searching for a brain of a boy with a diastema, which Omollo was, for experimenting cancer treatment. In his wisdom, there was no doubt about it that the professor was taking him to Arwing City so he could be butchered for body parts.

"He has never welcomed his own father in his Arwing home.

Now tell me how come he invites you, the 'Nobody from Nowhere?'"
Obongo posed a philosophical question that frightened Omollo even
more.

"You remember the story that spread all over the land some years
ago that Professor Girado's wife chased Girado's sister at night for
going to her home without writing her a letter in advance?" Obongo
complicated the issue further.

And indeed his words triggered Omollo's memories of his father's
old wooden radio – the one whose volume-adjusting knob had jammed
at maximum volume a year ago, causing it to be the loudest radio in
the whole of Rabar Village, especially when it had just been fitted
with a new pack of batteries and had only short wave and medium
wave modes, swingingly announcing all sorts of things amidst extreme
buzzes and cyclic flutes. Now, Omollo remembered having heard the
same radio broadcasting that parts of albinos and gap-toothed people
were hot cakes among witches in the cities. He now connected the dots
that the professor and his father were plotting to use him in a fishy way
for gain.

"I am not going to allow this to happen to me," he vowed upon
reaching this conclusion, "I will confront my father this evening, even
if he is purging fire," he swore.

True to his word, Omollo confronted his father in his private
hut that night with tears pricking his eyes. He thereafter narrated A
to Z what his fellow shepherd Obongo had leaked to him – namely, a
wicked plot against him. He even told him about what he had himself
learnt from the radio regarding such a plot.

Luckily, that day Omollo's father understood the mood of his son
and acted contrary to expectations: he spoke to the boy humbly and in
friendly manner, perhaps in a way he had never spoken to him before.

"The boys who tell you such tales of woes are jealous of your
journey to town," he explained in a parental tone.

"Have you forgotten that you are my heir, Ndemra?" He asked,
this day addressing Omollo by a name Omollo was hearing only for the
third time since his birth. Omollo was truly relaxed by these soothing
words from his father and agreed to take the journey, regardless of its
perceived dangers.

Eventually, the day of the journey arrived and Omollo was in
best clothes and shoes ever, most of which he had borrowed from
his peers. He was, of course, looking smart and gorgeous in his new
attire; though, he was, inwardly experiencing some discomfort: the
underpants his mother had bought him for that special journey were
giving him a hell of a strange feeling in his lower anatomy, whereas, his
first pair of shoes did not feel right on his feet. In his own description,
they deprived his feet of the freedom they had enjoyed since birth.
Even more, he was so embarrassed when his two years old sister, who

was naturally very fond of him, cried inconsolably when he tried to hug her goodbye – allegedly, for mistaking him with a stranger because of his strange appearance.

As soon as the professor started the engine of his car, Omollo's heart leapt and he felt as if various organs of his body were acting in isolation. He now considered shouting 'uuuwii', but the fear of being jeered as mshamba by fellow age-mates standing by each side of the car stopped him. Worse still, the road from his home to the highway was undulated and thus caused the vehicle to keep on tilting this way and that way. As Omollo had heard a lot about car accidents from his uncle Ongoro, he now felt he had to do something about the swaying of the car. That is, as the car would tilt to the right, he would innocently pull it hard to the left. Soon, it would tilt to the left and Omollo would resume the job of pulling it to the right, all in an effort to assist it to attain an upright posture. The professor, of course, noticed him struggling with the car and asked him to stop worrying about the imbalance of the vehicle, but he could not believe that the man was honest.

As he peeped outside the window, he perceived that trees and people on the roadside were rushing in the opposite direction as on the apocalypse he had heard from Pastor Okiero – the perception that caused his bowels to protest by ejecting all its contents.

"Ooooooooogh!" A squawk of vomit alerted Professor Girado, who at the time was concentrating on the steering wheel. He thus quickly pulled up to assess what was going on. This frustrated Omollo even more and he now braced himself for a stinging slap from the professor; so he was indeed dumbfounded to meet only a smile from a man whose expensive car he had just soiled all over with vomit. He was further astonished to hear the man telling him sorry – a word he had never heard an adult man in his land saying to a woman or a child. Even more, he was puzzled to see the professor helping him to clean up his vomit in a friendlier way than his mother could have done to him when sick. Now he learnt of the deep love and understanding in that man's character which almost everybody in his village had exaggerated tenfold. As a result, his heart relaxed and he found himself opening up for conversation with the most respected kinsman. Thereafter, Omollo could ask Prof. Girado a question and he could give an elaborative answer, just as he liked to do. The subsequent sense comfort then enabled Omollo to begin the discovery journey of his life.

Omollo's first shock in that trip was finding out they had crossed the hills which he had long thought to be the end of the Earth. But as soon as they entered the outskirts of the city, he was fascinated even more by a sight of a long bus with a giant head gushing out black smoke and running on an iron road – his description of a train. A few moments later, he witnessed a plane taking off at the airport beside the road – a mind-blowing experience in his life.

Concisely, he was now so happy with the journey, except that an anticipation that he would soon meet the professor's wife turned his stomach. That is, everybody in their village said that the professor's wife did not want any of his relatives to visit their town home or rather that a visitor was required to write a letter at least three months in advance, which he had not done. But as fate would have it, the feared woman was on holiday in her homeland with her two children – implying that Omollo could now stay with the professor and his two workers without worrying about anything.

The professor's house was a self-contained house inside a fence of a clay brick. The physics of the house indeed gave Omollo something sweet to tell to his colleagues in his return.

"In that house, a man twists an iron bar and water gushes out as from a spring on a mountain rock," he one day told his siblings congregating around him to listen to his escapade in the city.

"You touch a knob on the wall and the light from the sun fills the room; touch it again and the darkness from the hell bounces back in full force."

"More marvels are in the dung house that our uncle used to talk about," he added.

"A man helps himself while seated on a white shining basin; and he cleanses himself not with tree leaves as we do here in our village, but with soft cotton tissues hanging on the wall. Next, he pulls a handle besides him and water steals away his dung, leaving a shit basin as shining as cat's pupils for the next reliever to enjoy," he narrated and raucous laughter now radiated from his audience.

"In the bathroom, you twist an iron bar and hot rain falls on your back,' he added.

"In the sitting room, a magic wooden box is fitted with a mirror in its front view and it shows pictures and sounds of all-important events taking place in the whole world."
He said and his relatives claimed that he had inherited his Uncle Ongoro's trait of lying about life in the town.

In a brief, the eight days that Omollo peeped into the professor's life instilled in him a completely new standpoint – he now aspired for education and modernity, symbolized by Professor Girado's life style.

A few days after his return from the city, he asked his father to allow him to resume schooling, to which his father unexpectedly did not object – probably because he was still celebrating the acquisition of free bullets.

This time Omollo was determined to obtain the knowledge and wisdom of the marvelous white men he had witnessed in town at school. To draw inspiration, he would hence look at the splendor of the professor's magnificent house from a distance every morning on his way to school.

All the same, Omollo knew clearly that his father never wanted him to abide by modern education. He further knew very well that all the conservatives in his community were looking up to him to take over the baton of the healing profession when his father was gone. In the view of the above, he skillfully masked his new faith in education by doubling his hatred and criticism of Christianity (to fool everyone that he was not a changed man).

<<<*CHAPTER TEN*>>>

The Christianity that Omollo was then a champion of challenging was very old in Malaland, although it had never ceased to be at loggerheads with the traditions of the Malans. Almost every day, priests of Jesus Christ in Malaland would rubbish the Malan way of defining the world and would persistently refer to those Malans who were not following their faith as infidels destined for a furnace during the apocalypse: "The day that mountains and rocks would jog around like footballers training," they would say.

Omollo first heard about the dawn of Christianity in Malaland from his old black grandmother, whom they preferred referring to as *Dani*. In the year Omollo was born, *Dani* was celebrating her ninetieth birthday, after which she only lived for fourteen years more. This is to say, *Dani* did not live with her grandson long enough to see whiskers growing on his chin. Be that as it may, Omollo never forget her wisdom and, of course, her oddities to the day he bored his chest with a kitchen knife.

Dani was a troublesome woman with a strong deep voice that scared even soldiers in uniform – and apparently, Omollo's father owed his fighting spirit to her genes. As a total anthropological and traditional conformist of Rabar Village, *Dani* would not talk with anyone even for three days upon learning that the villagers had adopted something she considered 'uncultured.' In extreme cases, she would even undertake a hunger strike to protest against such things – on one memorable occasion, she had threatened to strip naked after learning that one of her granddaughters had eaten hare, a taboo food amongst Malan women; this caused her whole family to plead with her for six hours to dismiss her intention.

All the same, her family gradually learnt how best to handle her in her old age. Firstly, they learnt that many of her organs ached so wildly and that she needed pain-relieving ointments even more than food. Secondly, they learnt that *Dani* would forgive every sin upon the receipt of a *snuff bribe* and might even open up one of her rare talks about the disgusting intrusion of new things in Malaland. On such precious occasions, she would be heard saying something like:

'Thank you my grandson. Thank you for giving me 'brain charger.'

May our great God 'Obong'o Nyakalaga,' bless you abundantly,' she would chant her blessing. 'You are quite different from all your fellow young men of today. Let our gods be with you. You will prosper, marry many wives and build a big compound.

The generation of today is cursed. You are living in bad days, my grandson. This generation has destroyed the Earth. Now you have nothing to eat, my grandson. You are as thin as needles and as weak as lambs. When I was your age, the Earth was good: fish, milk, meat, geese, honey, you name it, ooooh!

Down the valley there: rhinos, elephants, buffaloes, wildebeest. My grandson, what a plentitude of food! Potatoes, maize, groundnuts, beans – all in abundance. The Earth was pure and our gods were happy with us. No young men died prematurely as today. The sun was not as hostile as it is today, for our benevolent gods gave us much rain. None of us would tire ourselves with the digging of large farms. A farm as big as this floor, filled granaries upon granaries. Today you have committed a terrible abomination on Earth. You have polluted the Earth in the name of modernity, schools, Christianity. As a result, the gods have removed the hedges of protection around you, my grandson.

My grandson, since when did a woman eat hare? Since when did a woman put on trousers? Since, when did a boy make his sister pregnant? Dahhhhhhhhh! My ears rebel whenever I hear what happens on Earth today.'

But just as even a broken clock is right twice a day, some days would see *Dani* in fine feather even without *snuff bribe*. On such days, one would hear her humming folk songs of her times or fluting and nodding her head in tune with her self-made melodies.

Omollo and (of course) all the other grandchildren of *Dani* could easily notice such days and would quickly congregate around her for novel stories and accounts. One of the most interesting accounts *Dani* had ever told her grandchildren was about the debut of Christianity in Malaland, something she claimed to have literally witnessed as a young girl. That day, *Dani* in her usual croaky voice broke out into a story from her childhood:

"My grandsons and granddaughters, in my youth all people were united, people were one. All followed the genuine ways of the land. Our gods were happy and life was joyful. But that was long before the white men started sowing confusion among us with their schools and Christianity," she said and wanted to confirm their attention.

"Do you hear me?" Asked *Dani*, "they had not come yet to disorganize our worthy systems of life. They had not come to soil our earth and disunite clans," *Dani* continued. Then came an unnecessary interruption from a naive girl.

"*Dani* is our clan divided now?" One granddaughter asked.

"Of course, that is as obvious as a standing elephant," answered *Dani* in her usual croaky voice.

"Now our society is as spotted as the leopard's skin: some people follow the white men's school, others follow the religion of Kirisitu, and others are like bats. Only a few people like your father have held steadfast to our ways of life. Oh! Obong'o Nyakalaga, our God, save your people!" Prayed *Dani*.

"My grandchildren, do you know the reason every foolish being in this village is often nicknamed Andaro Nyokelo?" She posed a question to her audience.

"Noooo, *Dani*," the grandchildren responded in chorus.

"Naam, I was a nubile girl when the people of Rabar Village one morning wondered at seeing a peculiar two-footed creature with a heavy sack on his back. In features, he was very much like us but his colour was different.

"*Dani*, do you mean a white man?" One child cleverly guessed.

"Of course," answered *Dani* summarily and continued with her story, "because of his peculiarity, therefore, uncountable children trailed the organism whenever he passed. Sane adults too stared at him motionlessly, yet insane ones involuntarily joined the children in trailing him."

"But *Dani*, why were they trailing the white man?" One grandchild asked for clarification.

"Hahahahaha, back then, not even Ombuoro, the most widely-travelled villager, had seen a white man," said *Dani* and laughed heartily. "Ombuoro had, of course, seen an albino in Kinesa before – and had told everyone about what an albino was like. So we called him to come and inspect if that man was the albino he had been talking about,"

"Eeheheheh!" The grandchildren encouraged *Dani* to speak.

"He, of course, came around, inspected every part of the creature and eventually declared to the itching audience that the biped was from a different seed altogether,"

"Hahahahaha," the grandchildren laughed briefly and then one of them chipped in a question.

"But *Dani* what was his name?" He asked.

"Hahahahaha," *Dani* laughed long and joyously before

continuing, "did anybody know his name?" She asked back in a transfigured voice that made her listeners laugh, "his skin was soft and red and therefore everybody supposed he was no different to a newly born baby, who is not strong enough to lift up a calabash of porridge. Out of this thought, they named him Orembe or an indolent man, ahahahahahahahah!" *Dani* laughed.

"The irony was, however, that he arrived with such a heavy sack that only real men could lift up."

"*Dani*, did he talk with you?" Another curious listener asked.

"Yes, he did, through sign language, of course; back then he did not know even a single Malan word. And no one knew his language either. Talking to him was therefore like talking to a dumb person, but only for the three months it took him to learn our language. The crowd followed him on that first day until he camped at Aheko Hill, which was densely forested in those days," said *Dani* and temporarily diverted her talk to one of her granddaughters in particular:

"You gigantic-eyed cow, sit like a woman!" Exploded *Dani*, while pointing at a granddaughter she considered to be sitting like a man.

"At Aheko Hill, the masses viewed him reverently for two days, and on the third day, the crowd started experimenting on him," *Dani* continued.

"*Dani*, how?" Asked one of the grandsons.

"Touching his skin, opening his mouth to observe his dental formation and even trailing him whenever he went to relieve himself in the bush."

"Did they see his dung, *Dani*?"

"He had a small hoe with which he buried his dung," said *Dani* and grinned widely "But people who exhumed his dung claimed it was smaller than the typical dung of the villager and was also as multicolored as the excreta of an imbecile: the one who shows up in every house for a share whenever its dwellers are eating something."

"Ah! Ah! Ah! Ah! Ah! Ah!" The children bellowed with laughter again.

"And did his dung also stink, *Dani*?" Another question was thrown at the old woman.

"Ahahahahahaa!" *Dani* could not help herself from laughing this time, "dung is dung, no matter which mammal species produces it," she said and the children cut in with more laughter.

"Eeeehe," the children encouraged *Dani* to keep on narrating her story.

"But most important was that these villagers' harassments often changed his color," said *Dani* with confidence, "he would be white in the morning, but blood red after the onset of the locals' experiments."

"Really, he turned red, *Dani*?' One grandchild wanted to confirm. 'Did you witness that yourself, *Dani*?" He added.

"Of course, I saw it with my own eyes. His face and ears would be either blood-red or milk-white depending on the context he was in," said *Dani*, "and that is the reason people changed his name from Orembe to Kamiriona - chameleon if you like," said *Dani* and the children laughed even more.

"Did he not resist being experimented on, *Dani*?" Asked one granddaughter.

"He bore the harassment until one day the locals got on his nerves and he showed them what he was capable of,"

"How, *Dani*?" Asked a granddaughter.

"One man travelling on foot via Rabar Village found people viewing and investigating the biped on Aheko Hill."

"Eeeehe," the children encouraged *Dani*.

"The man then lied that he had met many such bipeds on his previous travels and sensationally claimed their balls were no different than the vervet monkey's balls - vivid blue in colour, to be specific," said *Dani*.

"Ahahahahahahah!" Children laughed like hyenas, "is it true, *Dani*?" One of them eventually wanted to confirm.

"Of course, just like you now, as soon as the man had proceeded on his way, everybody wanted to prove the assertion," said *Dani* and coughed a bit, "the white man then had a very hard time protecting his balls from viewing by an appetitive crowd," *Dani* said and the children were almost rolling on the ground with laughter.

"Ah! Ah! Ah! Ah! Ah!" They yelled joyously.

"And when Waringa and Oruba tried to strip him naked to expose his balls to the audience, the white man became angrier than ever. He now got into his hut and came out with a long wooden spoon that everybody laughed off hysterically."

"A gun, *Dani*?" Omollo's nephew suggested.

"Of course, it was a gun; but back then the idea of a gun was still no more than a rumour.

"Ah! Ah! Ah! Ah! Ah!" The children laughed.

"He next fired the thing with a loud bang – after which Oruba and Okello were in a cesspool of blood," said *Dani*, "since then, no one heckled Kamiriona or any other white men who later came to Malaland. People accorded them the respect of fear – actually as supreme witches. And for that reason they lived comfortably in our land afterwards."

"*Dani*, what did he eat?" Another granddaughter threw an interesting question to *Dani*.

"He just ate, rech, atipa, dek, ochiago and their kin."

"Ah! Ah! Ah! Ah! Ah! Ah!" The children laughed uproariously and long (at the idea that the white man could have eaten dek and atipa).

"Eeeehe, so what happened to him next," the children encouraged *Dani* to tell more.

"After getting used to the land, he would now move from one village to another, spreading the words of their imaginary prince who was assassinated for self-aggrandizement. The first convert he got was, of course, a bewitched woman going by the name of Nyandiri Nyobala. Everybody in the village now laughed to hear Kamiriona saying that the prince sent him to look for haunted people like Nyandiri Nyobala."

"*Dani*, why was it ridiculous for their prince to want Nyandiri Nyobala?" Omollo's sister asked logically.

"*Eeehheheheh*," *Dani* laughed and cleared her throat in her usual scary style before continuing with her story. "Nyandiri Nyobala was long haunted by spirits after committing a grand abomination in Malaland," she said and coughed again, "one day, she and her co-wife, Matata Nyotato, were going to pick vegetables in the field – just as all women still do here today. But before reaching the intended field, the two women encountered a buffalo that was fast asleep by the path they were following. And because Matata Nyotato liked meat as a cat likes milk, upon seeing the sleeping buffalo, the idea of serving a meat sauce instead of vegetables that evening crossed her mind like a flash. Accordingly, she pronounced the buffalo dead and hence a possible source of meat. On the other hand, Nyandiri was somewhat wiser, and thus strongly warned her of the likelihood that the beast was just asleep. All the same, Nyotato, under the influence of greed, did not agree with her," said *Dani*.

"Nyotato rather proposed a test of throwing stones at it to check if it was alive. Indeed, the women threw several stones at the beast yet it did not respond to any of them," she said and grinned widely, "thereafter, the meat maniac proposed to a hesitant Nyandiri that they harvest the first fruit from the dead animal before alerting the rest of the villagers." *Dani* now cleared her throat and picked her nose before continuing the narration of the story to her attentive listeners.

"Still doubtful, Nyandiri pointed out the hurdle of the lack of a knife for the exercise, but Nyotato would not give in easily on meat. She said she would try something and gave Nyandiri her basket to hold for her. Thereafter, she knelt down behind the animal and inserted her right arm into its anus – evidently intending to pluck out its tasty liver for soup. But no sooner had she started pulling the buffalo's liver than the beast flexed the muscles of its anus and dashed in bewilderment, with Nyotato's arm stuck up at its backside.

"Eeeeeeeeeee," the children sympathized with Nyotato as *Dani* threw a snuff-laden spit, as she often did.

"Eeeeh, it started dragging the woman behind her, literally bashing her in the thorny thickets and bushes it was bushwhacking in its bewilderment at what was sticking up on its rear. As the woman cried, the timid animal sped up in fear of the queer thing making a noise on its rear. But Nyandiri, instead of calling for help, only laughed and laughed, as the beast towed Nyotato up and downhill at the speed of a tornado. In fact, Nyandiri would lie down on her stomach with laughter as the beast descended with its captive into a valley, and would only stop when the beast and Nyatato were out of sight, usually when they would be in the middle of valleys. But as soon as she would stand upright, the beast and Nyotato would be now ascending the next hill with Nyotato on its rear, and the sight would plunge Nyandiri back to her hysterical laughter for at least ten minutes. It was said she laughed until tears were now rolling down her cheeks and, of course, continued laughing over the event for two more days without stopping. Even afterwards she could never prevent herself from an intermittent baseless laughter that eventually qualified her as a madwoman of the village," *Dani* said and stopped to add some snuff in her mouth.

"The dead body of Nyotato was later found leaning on a dense thicket through which the buffalo bushwhacked with her in fear of the strange noisy object at its posterior," she said.

"Nyandiri was then an old woman living alone at the edge of the village when she became the first convert of Kamiriona. Later on, other lunatics followed suit and laughter about the reasoning of Kamiriona's god dominated the village."

"*Dani*, what happened next?" Omollo's elder brother yearned for more.

"Kamiriona would in the morning move to Rabar Village to preach his new faith; then go back to Aheko Village in the evening to sleep. One day, as he was passing by from Aheko Village to Rabar Village, he noticed a small girl on a branch of a tree by the path he was using – actually wearing nothing but an honest smile – and it is like he saw that red button at the junction of her hind limbs and thus pitied the nude girl," *Dani* spoke euphemistically and now the amused children broke into a thunderous laughter.

"Hahahahahaha!"

"So, what followed in short order, *Dani*?" Another grandchild asked.

"He asked the naked girl to climb down, whereupon he gave her a coin, and ordered her: 'Go and buy pants for hiding your firefly,'"

"Hahahahaha!" The children burst into more big laughter.

"The happy girl then took the coin she had been given by Kamiriona to her mother, who was Andaro Nyokello, and, of course, told her mother how she got the money from the white man. From what I heard, the story moved her very much and even enlightened her to use the same trick to get some money herself from the same man," she said and paused to throw away the saliva that had gathered in her mouth.

"*Dani*, how?" The children said together.

"The following day, as she saw the white man coming back the same way, Andaro took off her clothes, ran and climbed the same tree as her daughter had done on the day before."

"Eeeehee," the enthusiastic children wanted to know what followed.

"On reaching the tree, the white man was quite astonished to see a nude woman on the tree and could not understand why. All the same, he ordered the woman to climb down – as he had done to the child on the day before."

"Eeeehee," the enthusiastic listeners encouraged *Dani* to carry on.

"Andaro Nyokello now climbed down from the tree quickly with a full-grown grin across her face, reasoning like this: 'If a child got a coin for being naked, then an adult like me must get at least four coins for being naked.'"

"Hahahahaha," the children burst into a booming laughter again.

"So, how many coins did she get in the end, *Dani*?" A granddaughter chipped in.

"Are you talking of coins?" *Dani* asked back and broke into a light laughter, "Kamiriona, dipped his hand in his jacket pocket, fished out a razor blade, gave it to the woman, and landed a resounding slap on her cheek: 'Go and shave yourself. You are as bushy as Gagamoya Hill,' he roared." *Dani* imitated the white man artistically.

"Ah! Ah! Ah! Ah! Ah! Ah!" The crowd of children laughed long, some even rolling on the ground in hilarity.

"Did any man join Kimiriona's religion after that incident, *Dani*?" One granddaughter asked her a related question after the marathon of laughter

"Yes, of course," said *Dani* thickly, "there was this senior bachelor who did not see eye to eye with the women of Rabar Village. Nothing thrilled that man so much as learning that a woman had been beaten, injured or killed."

"Eeeehee," the attentive children encouraged her to speak more about this strangely behaving man.

"Women would reciprocally celebrate upon learning that that man had been beaten, injured or killed," she narrated.

"*Dani*, what is his name," asked one grandchild.

"His name was Salamba, though women unanimously nicknamed him a Terrorist – allegedly, for possessing an oversized third arm of a man that would indeed send whichever woman who happened to catch sight of it sprinting like a racehorse," she said and the older children started laughing; the young ones, of course, remained clueless.

"So, the Terrorist instantly joined the church after being convinced by Kamiriona that he would get so many fitting and non-stigmatizing women in Heaven," finished *Dani* and ordered the dispersal of the children as it was getting very late.

And Because of this story, whenever Omollo came upon any motivated Christian preacher, he would always grin and instantly remember his grandmother. Omollo would from time to time also remember his grandmother for her act of great kindness to him a few weeks before passing on. That particular night, his ailing grandmother awakened him when everybody else was asleep. Next, she ordered him to take a hoe and led him to the Sacred Rock. Upon reaching the place, she asked her grandson to dig a deep hole under it. When the hole was about two meters deep, she handed Omollo two golden bangles and said:

> *"I bequeath you these bangles, which I myself was bequeathed by my grandfather. Fortunately, I have lived all my life in such plentitude that I did not have any need to sell the bangles. Bury them in this hole, and when you are ripe to marry, dig them out, sell them and buy as many cows with which to marry as many wives as possible to perpetuate our noble clan."*

She recited in a very lovely voice – more lovely voice than ever before.

<<<*CHAPTER ELEVEN*>>>

All the same, the events that marked the dawn of Christianity – like the shooting of Oruba and Okello – had happened even before Omollo's father was born. That is, Omollo grew up to find that many churches were already well-established in Malaland and had many followers. One such well-established church in Rabar Village was the one run by Father Kamiriona – the man who, in *Dani's* accounts, had slapped Andaro Nyokelo for stupidity. Kamiriona's church had many followers, both active and dormant, and owned a primary school and a dispensary in the village. According to the Malans, the church was more tolerable than other Christian churches in their village, as it was the only Christian church that allowed its members to drink wine a bit, dance *arutu*, go to *teng'o*, and eat pork.

The story went that after reaching old age, Father Kamiriona passed the torch to Omiesa Senior, who later on passed it to Omiesa Junior – actually, a man who once had disgraced the church after he was identified as a witch by Ghati, *the Magician*. All the same, Kamiriona's relatives would still visit their kin's church during their princes' birthdays and deathdays – the days when many dormant followers of the church would turn out – and Omiesa would prove he had made a kill in collecting God's taxes by replacing his old bicycle with a brand new one. Nobody, nonetheless, complained about this – owing to the fact that it was clear in the church's manifesto that Omiesa was God's mouthpiece, whereas, the rest of the church members were the baby sitter's hand that had to feed it.

Apart from Father Kamiriona's church, other churches were in bad odor in the land. The Malans purported that they were against all the natives' favorite things: funeral music, folk songs, *teng'o*, tobacco smoking and liquor drinking. Consequently, the churches had fewer followers, which was reflected in the slimness and shagginess of their leaders, compared to the sparkling Omiesa. Their services were also normally conducted in grass-thatched huts that looked like the villagers' huts: some Christian groups, in fact, did not have even a grass-thatched building and could only worship their god either under the shades of big trees or in primary school classrooms. Overall, all the churches had so far stood the test of time since their debut in Malaland.

In addition, new churches still kept on popping up in Malaland from time to time. In other words, some were younger to Malaland than Omollo himself. But as if they had all graduated from the same college, every church would enter Malaland with a loud bang that would definitely raise the eyebrows of the slumbering Malans.

The latest church in the land was then the one headed by Okiero – the one-eyed Malan who was as hard to interpret as a medical text.

Okiero's church was introduced to the land by a group of white men, who brought with them a good number of second-hand clothes and blankets for charming the Malans. These men declared an instant reward for whoever showed interest in their faith: whoever showed allegiance to their new church would instantly be rewarded with a bunch of clothes and blankets for allegedly choosing the light over darkness. With this bait in hand, three-quarters of Rabar villagers had frequented the classroom that the group was using for a church in its three months of existence.

One such new believer was, of course, Bongo Onduro, *the Iron*. This man attended the congregation for three days, collected his share of clothes and bolted out, never to return to the church again. Whenever someone asked him why he was not attending the fellowship anymore, he would give a long list of excuses, none of which held water.

"The three times I attended the church, we would always pray for those who are cooling their throats with beer at bars or resting under the shades of trees at home. So with that knowledge, need I waste my time going to church, whereas, absentees are prayed for?" He would ask you back persuasively.

"And the man was telling us to give our life to Jesus, imagine!" He would add amidst roars of laughter, "so! Give him my life and remain with what?" He would ask sarcastically, "and imagine! I went there and they wanted me to mourn for someone who was nailed on a cross for contempt. And you all know that I am still satirized in the village folk songs for failing to mourn for my own beloved mother, Auma Nyokelo," he would conclude, amidst howls of mirth from his listeners.

Three-quarters of the new believers, like Onduro, withdrew from the church within a few days. Some claimed that they dropped out after discovering that there were a number of hidden costs in following the church:

"Imagine offering money to feed and dress God whom they conversely told us is capable of everything," one of them animatedly claimed.

Others claimed that their throats were burning like hell for missing the cold beer at Ambalo Nyatiga, a revered brewer of Rabar Village. All the same, a few people like Okiero, miraculously hung on in spite of all the obstacles.

Okiero, of course, like any other, initially joined the church to collect his clothes and then vanish into thin air. Nevertheless, while there, some teachings of these foreigners stunned him so much that he chose to hang on for a while to get some more of it. However, in the course of this overstay, he encountered a verse that he considered outrageous. This was none other than Mark 12:31, reading, *Love your neighbour as you love yourself.* Completely disbelieving the possibility of the verse, Okiero publicly accused the white pastor of lying and even threatened to walk out of the church if that man of God could not admit he was joking when he read the verse to them. But as the trained missionary had long known Okiero as an obstinate person, he chose to deal with him in textbook fashion.

"The joy of our faith is that you can test it yourself." He set a trap, into which Okiero easily fell.

"How can one love his neighbour like himself?" Okiero talked to himself as he mused about the teaching on his way home that day, "I indeed must test the possibility of this crazy idea of the whites' God," he concluded.

Now it happened that a stone's throw away from his homestead lived a wife of his jailed brother, a woman whom down the years he had treated just like any other villagers of Rabar. Unexplainably, out of all his neighbours, he chose to experiment the practicability of Mark 12:31 with this particular woman.

Okiero started his experiment by visiting the woman regularly and helping her with manly household work in her compound, like clearing the land and mending the fence – just to see how much he would begin to love her like herself. Before anybody suspected anything, he was already eating and sleeping with the woman in the name of 'love your neighbour as you love yourself.'

As expected, Okiero's love-research irritated his second wife greatly. She in turn sternly warned him to stop the madness that Christianity was pumping into his narrow mind. All the same, the junior man of God turned a blind eye and a deaf ear to his wife's fuss. But eventually, Okiero's second wife could no longer stand such nonsense. In a fit of madness, one day she jabbed Okiero's left eye with a sword while he was asleep and took to her feet to a location still undisclosed to this day for betrayal of their marriage. Okiero afterwards suffered pain and depression beyond compare – and would not have overcome the depression, had the owners of his new church not been nursing him throughout his agony.

But upon his recovery, Okiero's faith catapulted to a degree that stunned even the church owners themselves. So, by the time that the proprietors of the church were leaving Malaland for evangelistic missions elsewhere, they gladly handed their thriving church in the safe hands of Okiero. That is, Okiero now became the de facto head of the church popularly known as *the Mourners and Dancers' Church*, due to their breathtaking artistic style of wailing and dancing for their slain prince. A few years after handover, Okiero took his faith to a notch that startled even his fellow shepherds. It happened that a cobra bit his daughter while collecting firewood at Ramar Valley. The girl thereafter ran home madly with her life-threatening bite for her father to rush her to a snake-healer. Conversely, Okiero stunned even dogs by refusing to take his daughter to Omwanda, the revered snake-healer of Malaland – asserting that their imaginary prince would cure the girl of snake venom to prove to non-believers that he was a capable god. According to the story, he immediately summoned his followers and all of them started exorcising the alleged demon in the form of snake inside the girl:

"Go away, go away, go away!" Some shouted, while others chanted unintelligible slogans in the name of extorting a demon in the form of snake out of the poor girl. Whenever the girl cried: "I am dying, you people!" The animated Okiero took the girl's voice for that of the demon and would therefore just roar back, "die, the deceiver of mankind, the destroyer of the decent, the demolisher of the built!" Some months later though, one of his deviant followers spilt the beans that they were instructed by the girl's father to pinch the girl as hard as possible to put the expression 'I am going now' into the alleged Devil's mouth through the mouth of the girl.

In the end, the poor girl silently passed on, actually depriving villagers an opportunity to witness the power of Okiero's Father in Heaven. A persistent rumour had it that the inconsolable mother of the girl later claimed she visited a soothsayer and that he had told her that the cause of her daughter's death was a combined team of venom and the noise pollution of the saints. Okiero nonetheless rubbished the soothsayer's observation and accused the Devil of infringing into his spiritual life through his wife.

From what I heard, no sooner had the colonial police officers, who were still at large on the land, received the news about the death of Okiero's daughter than they stormed into his compound like a flood. Subsequently, they arrested Okiero and his followers and allegedly gave them some free social tuition whose details have never emerged since. Even so, the scars from whips seen on their backs whenever they took off their clothes for bathing at the River Ramar suggest they had serious teachers. In addition, the fact that they would subsequently rush their colleagues to medicine men, even for influenza, implied that the lesson was a success. But when themselves were asked the reason for switching from their old practice after the incident, it was claimed, they would unanimously quote Christ's famous words to the Pharisees: "Give back to Caesar what is Caesar's and to God what is God's"

Overall, all Christian churches in Malaland were more or less the same. That is, they all used the Bible and believed in the same Father and Son. Equally, they strongly criticized one another for petty reasons – some accused their counterparts of baptizing with too little water, or of eating uneatable things. Others accused their fellows of showing insufficient grief towards the slain prince. Furthermore, they all used similar vocabularies such as "running from the world," "seeing in spiritual eyes," "everlasting life" and so forth. Likewise, they all forced their faithful to find themselves hard-to-pronounce names for heavenly purposes. Accordingly, everyone who joined them came out with a peculiar name. Okello got for himself *Sakaria*; Omwanda was *Atonia* and Ombalo became *Tito*. When asked about the change of name, they reported that their preachers had told them that God was not used to local names and they would miss out on many events in Heaven if they retained such names that God could not pronounce. Further, all churches forced their lying members to tell the truth, selfish ones to be generous and womanizers to see all women as their mother-in-law. People even laughed themselves sick upon hearing that Jamba, the chronic rustler, had vowed he would not steal anybody's cow again after joining *the Mourners and Dancers' Church*.

Omollo, like any other Rabarian, of course, found the teachings of these people weird, let alone the hurdle of his obedience to his father and his tradition. As a person, he strongly believed in following his heart – *kuipa roho ile kitu inataka'*, unfortunately an antonymic perspective to that of Christianity. As he always told his friends, his heart haboured an unimaginable thirst of dancing with pretty girls, attending traditional ceremonies, eating pork and mating at will – actually the opposite of what Christianity demanded.

Omollo also hated the way Christian preachers pounced on everyone with their so-called good news. One Christian, whom they nicknamed *Hitchhiker Weed*, would, from time to time, pop up at the spot they would play *bao*, allegedly, for trying to save them from the fangs of the demon. Omollo would, of course, get into an argument with him almost every day, yet the city made of jewels the man kept on talking about appealed to his senses. Arwing City, the only city whose beauty he could not fathom, was not even a quarter as good as that hypothetical city that Hitchhiker Weed would talk about with every enthusiasm known on the planet Earth. As far as he could recollect, Arwing was full of accidents, robberies, and murder – he himself became a victim of a fraudster on only his third day in Arwing City. That day, he was playing with a ball in front of his host's compound. Now it happened that he had taken off his pair of new rubber footwear, as he was not used to playing football with shoes on. At that juncture, a trickster approached him and greeted him in Kilayi. But as soon as Kilayi words curiously rolled off his tongue in reply to the greeting, the con artist recognized by his accent that he was a new entrant in the city. Realizing this, the conman fished out fifty cents from his wallet and asked Omollo to go and buy him a packet of cigarettes at a kiosk about one hundred and fifty meters away from where he was playing. Meanwhile, the man offered to watch over his ball and shoes while he was away on the mission. As Omollo had been brought up in his village to obey adults' orders, he did not doubt this man even a little; on the contrary, he quickly ran to the shop, only to encounter a rude shock on his return: not only was the man who had sent him no longer there but also his belongings where nowhere to be seen either. Shocked like a scolded schoolchild now, he remained there stranded with a packet of cigarettes in his hand – actually as useless to him as a rake in a canoe.

Besides, he saw many dirty children wandering and begging in the streets of Arwing; his host had referred to them as "street children." Here, however, the likes of Omiesa and Okiero were talking about a city that was too good to be true: a city where the lion shares a taxi with the antelope; a city where rivers flow with soda; a city where trees bear cakes; a city where cats sing in chorus with rats; a city without wails, hospitals, bandits and fraudsters. Omollo even liked the part, which stated he would only be required to click a button and a machine would do his washing for him.

"That city is the place to be, ooooh," he thought to himself one day.

"No," he quickly corrected himself, "Okiero claims that saints populating that city sing songs of praise to God day and night." He voiced his thoughts aloud and giggled alone like a madman, "how can I, Omollo, son of Nyamngwegre, afford singing for such long time?" He soliloquized, chuckled again and continued thinking. At that juncture, he flashed on how their schoolteachers would punish them for boycotting singing their monotonous national anthem – and now the thought made him chuckle even more, "what will happen if the same scenario occurs with such heavenly songs of praise?" He now asked himself audibly and again grinned from ear to ear.

<<<*CHAPTER TWELVE*>>>

One cool night in June of the same year, Omollo was fast asleep in his hut when he heard wails of misery from a group of women. The sound of such wails would normally proclaim the death of a person or an alarm of cattle rustling in his village. But since nobody had been ill in his village the previous evening, he instantly concluded that the cattle of one of his kin had been rustled – a conclusion based on the fact that cattle rustlers would, from time immemorial, frequent their village to steal from his people. In his land, herdsmen would regularly check if their cattle were still safe in the kraal: if not, they would swiftly search for them in the immediate surrounding area (if by chance, they had broken the kraal). If not, they would rouse their families to join them in awakening the whole village through wails like the ones Omollo had just heard.

Since antiquity, cattle had been among the common wealth of Malans. It was therefore the duty of every young man, such as Omollo, to pursue cattle rustlers whenever an alarm for such thieves was raised in their village. With this in mind that night, Omollo jumped out of his bed like a warrior in survival mode, scrambled into his trousers and thrust his feet into tire-made sandals. Next, he rushed to the corner of his hut and fumbled in the darkness for his spears, shield and a dagger; then ran madly out of his hut – all the while envisioning a daring cattle chase ahead of him. Now upon crossing a perimeter fence of their compound, he swung his ears this way and that way in an attempt to ascertain the location from which the wails were coming.

Contrary to his anticipation, the wails were from the opposite hill of *Chikiti* and were in the company of dim sounds of drums and horns – an apparent clue that someone important had departed for the next world. Safe in the knowledge of a false alarm, he sighed deeply and hurried back to his hut to try to re-gather the dear sleep he had unnecessarily blown away due to a lack of keenness. Deep down, he thanked his hospitable gods for sparing him the daunting task of pursuing stolen cattle he had originally anticipated that night: it would have taken him and his colleagues at least a day or two to catch up with the blood spillers – which the cattle rustlers were, during which time he would be hungry, thirsty and sleepy. If lucky, they would restore the cattle to their village and end up at a big heroic banquet in their village. Otherwise, the normally armed rustlers would carry the day in their battles with the villagers and, instead of stolen cattle, the surviving cattle pursuers would bring back to the village the dead bodies of their colleagues.

The next morning revealed that the midnight wails had been proclaiming the death of a clan member by the name of Nyambeu

Girado, *the Rooster* – a nickname that reads in full as *the Rooster* – *the Giant Fowl that Meets a Crippled Man on a Foggy Day and Supposes that it is a Frog. It thus Amazes Honestly and Audibly, 'My God! What Do Frogs Feed on these Days that they Grow this Big?'*

Girado, *the Rooster*, was well known throughout Malaland and its environs, especially for fathering Professor Girado, Mr. *Tell Them*. In this view, his death would consequently give the land a rare opportunity to eat, drink, dance and mate in a fit of madness. Food lovers in Rabar Village specifically referred to such famous people as the baobab, an analogy of a tropical tree whose fall enables villagers to pick its abundant fruits while seated on three legged stools.

People thus expected that Professor Girado would bring them much food and drink at his father's death ceremony. Many people likewise anticipated watching Girado's learned sons and daughters weeping for their kin in a style never seen before in the whole of Malaland. What's more, at the event, Malans expected to rub shoulders with VIPs coming from distant lands to console the professor for having lost his father.

Much more than was expected, a chain of hooting cars, the like of which the village had never seen before, was noted on the very next morning. The spectacle thus took the village by storm: every villager who became the first to note what was happening rushed to call the attention of their clueless colleagues also to stare at the rare spectacle unfolding on their home territory.

"Irrespective of how hot the water becomes, it does not forget its coldness," one village newswoman now said in projecting Professor Girado as a true son of the land whom white the man's education and civilization had not maddened like his counterparts.

"Even I, myself, marvel at the efficacy of the medicine which Girado gave to his son," her colleague in the conversation contributed.

"While the main occupation of every young educated Malan is to despise our folk way of life, this son of Girado has visited all the classrooms one may think of. And, yet, still he has, for all this long time, outsmarted all the white men's intoxications to continue cherishing our every esteemed custom just like you and me," she strongly complemented Professor Girado.

As expected, the arrival of Professor Girado stirred up his father's homestead, just like swimmers racing to dive in a pool. Animated horn-blowers now blew their horns like hell, drummers beat their drums to their level best and old mourners sobbed for the dead man with all their heart and soul – all so as to join hands with the professor in order to mourn for his beloved father (who happened also to be one of the three earliest teachers at the first white men's schools in the whole region north of Damasawa City). As a rule, such bewailment would be cyclic until the burial event, after which the death ceremony proper of the deceased would begin.

As prophesied earlier, the death ceremony of Girado senior appeared promising from the start. Professor Girado brought with him plenty of rice, maize flour and drinks, making every mourner feel blessed for being able relate to Professor Girado, Mr. Tell Them, in whatever way. Apart from food and drinks, the professor had also brought with him a record player and a movie projector – probably to immortalize the death ceremony of his beloved father.

But in a sharp turn of events, an unfounded rumour began to emerge on the second day that the professor and his wife would not be staying at their father's funeral for the minimum of seven days required of them by the Malan funeral law. The persistent rumour added that the professor would leave for a distant land on the morning of the third day – suggesting that he would leave the land even before his father had been buried. Given the peculiarity of this news, the elders dismissed it outright because in their ears, it sounded akin to destroying a temple and rebuilding it in three days. As they had known from birth, violating the obligatory funeral rituals and protocols of Malans would invite inconceivable penalties from gods of the land.

The first outstanding funeral ritual was known as *the ritual of shaving-off*. This meant a goat would be slaughtered for members of the dead man's household before each of them was shaved bald – a symbol of casting away the bad luck that had befallen the family. Another outstanding ritual was the *teng'o* ceremony – a feast held in homage of the fallen hero. It was said that any deceased to be denied the ceremony would disrupt peace among his living clan members from time to time. All the same, the most important ritual was the *ritual of bones*, in which children of the deceased, among others, would pitch a tent at the home of the deceased for a minimum of seven days. During this time, they would most importantly abstain from taking a bath and getting into other people's pants for seven days. On the seventh day since the occurrence of the death, a cow would be slaughtered and a senior elder of the clan would distribute its meat to all the children of the deceased. Each benefactor would now smoke their share so that it would not go bad before their turn came to depart from the compound. Thereafter, dispersal from the homestead of the deceased would kick off but in turns: the first child, or *kayo*, would be the first to leave their father's homestead, alongside members of his or her household. On reaching home, he or she would cook the smoked meat and eat it with members of their family. That would now mark the end of the funeral abstentions. Following on the list would be the second born, then the third, to the last born or *chogo* – a.k.a the beloved child of its mother.

As everyone in the land knew, violating this custom would invite a taboo-induced disease known as *chira* to members of the family in question. It was said that a victim of the disease would grow thin like a rope and easily catch opportunistic infections that would eventually wipe him off the Earth's surface like a wind to feather. That would not be the end of the story, though: *chira* would soon jump on the next of kin until it was done with everybody in the clan. Worse still, it was claimed that neither medical doctors nor traditional healers could cure a victim of *chira*, considering that it was gods' punishment for disobedience. Given this anticipated ferocity after breaking the bone ritual, not even adamant Christians like Okiero and Omiesa were ready to test the depth of the river with both feet by violating the norm. They would always find a way to conduct the ritual secretly and they would gossip among themselves that the bone ritual was only the taboo in Malaland that the cleansing blood of Jesus had failed to clean.

Omollo, like everybody else in the village, was thus chilled to the marrow over the gossip that his role model was about to commit this abomination on the land. He even prayed to the gods of his forefathers to divert the imminent curse from the man he had long before admired.

As the news became persistent to the ears of clan elders, they consulted amongst themselves and resolved to hold a meeting to establish the facts surrounding the rumour before it was too late. And in implementing the decision, senior clan elders summoned an extraordinary public meeting at the bonfire in the middle of the deceased's homestead. Given the sensitivity of the issue at hand, most elders of the village turned up for the meeting. Likewise, Omollo, of course, like any other villagers, was enthusiastic about that meeting and thus took a strategic position to follow everything fully.

Eventually, the much-awaited time to commence the meeting came and Elder Ombui Pangla was appointed by his colleagues to chair it. He stood up, called for the attention of the murmuring gathering and immediately set the wheels in motion:

"The Malans," he addressed the meeting in a sonorous voice, "the grandchildren of Omollo Chunga." Here he paused to survey the gathering professionally.

"We are lucky compared to the people of other lands. Ours is a blessed land, which readily rewards its sons and daughters who can do things no one has ever done before or which others have done only in inferior fashion." He now cleared his throat before continuing in a fast and unique pitch, "...but mind you, young men, don't go around the village stealing wooden spoons, thinking that the land will reward you for discovering a new theft." he said.

The audience now burst into laughter and Elder Ombui generously allocated them ample time to exercise their joy to its full extent before proceeding: "Tonight we have called this meeting because we have been hearing a rumour, which disturbs our ears, for two consecutive days. Specifically, we hear that our most talented son – I mean Parafesa Jojo – plans to go back to his work even before his father has been laid to rest." At this juncture, a whole array of exclamations could be heard from the audience.

"Clansmen, this information has given us a hard time, especially we, the old men," Elder Ombui said and paused, looked here and there to register people's reaction. Then he continued:

"So, we thought, well, we might be fighting a shadow, which is, of course, a madness," he added, thus provoking light laughter. Once more, he granted the audience an opportunity to exercise their emotional right.

"We then thought: what would be wiser than getting the information straight from the horse's mouth?" He posed a rhetorical question.

"Jojo," he suddenly called the baptismal name of Professor Girado, erroneously, "tell us the truth about what we have been hearing." Here he finished his speech and sat down on his chair of authority, literally higher than anyone's chair at the bonfire, to wait for the response.

Professor Girado, who appeared to be very drowsy, now stood up and started addressing the mourners in a style of speech that was quite alien to the context of the funeral in Malaland. Honestly, the audience would have jeered him, had he been a commoner – thanks be to the fact that he was the most learned man in the whole village and its environs.

"Thank you, Mr. Chairman; thank you, esteemed elders of Rabar Village; thank you, distinguished guests from all corners of the country, ladies and gentlemen," he said and everybody was flabbergasted.

"On my behalf, and on behalf of my dependable family, I am very glad to take this opportunity to talk with you, my friends and relatives tonight. Foremost, kindly accept my heart-felt gratitude for coming out in multitudes to take part in my father's funeral." He now paused, and an uncontainable laughter escaped from a fourteen year-old boy – actually because of the funniness in the man's speech. Adults, for their part, now glared at the boy hypocritically – in fact because they would also have laughed, save for the fact that they considered the man too intelligent to laugh at. The professor himself did not mind the boy, probably being convinced that he was merely foolish; consistent with this view, he continued to deliver his speech in the same style,

"I want to assure all of you that I and my wife Lora are quite humbled by this friendly gesture you have shown to me and the family," he said. People who had just heard the name of his wife for the first time now looked at each other but did not say anything.

"The problem," Professor Girado continued, "is, however, that I am too busy to comply with your demand of staying at this single event for more than four days. Just to let you know, I have been out of the country for four months. In fact, my last-born had even forgotten me when I returned home last week," he bragged, "imagine that the boy told his mother, when she came back from work that evening, that his uncle was in the house. His mother, eager to know which uncle was in the house, was astonished to learn that I was the one our son was talking about," he added and the assembly now burst into a delighted laughter at the imagination of "body by God, mind by Mattel."

"Anyway, it is not a big deal; we know how funny children can sometimes be," he said after the laughter had ceased and cleared his throat for the sake of style.

"Of course, I am saying this to prove to you how busy I am. Personally, I don't like this kind of life but I am doing it for my country," he added cunningly.

One young woman now murmured a question to her colleague:

"Auma, has that man a second wife called Country, for whom he is ready to slay seven Goliaths?"

But even before her colleague could react to her canny question, a firestorm of disapproval engulfed the audience over what they had just heard from the man they had been considering wise. Opportunely, Elder Ombui intervened to rescue the situation,

"Let us be patient and listen to the son of Girado's argument in full," he calmed the meeting to allow Professor Girado to continue his infuriating speech.

"My clansmen, you don't have to worry about my departure. I assure you that nothing will go wrong even in my absence," he said and an uproar of disapproval resounded from the assembly.

"I will make sure that I leave everything required for the funeral as I leave you tomorrow," Professor Girado added.

"Heyyyyyyyyyyiiiiiiii, Jajajajajajaja!" Many people now exclaimed in traditional fashion to oppose what the professor had just said. Then Elder Ombui Pangla interjected his conversation with a friendly question, actually, for the benefit of everyone around:

"Where will you be heading to, young man?" He asked shortly and the professor took the opportunity to respond to his question in his usual alien style.

"Ladies and gentlemen, I am heading to Parani for an international conference on the conservation of rare lizards, for which I am the main speaker of Gondwanaland," he said, again provoking the audience into an array of angry exclamations. All the same, Elder Ombui Pangla put on a brave face and continued steering the meeting, as if he was not himself hurt by all that the professor had said that night.

"Thank you, my son. At least we now know what you are saying. But be that as it may, my son, while it is true that you have been away from our land for a half a century, it is the worst kept secret that you spent your childhood and youth among us here. And for that reason, we had hoped you would at least know the *a, e, i, o, u* of our customs," he said, whereupon the audience burst into a hard-to-stop laughter,

"I mean, I did not expect you to fail to know what to do at the funeral of a father. Actually, what you are saying stirs our stomachs with forks, 'I ask those who are sitting there on the passage to clear it for me. I might gallop to the bush to relieve myself any moment from now'," he said lightheartedly (in a transfigured voice) and the group laughed even more. He now switched back to a serious tone and continued:

"Look here, my son, the issue here is not about you leaving us with enough food and drink. Your elder Nyambadre is already rich enough to feed the funeral without help from anyone. Our concern is on the observance of the noble taboos founded by our esteemed ancestors. My son, you and I know very well that fingers were made before forks," he said, and paused for a moment, "we have stayed in this village longer than you, yet, we have never even dreamt of anyone committing the abomination you intend to commit," he added.

"Not even Okiero, who is maddened by Christianity." The sound of a young woman spilt from the audience to cement the point and provoked rapturous laughter once again. Then Ombui continued.

"If you commit this sin, be very well aware that you will have invited doom to all of us with your own hands. My son, if it is only reading a paper that takes you to Pumuni at the expense of your father's funeral, kindly send someone to read it on your behalf."

Here the assembly broke into a derisive laughter – to Elder Ombui's amazement, considering that he was sure he had not spiced his talk with anything this time around.

"What is the matter with you guys?" He reacted seriously.

"It is Parani, Sir, not Pumuni," one young man explained what had amused the audience in his speech.

"Okay, be it Rapani or Paroni," he said, and people laughed lightly this time, "the point I am making is that the head teacher of our school knows how to read very well. You all remember how well he read the village message to the Minister of Education last year! After all, you all know how well he speaks Linglish after the fourth beer or at the sight of pretty ladies," he joked lightheartedly and, the gathering exploded into hysterical laughter.

"Listen, listen!" He called for their attention, "I am suggesting that he sends the head teacher to read that paper on his behalf in Pajani," he said, again, confusing the name of Parani for Pajani and actually leading the meeting to quote him as saying in the Malan language, *Send the head teacher to read that paper on your behalf on the thighs.* Everyone thus dissolved into howls of laughter, after which four hands were up in the air, their owners keen to say something to the audience.

Now it happened that one of the hands was Professor Girado's and Elder Ombui's thus denied others the opportunity to speak and re-gave the word to Professor Girado – probably supposing that he would this time heed the advice he had been given by the elders and the meeting could therefore be brought to a close. But contrary to his expectations, the professor stood up with a broad fake smile and incensed the assembly even more.

"My clansmen, what you are saying is very clear to me. However, you should read the signs of the times. Our world is rapidly changing and an old superstition like this one will take us nowhere. We should abandon these things of yesterday, if at all we want to sail in the same boat with others."

As was to be expected, Professor Girado's words clearly irritated many foot soldiers of the Malan traditions; the most annoyed of all was Old Nyamkwa, who was sitting in the front row at the fireplace. Popularly known as *Kisikang'ino* or *the Log of Black Ants that you cannot Carry Away on the Shoulder*, Nyamkwa had never censored her speech when angry. In preparation to take on Professor Girado, so that she could assuage her anger, she first jetted out a snuff-laden spit, which had been occupying her mouth for over fifteen minutes. Now with her oral cavity empty, she chipped in an awesome question, which, however, only increased the level of amusement rather than offering a solution.

"My clansmen," she called for the attention of everyone, "have those views come from somebody's head or butt?" She derisively asked and the audience burst into heterogeneous long laughter once again.

"You laugh eeeeee? But if the ideas are not from the butt, how can a sober man leave his father's body on the grave-mound to attend a lizards' wedding?" She asked in astonishment, causing the audience to resume their laughter.

"It is not a lizards' wedding, Elder Nyamkwa; it is a meeting about lizards," one young woman corrected her.

"Does either of the events make sense anyway?" Nyamkwa asked inventively and the audience exploded in hysterical laughter again.

After a while, Professor Girado stood up and took the podium again, the fire in his eyes now indicating beyond reasonable doubt that he was an injured man. Inwardly, he had now affirmed that his kinfolk were a bunch of chronic conformists of stupid cultures and he felt obliged to get the jungle out of them once and for all.

"My clansmen, you exhibit all the symptoms of backwardness," he stated in disgust, "may I share with you an experience of my colleague, Professor Oksaru. His father died last month but I assure you that he only stayed at the funeral for thirty-five minutes and then went back to work. This is a ..."

Again, Professor Girado could not finish his sentence due to a rude interruption from Elder Omwanda, a.k.a *the Uncastrated Bull* – a nickname derived from an assertion that he was as hard to restrain as an uncastrated bull, a creature that rarely spends a night in its owner's kraal without jumping over it into other kraals that are full of cows on heat. This Omwanda man would always take on whoever was bending what he considered the sacred rules of his land in his presence.

That night, he had, of course, missed what the professor had been saying for at least two reasons. Firstly, his hearing ability had long faded; and, secondly, his main priority was sucking his smoking pipe rather than listening to the professor's long formal speech. Even so, he had caught a word that sounded to him like *oksaru,* which in the Malan language would mean, *can't you be circumcised?* Without checking the exact word the professor had delivered, Elder Omwanda concluded beyond reasonable doubt that the professor was drunk with power and was thus abusing the Malans, who, traditionally did not practice genital circumcision and did not like to hear anyone lecturing them about its goodness. With this supposedly screaming evidence of contempt in his hands, Omwanda now felt obliged to cut the minor down to size for his "lack of respect to elders."

"Onang'o Jamicola, *the Only Malan who Defecates Seated on a Pot Like a White Man,*" Elder Omwanda erupted, causing everybody to look in the eyes of their neighbour in disbelief, "so, you have all of a sudden become so important that you are now demanding to know why we are not circumcised!" He roared and the audience now struggled with their suppressed laughter, realizing that Elder Omwanda was reacting out of context. Nonetheless, their reaction did not stop Omwanda from continuing to spit fire at the man he now considered to be the stupidest descendent of his clan,

"Onang'o, are we the Kombia tribe? I ask you!" He exploded like a thunder of the first rain and forced Elder Ombui again to try to rescue the situation.

"In fact, he did not mean what you have understood, Elder Omwanda," Elder Ombui tried to pour some oil on the already troubled water: though his intervention charged the hero of the Kubuya Civil Wars even more:

"Don't treat me like a kid, Elder Ombui," he scolded his junior colleague, "I was already old enough to graze my father's calves when you were still living in Scrotum Street," he added and the audience exploded into hysterical laughter at the funniness in this response.

"I have, with my own ears, heard him mocking us, *oksaru, oksaru!*" Elder Ombui asserted, now sending everybody who had understood Professor Girado into a wild laughter. This made Elder Omwanda pause and wait for the laughter to fade away.

"Onang'o, do you consider yourself cleverer than your fathers?" He resumed his scolding to Professor Girado, "we, your elders, tell you the right thing to do and all you do is to refute everything we are telling you. Where did you get such authority to lecture your mother's husbands? When did a chick become cleverer than a cockerel? Now, let me ask you, aren't we the ones who nursed you when those mosquito's legs you are walking on were a metropolis of rushes? Tell me, aren't we the ones who helped you with your running nose in the days when they nicknamed you *the Sheep, Owner of Nasal Discharge?* Now, leave the land tomorrow and we will see if it is possible for feet to clap while hands sing," he concluded and thereafter sat down with a white foam of anger having gathered at both sides of his mouth and his eyes glowing red like a firebrand.

But even before everyone had recovered from the devastation phase Omwanda had created, the ensuing quietness was disrupted by a wail as loud as a baby's in an injection room. Stunningly, it was Professor Girado who was the source of so much sobbing, allegedly, after Elder Ombui and Elder Omwanda had rubbed him up the wrong way with their series of pronouncements. In his later accounts to his friends, Professor Girado mentioned how Elder Ombui had referred to him, in his speech as *Onang'o Jamicola* – connotatively, someone who eats like a cow. Onang'o senior, from whom this nickname derived, would eat for several days without stopping and even died of overeating before his name become part of the tribal slur. Omollo's aunt, by the name of Owalo, was the first person to tag him this name: allegedly, after his impressive performance in eating among his peers at the end of that year's feast. Owalo later claimed that George's mouth was as busy as cow's tail that keeps chasing flies from one side to another whole day long. Further, Omwanda had referred to him as *the Sheep, the Owner of Nasal Discharge* – a tag deriving from a joke that his nose used to run all day and night when he was young. Additionally, Omwanda had exposed the state of his razor-thin shanks, which he had successfully tried to mask from the young generation with his trousers. Above all, the ultimate insult was his epithet of *the Only Malan who Defecates on a Pot Like a White Man.* The story behind this epithet was a sad sleepwalking incident that occurred when he was a teen. He had joined a secondary school in the metropolis, where his late uncle had been working as a chef for many years. The story went that, back then, this secondary school was very prestigious in the country because it had flush toilets, while many residents of that city still used pit latrines. In this light, access to flush toilets gave Girado a sense of pride that would, unfortunately, haunt him in his sleeps. Now it happened that he was at his uncle's place during his first holiday from school. A few days before going back to school, he dreamt that he was sitting on one of the school's flush toilet pots and saw himself defecating and appreciating the rare opportunities that life was giving him, compared to the rest of his kinsmen.

'I am the only Malan out here, who defecates while seated on a toilet pot like a white man,' he shouted in his awful dream, causing his uncle to rush to where he was shouting from – just to find out that the fool was defecating on his pot of chicken and shouting irrelevant phrases. According to the story, his uncle now avenged his soiled pot of meat by tagging George as *the Only Malan who Defecates Seated on a Pot Like a White Man.* All the same, his uncle died some fifty years ago and Professor Girado thought the epithet had been buried with him.

What's more, Omwanda had reprimanded in a way not even His Excellency, President of Kaya would do. After this choking sob, Professor Girado now lost control of himself and threw his weight on a chair behind him with uncontrolled violence. The wooden chair avoided confrontation by crumbling down with the man to the ground, bringing him to rest on granular dusty ground, forehead first. And with the thick lotion he had applied to his face a few minutes before the meeting, the sticky dust on the ground where he fell enjoyed some lifting. Honestly, he now looked no different from an animated Gondwanian witch doctor, an image that, as expected, sent the audience into uncontrollable laughter.

Ashamed and visibly angry, Girado now gathered himself lazily off the dusty ground and fished out his pistol, threatening as if he was about to blow Omwanda's brains out. Realizing the development, his accompanying friend, who had all the while remained speechless beside him, quickly grabbed Girado's arm in an honest attempt to prevent him from shooting the old man. Unluckily, in this tumult, two bullets accidentally discharged from the pistol with audible bangs. Sensing danger, everybody now ran amok for dear life at the speed of a bomber.

When the turmoil finally ceased, one old woman had blood oozing over her face, having been cut by a stone she bumped into during her escape; Omwanda, *the Uncastrated Bull,* who was at the center of the rampage, had dislocated his femur and could not stand up again from that day until his death six weeks later; Girado's uncle from a distant village also had blood draining out of his eyes after running into a sharp pointed sisal fence; Dwardy was permanently disfigured after running into a pot of meat on the stone stoves, which, in turn, retaliated against his disturbance by streaming hot sauce all over his face. The rest had small to medium injuries – all due to the uncalled-for rampage caused by Professor Girado.

To rub salt into the wound, the professor who had caused the tragedy was not even sorry for it. Rather, he selfishly felt he was the one who had been humiliated by illiterates. In a display of anger to his kinsmen, he left his father's compound the next morning in a convoy of his friends and nuclear family – an act that was considered treason by Malans.

At around 10:00 a.m. of the same day, a few members of the community gathered uncoordinatedly to give a send-off to the father of the man whom they now all claimed to "have died from the neck up."

Contrary to earlier expectations, Girado Senior now became the first VIP in Malaland to be buried without noise. A few minutes after he was buried, his clan called a meeting at which they unanimously cursed Professor Girado in an array of styles and excommunicated him from their clan for as long as he lived.

All the same, many years passed and the curses and wishes against Professor Girado did not come to pass. He continued to make headlines for another six years after this incident; then came a new chapter in his life.

<<<*CHAPTER THIRTEEN*>>>

Six years later, pieces of news started arriving at Malaland that a gang had attacked Professor Girado, shot him in the back and chopped off his feet. A different version of the story claimed a heartless gang had invaded his house and beheaded him but, fortunately, he was rushed to the white men's hospital, where his head was re-attached. Another rumour went around that the gang went to his house with a cruncher, crunched his genitals and feet, barbecued them and shared them with the Girados. A further nasty rumour described how three lustful gunmen invaded his house and gave members of his family the option of getting some hot showers from their hide muzzles or bullets in their O-rings. According to the story, all – including Professor Girado – chose the hot shower option, yet the evil men still mutilated the man afterwards.

All the same, nobody made a big deal out of these rumours; the fact was that a rumour-spreading tradition had been in the villages from time immemorial.

As long as Professor Girado had generated uncountable enemies per square meter in the villages, it was only to be expected that the sad tales about him were no more than wishful thinking, just as it was known that every hen would wish for a hawk to become bread and drop freely on its dining table. Equally logically, haters of Professor Girado were as usual wishing him the unthinkable, due to the loathing towards him that they harbored in their evil chests.

After a while though, all the rumours died away as they lost their flavour, or rather the people of Rabar Village found something else to talk about. But one evening, six years later, the villagers noticed a lorry digressing from the highway towards the professor's home. As they had long cursed Professor Girado, nobody cared whether he was going to his home by lorry. All the same, one freelance village journalist was moved to action by the knowledge that the lorry was offloading things from its rear, as if someone was moving into house. In a quest to be the first to report what was happening at the cursed man's homestead, he went and peeped behind the euphorbia tirucalli that was fencing the building. In a strange revelation, he was astonished to see that one of the items that had been offloaded from the back of the lorry was a mutilated man in a wheelchair. In possession of this dramatic news, the journalist rushed towards the village to share the story of a rich crippled man who had leased the house of the estranged professor. The news quickly reached the village leaders, who took offence at the knowledge that there was an arrogant, rich, crippled man who was joining their village without reporting to the village authorities.

They thus hurried to scrutinize the incident but soon realized that the crippled man was none other than the once famous man in all the lands, Professor Girado, a.k.a Mr. *Tell Them*. The news that the erstwhile most revered man in the land had been brought back to the village on a wheelchair now spread like wildfire to Rabar and its neighbourhood. On the second day, therefore, a multitude of people, from as far as the fourth village, flocked around that man's homestead, allegedly, to witness a tragedy they would otherwise hear only from tribal folktales. One by one, they took turns to peep at the terminally ill man on his dusty couch in the sitting room.

Whenever the man cried for help, he would receive mockery tailored around the last words he had uttered to the villagers during his rebellion. That is, he would cry for water, and people would ask him if he wanted *oksaru* – in reference to a learned man he had mentioned as his role model in matters pertaining to handling funerals.

When Omollo's turn to peep came, his eyes caught sight of a needle-sized man who could neither sit nor stand upright on his own for his spinal code was broken beyond repair. The man spoke dimly and breathed by panting like a dog in a hot desert. This caused a grief-stricken Omollo to reflect on the history of this man in his mind.

"The same man who used to cause a sensation in all Malaland is now being treated like fresh shit by his own people in the name of reprisal?" He thought but did not give voice to his musings. Tears now welled up his eyes but with great effort, he managed to conceal his feelings.

The true version of Professor Girado's tragedy now come to light. At some point, he developed a habit of sucking breasts of young girls – those that would be still pointing to 9:00 a.m. if they were the hands of a clock. The story went that his wife, who was soon fed up with the habit, warned him several times of the possible consequences of his actions, yet the man of books thought he would die if he abstained from sucking young girls' breasts. Eventually, his wife was so pissed off by the habit that she retaliated by hiring hit men, who mutilated the professor to his current state. Next, she stole everything from him, before jetting back to her homeland in Laurasia – sadly along with their three sons. His employer later tried hard to treat him in every prestigious hospital in the country; but eventually gave up after realizing that his body had turned deaf to every best medication on the shelf. As a result, all the people who used to stick around him, be they friends, relatives or sycophants in Arwing town, also gave up in their support to the ailing man – actually after waiting far too long for the man to reclaim his glory.

A neighbouring pastor finally helped the situation by hiring a lorry to ferry the man and dump him where he truly belonged, Rabar Village. In short, this is the story that culminated in the very day the man was offloaded from the back of a lorry like a post parcel.

To execute their policy of exclusion, all the villagers unanimously agreed that nobody in the village should pass Professor Girado even a glass of water to quench his thirst. Whoever tried to do so would be cursed and excommunicated alongside him.

All the same, Pastor Okiero publicly vowed that he would not be cowed by anybody to stop helping a dying man of God, no matter what sin the villagers attached to him. He even shouted at the top of his voice that God forgives sins and that this man's sins had been forgiven a long time ago – which was a funny joke to most of the villagers. Even so, nobody cared about what Okiero was saying or doing with his life since the villagers had long classified him as a staunch deviant and devout rebel of their clan.

Unlike Okiero, Omollo did not have the stomach to declare his attitude towards Professor Girado. He knew very well that his father's knowledge of his sympathy and feeling for the man would straightaway enrage the old man with a long history of vengeance. In any case, he did not know even how to approach the man and talk with him.

Nonetheless, it soon happened that the villagers would encourage members of the community to visit the man's homestead to witness how he was suffering, embellish their observations and share it with like-minded villagers at the village's swimming pools or *bao* playing stations. Omollo would now use the excuse to visit and cry secretly behind the man's window, as he had not yet summoned enough courage to face and talk with him.

But one evening, Omollo chose to go an extra mile in sharing the agony of Prof. Girado. On this occasion, he took an elaborate detour through the forest to get to the man's house from the opposite side of the villagers' residences, where no one could know about this special visit to the dying man. After sneaking into the homestead, he went directly to the main door, which fortunately was unbolted. Straightaway from the entrance, he could hear the once renowned Malan breathing deafeningly like an old man suffering from tuberculosis.

As he peeped inside the bedroom, he almost collapsed after discovering the bed where the man was expected to be lying was empty. On the floor he was standing on, a liquid, he supposed to be urine, had simulated island and dry land scenery, and was inhabited by flies of all kinds. As if that was not enough, a big whiff of stench, akin to that of a rotten carcass, was wafting freely from the room and Omollo had a struggle not to wrinkle his nose. In this situation, his mind now lingered on the stories associated with dead men he had heard from elders, which heightened his anxiety and accelerated his heartbeats. His inner voice now told him to retreat discreetly rather than witness a man dying, yet his feet resisted against turning his body towards the opposite direction. As time was elapsing quickly, he now chose to knock at the man's bedroom door – but more respectfully than he would have knocked elsewhere. Nonetheless, he did not hear any reply from the owner of the room.

As if he was looking for more adventures, he pushed the door wide open and caused a swarm of flies, whose peace he had disturbed by his unannounced action, to fly in a mass to all directions – so many of them that some were even getting into his nostrils. Perplexed with what was transpiring before him, he remained standing still on the spot, not knowing what to do. The snore he was hearing from the bedroom now increased his supposition that the room was inhabited by evil spirits. Breathing deeply like the last runner in a marathon, he chose to test the existence of the man in that room.

"Prof, Prof," Omollo called the man repeatedly. After the fourth time, he heard a faint reply, but in an accent that, to him, was too local to belong to the professor: "The voice lacked the Linglish twang that was professor's hallmark even in the Malan ballads he would sing or hum when attending the extensive orchard in his backyard," he would later narrate. Under the influence of this premonition, he galloped to save his life from the (supposed) evil spirits in the room. Unfortunately, he slipped on some oozy liquid that was all over the floor and bumped his head on a dressing table by the door, so hard that his entire body, except for his eyes, became paralyzed.

As he could not move, he remained inactive on the floor, thinking of nothing but pain. Seven minutes after his fall, he saw a hand of a man rising up behind the bed, but was neither perturbed nor thrilled by the vision; rather, he just fixed his eyes on the hand, no matter whether it was a demon or a human hand. Fifteen minutes after falling, he felt that the energy had returned in his muscles and hence he gathered himself up, albeit with the support of the wall – actually to ascertain whose hand it was that moved behind the bed. When he moved to the location, he met eye to eye with a thin amputee soaked in fermented urine that was several days old. At that sight, energy left his body again; and he fell heavily on the man's bed and wept inconsolably.

Having shed all his tears, Omollo next changed the man's bed sheets for him, changed the clothes he was wearing and laid him on his bed as comfortably as if he was a newly born baby. Omollo was quite moved by the stability of mind the man showed even in that state of despair.

This day, Professor Girado used most of the time preaching to Omollo that everything under the sun was worthless, save for obedience to God. He narrated at length about what he had undergone in his life and how he ended up in his present plight. He further described how he was in a situation where his education, wealth and influence could not save him: how his friends and relatives had forsaken him and how they were now projecting his negative side, while erasing all his good deeds to them. He further cited how teachers, whose favourite spot was his home whenever he was on holiday, were then as absent in his vicinity as water on Mars. Further, he told Omollo, in considerable detail, how a wife whom he used to address with all good names on the market had inflicted on him the pain he was now undergoing; and even how she had fled with his beloved children to an undisclosed location.

"My father and mother were strongly opposed to my marriage to a Laurasian woman, on the grounds of cultural and perceptual differences," he struggled to talk as Omollo listened keenly, "and I wish I had listened to them," he added and breathed noisily for a minute or so before resuming talking.

"I was actually almost bowing down to their pressure, save for the intervention of the first president of this country, with whom I went to school together," he said and gulped air thrice before continuing.

"He even politicized our marriage," he said and gulped air again, "he said that by marrying a Laurasian woman, I was forging North-South cooperation, 'vital for the development of our country,' in his own words."

Though he was struggling to speak, the professor continued: "In fact, he attended our wedding and congratulated us for materializing North-South cooperation."

He paused, breathing with difficulty, then went on: "Even when I had my first son with the woman, he resurfaced and this time he congratulated us for launching a long time project that would maintain the tensional North-South relationship forever," he said and sighed heavily.

"All the same, son of Orwa, look at me today," he added, looking at himself in a manner that a body builder does prior to a heavy lift contest, "where is that North-South cooperation? Where? Where are the long term projects we started?" He asked Omollo and now threw his hands asunder, actually as vigorously as if he were a healthy man.

"I am so ruined that even a mere rat behind that cupboard now pities me for what I have become," he continued and tears now welled up in his shrunken eyes.

Without exaggeration, Professor Girado was alone in his sufferings. His relatives who would have helped him just maintained, "no one deserves sympathy for injuries sustained from a botched suicide attempt." In this loneliness, his genuine companion now became the Bible.

Following Professor Girado's message on his deathbed and the Christian God's love messages from Pastor Okiero Omollo's faith was overturned beyond reversal.

Then one evening, Pastor Okiero and his members were heard wailing at Professor Girado's homestead – a clear indication that the man they had been attending at the location was no more. Contrary to what would normally happen if a man of Professor Girado's caliber died in Malaland, this time, the people went as far as extolling death for doing a praiseworthy job. That is, nobody mentioned how special, how smart, how kind the deceased had been - as was the custom in the village even for a dead rapist. Rather, they named Professor Girado's death "aggrandizement terminator" - making it the first death in Malaland to have a proper name.

Again, nobody bothered about the preparations for Prof. Girado's funeral, except Okiero and his adherents. Omollo even heard the villagers saying they would dump his corpse onto a donkey cart and throw it into Radieya Forest for the hyenas and vultures to feast on if Okiero and his followers did not keep their nose out of the matter.

In brief, the circumstance surrounding the misery and death of Prof. Girado did not allow someone like Omollo to participate in his funeral. He was even forced to conceal his grief before the hostile and unreasonable men around him. That night though, Omollo sneaked into the dead man's compound at least to pay his last respects to the neglected hero of his village. As expected, he only found Pastor Okiero and his devotees at the bonfire at the homestead of the once most magnificent man in the land. At that meeting, he learnt that the dead man stated in his will that he, Omollo, be given his big radio cassette and a suitcase as an inheritance, a message that humbled Omollo deeply and made him learn a gratitude and a humility inherent in the dead man. Likewise, the deceased stated in his will that his house and everything in it go to Okiero's church - actually, for the good will they showed him in his last hours on the planet Earth. Movingly, the dead man had stated in his will that his big farms around the Nyamori Valley and his approximately 400 cattle be reserved for his three children - if they should one day remember to return to their ancestral land.

Three days after the burial, which was attended by only about ten people, Omollo's clan members convened to discuss what to do with the dead man's compound, cattle and land - completely ignorant of the dead man's comprehensive will. At that naive meeting, the congregation resolved unanimously that his house, along with everything in it, be burnt to ashes and his compound be donated to the village government within seven days, allegedly, to cleanse the clan from the curse that the man had thoughtlessly inflicted upon it. His cattle and land, however, would be counted and divided among his many brothers in the village.

Omollo thus heard this new arrangement and knew very well that these people, whom he now considered evil men, were up for torching the luxurious house that none of them had or would ever build in their entire lives. He equally knew that in this process, they would equally burn the big radio cassette and suitcase that the professor had bequeathed him in his will. Especially for this reason, he resolved to do something to stop his clansmen's plan. Many possible solutions crossed his mind; but after processing them for a long time, he settled on engaging Okiero in his mission.

"Okiero is the right man for dealing with an issue of this sort," he mused and smiled.

When Omollo tiptoed to Okiero's homestead that night, it was dead silent – save for a drunk who was occasionally singing the oldies out of key on the opposite ridge and, of course, the idiot dogs that were howling or barking at fireflies. All the while, his heart was pounding hard and loud in anticipation of what would happen to him if any of the Okieros spotted him and raised the alarm that he was in their homestead at that hour of the night.

"These devils will instantly brand me a thief, a witch, a fornicator, or a peeping tom, and thus lynch me right away," he thought and now wanted to back off without delivering his noble message: thanks to his body that did not respond in line with his thoughts. With a heavy heart, he further tiptoed and eventually managed to reach Okiero's hut safely. There, he knocked and was answered in a much friendlier fashion than he had expected.

Concisely, he informed Okiero of the mischief the conservatives were brewing over the possessions of the departed. Okiero, as expected, took the message seriously and resolved to act on it as swiftly and precisely as possible. Indeed, the very next morning, without anyone else's knowledge, he went to inform the police about the plot and its timing.

Then came the very day that the villagers would torch the home of the departed in the name of cleansing the clan. On this day, men and youths, including Omollo, gathered at the home of Girado's elder brother for performing the rituals that preceded the torching of a house of that sort. After all the key rituals were done, the army of tradition now started marching like a windstorm towards the homestead of the departed for the torching exercise – little did they know that police officers had come and hidden at the compound at dawn without anyone's notice. As the army crossed the gate into the compound with ululations and songs, four police officers with loaded guns emerged from different angles of the compound and ordered everybody to stand right where they were. As everybody dreaded the police in this part of the world, all took to their feet, unwittingly making the work of the riot police a walk in the park. The police equally accelerated the running by firing one or two bullets in the air and the result was most impressive. To prevent future incidents of that sort, they arrested eight elders (including Omollo's father) and took them to the district police station, later to be released on condition that they would never interfere with the will of the deceased, which was, of course, read to them against their will. With all these developments, the incident reignited the antipathy against Okiero and his group to the extent that they were now not even allowed to show up at the water dam during the daytime. Fortunately, Okiero was his habitual tough self, having survived so many catastrophes of a similar kind.

Even a month later, Okiero and his followers were still celebrating the finding of a magnificent church for their God. In a clear and booming voice, Okiero would tell everyone who cared to listen of how his living God, whom the villagers had once mocked for turning down Okiero's request to resurrect his daughter, had now come forward to provide the naysayers with proof of his omnipresent ability by securing for himself a prayer house that was far better than the district commissioner's house.

To launch that miraculous church, therefore, Pastor Okiero was determined to invite the most famous bishop of his denomination –none other than Bishop Massawe, the Tent Man. It happened by chance that Bishop Massawe was then in the same region as Pastor Okiero; so, having received the invitation, he was more than willing to come over to Rabar Village to receive God's special gift for his beloved church.

Bishop Massawe was highly renowned among members of his church throughout the United Republic of Kaya. His real strength was primarily in his proven ability to wear a handsome man by the words that came out of his mouth. At the time, he was the only preacher in the whole of Kaya who could act out his pronouncements with the required standard of preaching: he would roll, laugh, sing or cry in the altar if that was the only sacrifice that would transform a goat into a sheep. For this combination of qualities, he was capable of gathering a congregation of followers even in the heart of a desert at any time of his choice.

Omollo, who had been inwardly converted to Christianity, thus longed to meet Bishop Massawe in person, to discover why bubbles of saliva would always coalesce in both poles of Okiero's lips whenever he was praising that man. In this regard, he even started a countdown to the announced date of Bishop Massawe's visit to his village.

<<<*CHAPTER FOURTEEN*>>>

Bishop Massawe was internationally famous for the powerful messages he was so determined that day to pass on to the Malans of Rabar Village - people who, in his view, needed deliverance from the bondage of sin and the Devil, the Destroyer. With this mission in mind, he organized his crusade in an open space on the western side of Rabar Village, with the aim of creating enough room for whoever was willing to receive or witness God's miracles to attend.

But even prior to his arrival, propaganda had long since gone around Rabar Village that he was capable of making cripples race the cheetah and blind men repair the mechanical watch - which led to much discussion, with some people even placing bets on what would happen that day.

On the day in question, therefore, many villagers abandoned their works and moved closer to where Bishop Massawe's crusade would take place - all in a quest to witness how his alleged miracles transpired. But as if somebody had earlier on instructed them, they all reserved a pronounced space in between themselves and the preacher; lest anybody think they were a party to the ongoing activity. Fortunately, the bishop, out of his long experience in the service of Lord, had brought with him a powerful public address system that reached even people in the eaves of their houses.

In his preaching that evening, Bishop Massawe's message hovered around the tragedy that had befallen Professor Girado - a message that percolated deeply into the hearts of the likes of Omollo. That evening, the bishop purported that Prince Jesus had sent him to set free the Rabarians, who were still caged in a thorny kraal of traditions. He further stated that his god was the god of the excommunicated. He reiterated that human beings would only love you when you are healthy and rich, but would run away from you when you are sick and poor. He likewise stated that nothing should separate anyone from God, not even one's biological father. He stressed that one should rather pluck out one's own eye - if it stood between him and God.

When the bishop was now so sure that the hearts of the likes of Omollo were well soaked in his message, he summoned them to triumph over the Devil and his evil ways by marching onto the stage to give their lives back to Christ. He added that Christ would avenge whoever was ashamed of him that day in his father's palace. It was at this point that Omollo found himself answering the summons, actually to the surprise of every bystander. A few minutes later, two excommunicated women followed suit in giving their life back to Christ, which made Bishop Massawe very happy.

Even before an hour had passed, the shocking news – that the son of the real conformist had jumped onto Christianity bandwagon – had spread to the whole village. The news found Elder Orwa playing *bao* with his fellow elders, and it not only threw him down like a sack of potatoes but also caused him to lose consciousness. And after coming round, Elder Orwa overdosed himself with spirits and bhang – allegedly, to relieve his heart of the thorny input he had received. But all in vain.

At the end of that fateful day in his life, the central committee in his head passed a resolution to sweep that disgraceful boy off the planet Earth. In implementing this decision, he reached for his legendary gun, cleaned it with lion fat and loaded it with four original bullets.

After the end of the final prayer for the new converts, an ugly reality, that he had betrayed the trust of his people, now started mocking Omollo. He had been known as the true heir of Orwa Nyamngwegre's priesthood since birth but now, all of a sudden, had deviated from conventional values. This hurt him greatly and he wished he had recanted his submission to Jesus Christ. But it was already too late to jump off a moving train. In an effort to save the already bad situation, he instantly made up his mind to move for some time to his liberal sister in another region in order to allow things to settle down in his village.

Elder Orwa Nyamngwegre, for his part, wore his war gear and lurked in wait for Omollo in a shrub in front of the hut where the boy would always spend his nights. The sole mission in his mind that evening was 'to wipe the filth off his sacred land.' Be that as it may, hours elapsed and the boy did not show up in front of the hut. But as the old man was not known for leaving a job half-done; he kept on waiting with his barrel pointing to the door of the hut, almost unshakingly.

"I am at least going to carry out one last noble mission in my life despite this backslide," he murmured to himself as the waiting got harder.

On the other side, Omollo waited for everybody to sleep before sneaking into his hut to collect a few belongings with which to move to his sister's place – little did he know that his own father was planning to ambush him from the shrub on a shoot-to-kill mission.

Suddenly, Elder Orwa sensed something moving towards the hut where his son was accustomed to sleep. Accordingly, the slumber which had been tormenting him in that thicket disappeared and he now became more focused so as to execute his mission as precisely as possible. His eyes proved to him beyond reasonable doubt that the moving thing was actually the disgrace he had been longing to spot for the past six hours. He therefore prepared his gun and waited to take precise aim once the boy came within shooting range.

Omollo had climbed over the gate and was now tiptoeing towards his hut. All the while, he was shivering with fear of what would happen if his father noticed that he was at the compound. At one point, a dog barked at him and he tactfully calmed it down by calling its name in a soothing murmur.

Now he was right in front of the hut and about to touch the door handle. At that moment, Elder Orwa, who was sure the barrel of his gun was exactly pointing at the back of the head of his good-for-nothing son, fired a bullet that travelled to its target but, unfortunately, only tore the right earlobe of the boy, not the intended back of his head.

Startled by the explosion of his father's gun, the boy sprinted wildly towards the gate and this time did not even climb over it: he literally flew over it in a manner he did not understand until the day he died.

Realizing that his prey was escaping alive, Elder Orwa now tried to pursue it but, unfortunately, stumbled on a small stone hidden in the grass, lurched for a while and then fell down. His gun jumped above his head and landed some meters away. He tried quickly to recollect himself and reach his weapon for another attempt but found himself unable to get up: at the time, he was unaware that his spinal cord had been severed upon his fall. Angry but helpless, he hurled at his escaping son a curse that would follow him all his life:

> "A magnified piece of nothing, you have eventually killed your father to satisfy your evil heart. May the spirit of the Devil dwell upon you; let it cause you to eat maggots for food. May you vanish and die like a wild dog, at least to relieve the world of a hopeless creature, such as you are."

Supposing that his confrontational father was behind him to finish him off, Omollo accelerated his run every single second and soon plunged into the tent in which Bishop Massawe was spending his night like a falcon in a fishpond – and I wish you had been there to enjoy what happened next. As soon as he landed on Bishop Massawe's chest with blood and sweat, the man of God, who had earlier on preached about fearing nothing on the planet Earth, emitted a wail louder than that of a child whose nose has been stung by a wasp.

The pathetic wail of the bishop caused everybody at the compound to wake up in a hurry and sprint like mad, some even in their birthday suits. About fifteen minutes later, Pastor Okiero sneaked back into the compound with his old rifle, only to find out that what had dived into the bishop's tent was not a leopard – as the bishop had sensationally claimed – but rather Omollo, son of Orwa Nyamngwegre, who had been running for his dear life after his father had shot him with a rifle in his right earlobe.

<<<CHAPTER FIFTEEN>>>

Omollo was now in the same predicament in his village as Professor Girado. Given his apparent miseries, the bishop had no choice but to take him along in his non-sedentary evangelism. By the way, he was not going to be the only adoptee of that man, as Bishop Massawe had earlier on adopted two extremely beautiful girls who, he claimed, had more or less similar experiences as Omollo – specifically, they were victims of the defence of Christianity in the Kaya Republic.

Because of this decision, on the third day after the tragedy, Omollo and his colleagues embarked on a long journey in the bishop's lorry. A bandage was still wrapped around his head to protect his blown-out earlobe and a killing pain continued to radiate from the wound.

The last news about his family he heard before leaving his village was that his father had broken his backbone and could no longer walk on his own. The news genuinely hurt him, even if there was nothing to do over spilt milk.

The bishop and his divine family settled in a village about 92 kilometers away from Omollo's home. There, they preached for two weeks, during which Omollo acquired at least the basics of his new faith, a faith he would later defend with all his powers as per his character. It is also during this time that he was baptized *Eucalyptus Omollo Orwa*, a name he would later shed off for good after experiencing a great disappointment in the heart of an animal park.

When they moved to another village, Omollo was already 'a wise man' – a name given to a male assistant to the bishop. With this new title, Omollo would ascend the stage during evangelistic assemblies and movingly testify how their mighty God had delivered him from the bondage of traditions. Over time, he came to learn that his bishop liked his testimonies when they were spiced up with lies that readily moved listeners to join their faith in large numbers: from there on, he did his best to fulfill the wishes of his spiritual boss. Soon, he was very dear to the bishop for his vibrancy in the service of the Lord – so much so that the impressed bishop rewarded his actions by teaching him how to drive and repair his famous lorry.

In the sixth week since departure from his village, the son of the diviner-priest could now be seen driving the bishop's lorry on his own – which was in itself a miracle. Proud and happy for the achievement, he even wished he could drive the lorry through his home village, keeping his head outside the driver's cab and waving at the staring crowd on the square for appreciation. He would wave until everybody was able to recognize him beyond reasonable doubt.

"God has started blessing me, and this is just the beginning," he thought in line with Bishop Massawe's teaching on God's blessings to his followers. Possessed with young spirit, he would daily pray for his parents and his entire society so that they also might see the light he himself thought he had seen.

What followed in short order was preaching from one village to another, one town to another, and, worse still, the same stories every day. In this routine, the new or rather the committed faithful would give some money to the bishop to take to God, but the man of God would contrarily spend it on his luxuries. When Omollo and the two girls implied that they should also receive their share, the senior man of God would argue strongly that he alone was the ordained mouth of God in their group, something that did not augur well, at least for Omollo.

In this context, Omollo started doubting the path he had chosen to take and even wished that he had listened more to his father, who had warned him not to jump on those people's bandwagon.

"I would rather live in my village than be the outcast I have become for no good reason," he reflected one evening but did not reveal his thoughts to anyone.

Later that night though, Omollo violently rebuked and cast away the Devil, together with all his satanic ways. All the same, the Devil appeared to have migrated to stay in Omollo's soul forever – at least, if what transpired next was anything to go by.

That week, Omollo, the bishop and his two sisters in Jesus Christ, Wankyo and Bupe, pitched a tent in their seventeenth station since leaving Omollo's village some three years previously. On this spot, they had three tents: one was Omollo's, another was for his two sisters in Christ and the third for the senior man of God.

One morning though, the evidence was screaming that supplies were drying up in the camp and that something had to be done quickly to ensure continued livelihood in the camp. In view of this, Bishop Massawe ordered Omollo and Wankyo to go by his lorry to a nearby town to buy supplies. On this mission, Omollo would serve as the driver and turnboy and Wankyo would be the procurement officer and cashier of the mission. Bupe would meanwhile remain in the camp to take good care of the man of God, alongside spreading the word of God to the lost sheep of their host village.

According to plan, Omollo and Wankyo left their campsite in the lorry and headed for a small town about seventy-five kilometers away. By the end of that day, the duo had managed to buy everything they wanted and were on their way back to the camp. All of a sudden though, their usually loud lorry came to a halt in the last valley to the fourth village from the town. Omollo tried very hard to solve the problem, but in vain. Worse still, the sun was quickly rushing to its nest and the two travelers would soon need food and shelter for the night. Another impending concern was, of course, the security of

God's lorry. Omollo thus left Wankyo with the lorry and walked to
the center of the village to look for where they might sleep safely and
how they would guard the lorry at night.

As Omollo's physical appearance portrayed him more as an
armed robber than an evangelist, it took him a while to get help from
suspicious villagers. All the same, he eventually came across a catechist
of another Christian denomination who would provide the two not
only with beds for the night but also young men to guard their lorry.
Happy and relieved, Omollo quickly returned to the site to collect his
sister to the Good Samaritan as the sent guards took charge of their
lorry.

That night they ate, sang and prayed in the style of their host.
Thereafter, sleeping time arrived and the catechist assigned them a
house with a perimeter wall – the house that would be used by padres
on their rare visits to that rural church. To avoid the possibility of
strangers stealing everything in the house they had been kindly
lodged in for the night, the catechist padlocked the gate without their
knowledge and left with the key.

The house had two small adjacent rooms, each furnished with a
bed and bedcovers, so each had their privacy. Yet no sooner had the two
saints been left by themselves than Wankyo claimed she was too afraid
to sleep in her assigned bedroom alone – she was insinuating that she
and her brother in Christ sleep together – worse still, not only in his
assigned bedroom but also in his assigned bed. This was definitely a
great temptation to Omollo, so he prayed about it and believed that
the blood of Jesus would cover and protect them against the Devil
and all his ways. But to avoid leaving anything to chance, they further
placed a pillow in between them so as to prevent their bodies from
touching each other, lest any such contact spark the demon they had
learnt about from Bishop Massawe to be very active in the darkness.

But even with all these measures in place, each of them spent
most of that night fighting 'the demon of desire.' Omollo's spirit, for
instance, was genuinely willing to abstain from touching the tempting
body of his sister in Christ; nonetheless, his flesh did not approve of
such a decision. Wankyo, for her part, did not find it natural for an
angry healthy hyena to sleep alongside a juicy lamb without touching
it. All the same, seconds turned into minutes, minutes turned into
hours and soon the cockerels started announcing, by their crows, that
the darkness was losing its battle with the light.

Since Omollo wanted to fix their lorry as soon as possible, he
jumped out of bed at dawn, simultaneously awakening Wankyo, who,
of course, pretended to be fast asleep, to say they should set off for the
site of the lorry.

In spite of the fact that Wankyo was hurting inside because of
the stupidity her slow-learning brother in Christ had shown all night

long, she woke up and followed her brother out of the house. But now, upon reaching the gate of the house, the two discovered that it was padlocked from outside and therefore they could not get out of the compound without their host opening the gate for them.

"Sister, I have to fix our lorry as quickly as possible, "Omollo declared but Wankyo was unmoved.

"Let's jump over the fence right now," Omollo proposed excitedly, quite unaware that he was infuriating his sister greatly.

"Let us blah blah blah!" Roared Wankyo explosively, "stupid pig!" She blasted Omollo rudely, "you failed to jump over a mere pillow throughout the night; now, all of a sudden you are talking about jumping over a fence?" She scolded Omollo.

Omollo, upon hearing this response, was grinning widely as he retreated to the doorstep of the house, where he sat down with his back towards the door and face towards the gate. After a few moments, Wankyo followed and sat a few meters away from him. For several minutes, they kept mum, albeit stealing quick professional glances at each other – and pretending to be looking at something else whenever their eyes made contact.

As they waited in this tense condition, both of their minds, of course, wandered beyond the confinement of the perimeter walls enclosing the house.

Fortunately, their host appeared before long to release them from their voluntary confinement, forcing them quickly to assume the lively faces one would expect from the united children of God who had spent a very pleasant night in God-given accommodation.

Despite Omollo's efforts to fix the lorry all day long, it responded to neither spanner nor hammer. In fact, it did not move an inch on its own even after having been pushed for half a kilometer by cooperative villagers. This necessitated the children of God to remain in the same village – again sharing the same bed at the same place.

This second night they did not put the pillow in between them again. Rather, they prayed hard about the impending war with the Devil – under the pretext that the fight with the Devil is more spiritual than physical.

As the sleeping kicked off, each of the duo started rolling extraordinarily on their tiny-shared bed for reasons beyond their control. And as they rolled, their bodies at some point made contact and they pretended to be unaware of what was happening to them, at least for a while – because it felt good to them.

Then all of a sudden, Omollo alleges that his hand by itself started sliding over the body of his sister. And because his sister's hand also knew the biblical notion of 'a tooth for a tooth' it retaliated by also starting to glide on her brother's body. Shortly after starting its journey, the accelerating hand of Omollo came across two adjacent hills on the chest plain of his sister's body. These hills baffled Omollo, necessitating him to inquire what they were.

"Sister, what are these?" Omollo is said to have asked Wankyo, as he gently fondled the protruding mounds.

"Mmh, woman's testicles I suppose," Wankyo is said to have replied in jest.

"And you brother, which garden is this?" Wankyo asked Omollo while swirling the bushy hair on his chest.

"Hahaha, have you not read about the garden of good and evil," Omollo asked his sister jokingly as the swirl of their hands automatically descended to their protected areas.

The story went that the hands of each of them glided down their bodies under the pull of gravity – step by step to forbidden zones. As this was happening, friendly groans now started emerging and neither of them could explain what was ensuing between them. Then all of a sudden, Omollo's hand entered his sister's rift valley amidst the rain forest. Soon, he discovered a natural spring in that region, and he wanted to know what exactly it was called.

"Sister, what is this again?" Omollo asked Wankyo, his heart pumping as hard as the heart of a wildebeest that has just survived the chase of a lion.

"Mmh, can't you feel that it is a burrow?" Wankyo scolded him.

And on the principle of 'do unto me as I do to you', his sister's hand also reached in the same location on her brother's body and likewise fumbled on something she also wanted to know about.

"And, you my brother! What is this?" Wankyo asked him as if she was truly naive.

"And you my sister! Can't you just feel that it is a snake?" Omollo asked Wankyo back.

"And what the hell is a snake doing outside the burrow?" Wankyo asked him in fast-forward mode (as if she were a cassette player).

At that indirect command, it was claimed the one-eyed snake, whose muscles were almost tearing with anger, sneaked into the burrow and consequently set Omollo and Wankyo into vibrations at the same frequency: the snake would plunge in and then surface out of it, again and again; meanwhile, Omollo and Wankyo simultaneously cheered for it like lunatics would fighting harlots. But after a while, I heard that it spat out a white mucous of venom, then limped and stopped its commute into the burrow.

According to the story, the snake and the burrow became best friends thereafter and Omollo and Wankyo's eyes simultaneously opened to see the joy of serving Jehovah Shammah, the mighty God who created sweetness in 'the rift valleys.'

"Even before the return of Jesus Christ, I am already reaping big from serving the good Lord. Aiiii! Wankyo is sweet," Omollo thought when he next reflected on the episode he and Wankyo had engaged in the previous night.

"I have now solved the puzzle of why some church members would sing our most ambiguous church hymn so animatedly and with great gesticulation," he thought and grinned.

"From now on, I will equal them in singing of the hymn," he said to himself and burst out into singing the hymn whose chorus literally translates into Linglish as:

'Before I knew you, I was very dry; now I know
you, I am very much lubricated, AAAlleluia'.

Meanwhile, in a simultaneous affair, Bishop Massawe's snake was diving and rising into Bupe's burrow at will. At some point, therefore, each of the saints comprising that team knew clearly what was going on among themselves but did not open their lips to speak about it. Things, however, took a turn for the worse when Bishop Massawe's snake carelessly spat leavening venom in Bupe's burrow, causing her to start to swell like a balloon. Thus, it would soon become known that she was in the family way.

This development kept Bishop Massawe thinking creatively about how to save face – thanks be to his long experience in dealing with scandals of that nature. Six years ago, a fish bone had stuck in his throat in the week when he was spearheading his faithful in fasting and praying. It hence became very difficult indeed for him to account to the faithful of how the bone got into his throat during the fasting week. But, clever as he was, he later duped his believers that a falcon dropped the bone in his mouth while he was asleep with his mouth open – allegedly, a result of tiredness after praying all night long on a mountain. As if that was not enough, a year later, he was caught making love to a wife of an elder of his cathedral – but again convinced many of his believers to buy his defence that he did what he did at the Devil's gunpoint.

Considering this wealth of experience in dealing with scandals, he faced Bupe's issue level-headedly and soon managed to come up with the best solution ever – running away from Bupe's expanding gut as fast as a startled rat.

On the day he planned to execute his excellent idea, the man of God sent poor Bupe to the village shop, about two kilometers away from where they were then camping. As soon as she had left the camp, Bishop Massawe ordered the others to pack their things into the lorry – and off they set for a long unexpected journey. Omollo and Wankyo, of course, asked about Bupe's fate but the bishop animatedly insisted the Holy Spirit had just spoken to him and ordered him to leave for a different location immediately – and that all he could do 'as the servant of God', was to obey the voice of the Holy Spirit, just as Isaac and Abraham did in the Bible. Further, he lied to Omollo and Wankyo that the same spirit would guide the girl to a new location they were heading to without fail. The drive was, however, so long that Omollo and Wankyo inwardly questioned the capability of the Holy Spirit to guide that poor girl for that far. Even so, they kept quiet to avoid a derision for appearing faithless before the man of God.

Nonetheless, the fact was that Bupe never joined the team again after the incident. This meant that now only one mortar remained in the camp for two eager pestles. As was to be expected, Omollo soon started experiencing restricted access whenever he wanted to pound the yam – which had not been the case in the last five months – little did he know that Bishop Massawe was then killing his goose, eating it, wiping his mouth and keeping mum like a patient after an operation.

After a few days, the wandering missionaries moved to another community, and as usual, camped a few meters outside the mainstream village. They would have an evangelical assembly on the third day after their arrival – as usual, to warn the locals against the dangers of sitting and eating with the Devil throughout their lives.

In accordance with this mission, Bishop Massawe assigned Omollo to go to the eastern part of the village for the invitation, while the bishop himself would go to the western part for the same purpose. In the evening, they would meet, cook and pray together as per their tradition.

Omollo thus left with his Bible and hymnbook to sow the seeds in his assigned zone. Nonetheless, his evangelical day appeared tumultuous right from the morning. As soon as he left their camp, he came across a drunkard man lying by the road he was following. The sight instantly filled him with a desire to invite that man to attend their evangelical assembly, so that he could be saved from his drinking habit. Unluckily, Omollo started his task of persuasion erroneously: asking if the man, by chance, knew Jesus Christ.

"I am not a resident of this area, and I know none such around here," the man answered, causing a shock to Omollo's biological system.

Omollo now tried to explain that he meant Jesus Christ, son of God, who lives in Heaven – which in turn surprised the drunken man.

"How can you ask people who live elsewhere about a person in a different village then?" He asked but Omollo remained speechless for not comprehending the question, which forced the drunken man to clarify his response.

"I mean that, despite not knowing people who live here, I at least know that this place is not Heaven, and that you are looking for that man in the wrong place," he stated logically and Omollo now grinned at how ignorant the man was about God and his son.

Omollo next tried to put up a good show, as Bishop Massawe had previously taught him, yet his clinginess only angered the drunken man, who after taking enough of what he considered monotonous questions, told Omollo that he was as sticky as an old whore.

Now red with anger, Omollo considered beating the man up to please his heart, except that his inner voice reminded him that beating up someone was contrary to the good news he had just been preaching to the man. As a result, he left the drunkard untouched, and in a gloomy mood, continued with his ill-fated mission elsewhere.

At around 11:00 a.m., he met a group of men who were happily and noisily irrigating their throats with demon drink. Again, the Holy Spirit struck him with an urge to invite the men to their evangelical meeting – allegedly, to be saved from beer and laziness. Again, his start landed him in trouble.

"God is showing me that his angels are now crying in Heaven for what you are doing, my elders," Omollo told the men after the initial greetings. But it was as if his words delighted the men more than anything else.

"Let them weep," one of them replied amidst raucous laughter,

'I am not joking, my elders. God is truly showing me that Satan and his angels are now dancing and singing for every sip of alcohol you take,' Omollo added and the men now laughed together even more.

Briefly, Omollo eventually gave up on the men and sadly left them alone to continue their drinking spree. He went on with his evangelical mission – but on this day, it was fruitless and disappointing.

At around 3:00 p.m. he considered it wise to return to camp for he was tired, hungry, and dejected. As he reached their site, he wanted to go to his tent but realized he needed some water to appease his biting thirst before jumping on his mattress for resting. As water jerrycans would always be kept in the widest tent of Bishop Massawe, he turned and marched slowly towards that location.

As he neared the tent, a familiar wail struck his ears; yet he could not instantly figure out whose wail it was or what it was all about. Out of curiosity, he rotated his ears around the circumference of the point he was standing; still, he could not locate either the source of the wail or the nature of the wailer. But after a short while, he discovered that the wail was coming from the bishop's tent, and that instantly opened up his mind that he now strongly suspected who the wailer was – and what it was all about.

In this knowledge, his thirst and exhaustion melted away as quickly as butter on a pan, while his naturally blood red eyes glowed even redder. Possessed by a spirit of anger and revenge, he charged towards the tent at the speed of a buffalo on a rampage.

"Is it true that the motor I have been considering to be mine is communal?" He thought as he hurtled aggressively towards the tent, "It is like somebody else is pounding it mercilessly in there!"

Omollo now stormed into Bishop Massawe's as abruptly as a police officer would a criminals' hideout. As he had envisaged, Bishop Massawe was naked on Wankyo, and was pounding her yam as severely as if there was no hell fire for fornicators.

Very angrily, Omollo grabbed Bishop Massawe by his two feet and lifted him up until his long bent pestle unplugged completely from Wankyo's motor. Visibly displeased, Wankyo tried to chase the rising pestle with her motor but it became too high for her to reach. Omollo, of course, continued to raise the bishop's feet higher so that he was eventually standing on his head. Next, he pushed him forward so hard he fell on his back and disentangled a basin of flour on a stool in front of the mattress – which in turn took its revenge by scattering the flour on everything in the room.

When everything came to rest therefore, each of the three people present were powdered all over their bodies, save for their natural holes such as eyes, mouth and nose, which had been miraculously spared by the powder. Angrier now than he had ever been, Omollo did not say anything but rather hurried back to his own tent, somewhat happy with the initial punishment he had administered to those he considered a pair of sinners he had just caught on the act. He composed himself on his mattress, with a wrinkled face and curled lips, actually thinking about nothing but killing someone.

This episode then broke up the cordial relationship, which had been prevailing all those years among the hallowed men and women on an evangelical mission – and all the blame for this turn of events rested on Omollo's shoulders. His accusers said that he had wronged Bishop Massawe and thus by extension God, who had sent the bishop to the world on His behalf. They argued that Omollo should have known that the bishop was exorcising demons hiding in the girl's private parts – that he should have known that Wankyo had crafty demons that needed such sort of holy ritual from the powerful man of God that Massawe was.

"We cast out demons by placing hands, don't we?" The bishop started from the known to unknown, "and you might have heard that some demons barricade themselves in the genitals, right? How did you then expect me to place a normal hand in such a delicate part of the girl? How could I have sprinkled holy water in such areas with a normal hand? Don't special areas need special gadgets, my son?" Asked Bishop Massawe seriously and now gave Wankyo a room to also counsel Omollo.

"I supposed I was cleaning that black cudgel of Bishop Massawe the whole time you claim we were sinning," said Wankyo to Omollo, "I am convinced you saw a spiritual act with physical eyes, which does not work, my brother," she concluded.

All the same, Omollo rubbished what he considered a baseless defence of the duo, but Bishop Massawe and Wankyo continued blatantly to insinuate that Omollo was still naive about the teachings of the Bible and still lacked the spiritual eyes to see the purely spiritual ritual that the bishop was performing on the patient. On that account, Omollo was ordered to ask for forgiveness from the man of God – and, of course, by extension from God Himself. He was further required to pledge no interference in any similar pastoral ritual in the future that might involve either Wankyo or any other clients whose demons would barricade themselves in the genitals. All in all, a defiant Omollo was not ready to ask for forgiveness or make any promises with regard to standing aside in a context where a similar ritual would be performed again on Wankyo. As expected, his stand attracted more trouble: the senior man of God quickly tagged him a *demon* he would now fight by every possible means.

"We will see if an ear can grow above the head," remarked Bishop Massawe after the collapse of his peace talks with Omollo.

That night Omollo did not sleep for two good reasons: firstly, he was so confused by what he had seen and heard from the men of God; secondly, he did not want that man's pestle ever to get back to the motor he considered his own. To leave nothing to chance in protecting his territory, he would that night regularly check if the two suspects were asunder. In other words, he went to bed just around 6:00 a.m.

At around 8:00, he distantly heard sounds suggesting their loud lorry was setting off, albeit he was too sleepy to figure out what was exactly happening. Lazily, he went back to sleep until 10:00 a.m. – the time at which each of them in their camp were supposed to wake up.

As soon as Omollo opened the door of his own tent, he was shocked to learn that the other tents where nowhere to be seen at the site. Perturbed at the realization, he rubbed his eyes clean with his right palm, supposing that mucous might have blocked his vision; even then though, there was neither the lorry nor the other two tents that used to stand alongside his own.

In his bewilderment, he ran outside and checked where the two tents had been but now there was really nothing there. As he looked back, only his tent was standing there. Coincidently, he noticed a small paper inscribed in pencil at the location where Bishop Massawe's tent had previously been. It read as follows; *Don't bother to find the whereabouts of the men of God. Read Matthew 24:40.* With this new information, Omollo rushed back to his tent, opened his suitcase in a hurry and rapidly fished out the Bible with which Bishop Massawe had once rewarded him. He soon located the relevant chapter and verse and read it aloud; *Then two men will be in the field; one is taken and one is left.*

Upon learning this, he snapped the Bible shut and hissed venomously: "A naked lie!" They have just abandoned me on their own. Nobody has taken any man here, so who has taken the woman then? And who has taken the lorry too? And why should that man only take the evil man?" He was now yelling, as if quarreling with someone.

After a while, he returned outside and could now see the tracks the lorry had left behind

"So does this mean that the man has been taken inside the lorry by pulling? Are these not the lorry's trails?" He asked himself angrily, while hastily following the tracks.

After some time, he came across a young girl who was tying a bundle of firewood by the road he was walking on. Judging by the amount of firewood she had collected by then, Omollo supposed she had been gathering it at that spot for quite a while and thus might have seen the lorry passing by. Omollo thus approached her to ask whether she had noticed anything like a lorry passing by.

"Clean, sleeping Beauty in the woods," Omollo flattered her - by the way, she had a long chew stick toothbrush in her mouth at that hour of the day and far away from any source of water, a prototypical behavior of the cleanest village girl in the area. However, she appeared to like the complement, if the smile she emitted in response was anything to go by.

"Have you seen a certain lorry passing by here?" Omollo next asked her.

"Which lorry? The bishop's lorry?" Specified the girl.

"Of course," Omollo answered with enthusiastic haste.

"It passed by here about two hours ago," she answered jovially - unaware that she was touching a raw nerve of Omollo with her claims.

Upon hearing the time lapse since the lorry had passed by, Omollo lost all his strength, collapsed to the ground and broke out into a loud cry. This subsequently sent the timid young girl running for her life like a madman pursued by a deadly imaginary lion - a few minutes later she was narrating to anyone who cared to listen how she had cleverly escaped from a trap of a violent lunatic who had tried to rape her in the bush.

"That man has abandoned me in the middle of nowhere," Omollo lamented, "and he has stolen my two precious things: Wankyo and the radio cassette that Professor Girado left me out of love," he said while wiping tears from his cheeks with his palm.

"I will meet with you face to face Bishop Massawe! And on that particular day you will really learn the true colours of Omollo, *the Baboon!*" He swore in a traditional fashion.

Omollo was thus left alone in the camp and now had to learn how to fend for himself in the absence of the man who, for the past three years, had always been his patron. That same day, he went around the village and sold his tent to one of the schoolteachers at a throwaway price. Next, he collected small items in his suitcase and started walking after the trail of the lorry. He thereafter walked and walked, yet there was neither the lorry nor the anticipated sight of a camp anywhere along that path. At the end of the day, he decided to roost at a farmhouse he noticed beside the road. Unfortunately, the hut was dark and full of mosquitoes – thanks be to the strong stench from his armpits, a product of his walking in a hostile equatorial sun for over seven hours, which harassed the mosquitoes barricading in the hut.

At dawn, he resumed following the tracks of the lorry with great enthusiasm. At one point, however, he found that it had rained and flowing water had blurred the lorry's tracks. Confused and disgusted, he switched to asking people he encountered, if by chance they had seen the lorry he was seeking. But it was as if they were misleading him instead of telling him the right direction: the evidence being that he eventually found himself in the heart of the animal kingdom and, worse still, with only a suitcase on his head.

Now realizing how far astray he had gone, all the scary stories of predators that his father used to tell him long ago revived in his mind afresh and scared him to death. With such immense fear in his flesh and soul, his bowels protested and caused him to dash into a nearby bush to relieve himself.

But no sooner had he squatted for purging than his noisy emissions frightened a baby antelope that was lounging in that same bush. Supposing that Omollo's anal plosives were a hunter's bullets, the fragile animal jumped out of its nest in a hurry and started bushwhacking through the dense thickets – actually, so scarily Omollo supposed it was a lion coming for him for lunch. In life-saving mode, Omollo now jumped the hell out of his trousers with a solid bar of dung stuck halfway in his anus and sprinted naked like a rocket in the direction from which he had just come. But alas, he soon realized that he was running parallel with a baby antelope, which had itself been reciprocally frightened by his explosive intestinal gas.

Omollo now stopped, though his body was still trembling like a leaf in the wind. In the premonition of an imminent disaster at that place and, of course, also out of anxiety, he swiftly returned to where he had been relieving himself, to collect his dear suitcase and trousers.

But upon learning that his trousers were badly stained with shit, he abandoned them and started off with only a suitcase on his head and a T-shirt on his upper body in the animal park. And as he had also not cleansed himself because of haste and panic, a giant dung fly, its mother-in-law, and children started trailing him because of a spoor he emitted behind him. To make matters worse, they started singing horrible tunes in his ears, necessitating him to slap his ears once in a while to sandwich them to death – thanks be to God, he was done with the last one after a quarter-hour of compulsory self-slapping.

As he continued marching naked across the park, which was teeming with predators, he, at one point, walked into a pack of wolves, which in return physically charged at him like rugby players. Helpless and chilled to the marrow, Omollo now prayed to God more pleadingly than ever before – paradoxically with his eyes wide open like a pastor who is praying for a lunatic. Inexplicably, upon saying "Amen", the wise grandmother of the wolves intervened.

"Hey, kids!" She yelled at them, "from what I know, an unarmed two-footed creature should dread us like the plague. The fact that this one is strolling through the wilderness with the confidence of a military tank on a rampage – it must have denied itself."

Then she suddenly broke out into light derision: "With such gargantuan appetite, I am afraid that you guys will one day try to eat what eventually eats you instead."

Luckily, the cubs saw the point in their grandmother's wisdom – or maybe it was Omollo's prayers that saved him. Either way, the wolves retreated and left the Busy Malan to keep on hurrying amidst the predators that were rampant in all four cardinal directions.

Just when he was losing all hope of survival, he noticed a cassava farm beside the blurred path he had been following – an indication that he had arrived at some human residence. At the gunpoint of hunger, he hurriedly digressed towards the farm with every wild appetite you may know of.

"I am not stealing; I am just self-defending against hunger," he said, while uprooting someone's cassava with all his remaining vigor.

He ate the raw cassavas until he was full, and now only needed water to settle it down. Full and feeling a sense of relief, he moved to one of the sausage trees beside the farm and sat on an old log with his case next to him, just to get a bit of rest before setting off again to nowhere. But while relaxing under that shade of the tree, he sensed that something was rattling roughly in the thick grass behind the shrub. In the context of the jungle where he was, he supposed that a python was creeping up to devour him alive. He considered bolting but backed off, reflecting that he might only be repeating his flight from a baby antelope. In line with this new thinking, he decided to find out what exactly it was that was wagging the grass so forcefully behind the shrub.

As soon as he emerged on the opposite side of the shrub, he almost fainted to come eye to eye with a man holding the tail of a restless jumbo leopard with both hands. A thin sheen of sweat was streaming across the man's entire body and all his key muscles were above his skin, like the heads of hippos in a dirty pond.

Since both his hands were busy holding the beast's tail, the black pair of shorts he was wearing had sagged to just above his knees, and that had licensed his pestle, its associated balls and bushy environs to be on display for all wildlife to view at will. Shocked by what he was seeing, Omollo wanted to flee the scene as quickly as his tired legs could carry him, yet fear had long pre-paralyzed his feet without his knowledge. Worse still, the man holding the leopard's tail movingly intercepted his decision to sprint away from the location in a way he could not explain.

"My countryman," the man addressed Omollo sternly, before continuing in an extraordinarily touching voice: "Please, don't try to run away from a fellow countryman in trouble of this kind."

As if bewitched by these words, Omollo's muscles now declined the order from his mind to propel him away from that spot at the speed of a bomber. Deep down, he knew very well that he was in deeper shit than this man and would not have liked anyone to forsake him, Omollo, in the fashion he was about to do himself. As this soliloquy played out in his mind, he remained glaring at the sorts of dance that he supposed that the man was performing with the leopard, which he also supposed must belong to the man.

The leopard would bend to the right and the man would twist its tail to the left; it would next bend to the left and the man would twist its tail to the right, over and over again.

"My countryman, I want you to help me with something," the man burst out to Omollo in a very persuasive voice again.

"I am scared of your pet. Could you kindly move it away please," Omollo requested, somewhat unreasonably.

"Countryman, it is not mine," the man replied gently.

"But why are you dancing with it?" Omollo asked in astonishment.

"No, no, my son, you are missing the point here. I am not even dancing with it," the man answered in the same gentle tone.

"So, what kind of witchcraft are you performing with it then?" Omollo asked demandingly.

"No, no, no, my son, you haven't got it right. It is a long story," said the man, "I was plucking grass for my new hut in the village. And you can see how tall this grass is." He now indicated the thick grass all over the place with his lips, as his hands were engaged in holding the beast's tail, "I therefore did not realize the thing was fast asleep in this grass until I accidentally scraped its anus with my sickle," the man added and paused for a moment.

"And when my sickle pained it," he resumed his narrative, "all of a sudden, it gave a frightening roar."

Again, he paused, probably for the attentive Omollo to keep track of his story.

"And why are you holding its tail then? Let it go now," Omollo suggested, at which the man now smiled as joyfully as if he was not in any danger.

"Did I hear you saying that I let it go? I wish I could, but I am very sure it will first want to retaliate for the scraping of its anus; and I am also sure that it will overdo it," the man stated with a smile that infected even Omollo.

"Does it mean that if you hold its tail like that, it cannot attack you?" Omollo asked the obvious.

"Of course, it can't. I have been holding its tail like this for six hours – see for yourself that it can't do anything," the man said confidently.

"So, what are you going to do with it ultimately?" Omollo asked naively.

"I do not really know, my countryman, but God will find a way to bail me out of this situation – and, of course, he has found one by sending you here," the man said hopefully.

"No, no, no, count me out of your nightmare, please," Omollo strongly defended himself.

"No, no, no, my son. I am not asking you to fight the beast by yourself. I am just saying that you can go and call my people to come and save my life," the man forwarded a convincing suggestion to Omollo.

"Yes, that I can definitely do, where exactly are those people of yours?" Omollo asked him in a hurry, for he himself also needed people.

"But sorry, my son," the man appealed for Omollo's attention, "before you set off for the mission, kindly come and help me with holding the tail of this thing for a minute so I can fasten my shorts and take a cup of water. My throat is indeed on hell fire."

"But, I am very scared of the thing, you know it," Omollo forcefully defended himself.

"No, no, no, it has no means when its tail is held like this," the man assured him.

And as Omollo pitied the man to the marrow, he naively accepted a shift on the leopard's tail. The man now moved some six meters away from the scene, fastened his shorts and drank almost half of the water in the bottle he had with him. Then, instead of repossessing the tail of the beast, he walked uphill and mounted a high rock some twenty-five meters away from the scene. All the while, Omollo supposed the man was sneaking into the bush to perform that biologically important process. Nonetheless, he remained speechless when seeing him climbing a high rock and then looking on him, kind of enjoying an aerial view of Omollo and the beast from that high elevation.

"Countryman!" Omollo eventually called him after waiting for a little while, "please come back and repossess your tail! What are you doing noooow?" But the man just sat there, unmoved by Omollo's yelling.

"You wicked man! Were you tricking me? Is this how you repay my empathy to you, Eeeeh?" Omollo once more bellowed at him but again the man did not answer a word.

Shortly however, Omollo felt an immense relief after seeing the man climbing down the rock and starting walk in the direction where he and the leopard were. Now he felt guilty for what he had just told the man; (he had supposed the man must have been quite exhausted and was thus taking a brief break; and that now he was walking back towards him to resume his obligatory duty). Contrarily, the man was nearing the scene to just collect his shirt and sandals before setting off to a place unknown to Omollo.

"So, you are a witch, Eeeeh!" Omollo shouted to the man as the man walked away from the scene. Again, the man did not respond to his fuss; he kept on moving away, oblivious to all the commotion Omollo was making behind him.

"Okay! God is watching what you are doing to me; He is watching, I tell you. You will see, I say you will see." Yet despite Omollo dragging God into the matter, the man ignored him just as before.

With the man out of sight, Omollo burst out into a cry as loud as a baby's in whose butt an untrained nurse is sinking a giant needle. Unluckily, his wail did not auger well for the beast, which jetted diarrhea into Omollo's face, catching *the Busy Malan* off-guard and nearly causing him to let the creature lose. Then it was the head of the animal right and Omollo and its tail left; Omollo and its tail left and the head of the animal right ... and so on. Eventually, Omollo learnt that his wailing was of no use in such a context; hence, he composed himself and started praying inwardly.

After two and half hours of hopelessness, he heard a squad of people moving towards the location where he and the beast were "dancing". His heart now throbbed very hard, for he was not clear about what exactly was going on.

Soon, there emerged a group of warriors with all sorts of arms. Unfortunately, their sight horrified the beast even more and it now staged one last fight for its threatened life. Having noted this, the warriors warned Omollo to cling to the tail of the feline as hard as possible, *if he was interested in walking out of this potential catastrophe alive*, they told him. Omollo, however, became extremely frightened and started begging the true owner of the leopard among the warriors to take his rightful place – but again, the man remained as indifferent as ever.

Now realizing that he had no other choice, Omollo heeded the advice of the alien warriors by flexing the muscles of his body and becoming as tough as a bar of iron. But as the beast likewise wanted to escape slaying, it increasingly moved Omollo here and there. Then, all of a sudden, Omollo heard the bang of a gun that sent a bullet directly into the neck of the beast. Distraught and bewildered, the beast now wagged Omollo in the air like a flag in a typhoon and only fell on its side dead after running out of its kinetic energy, with Omollo ridiculously continuing to cling to its tail even long after its head had been cut off by the warriors.

In the next episode, Omollo was taken to Dongruok Palace to attend a heroic ritual that was a requirement for a man who had killed a deadly predator at Rabar Village. In this ritual, the king of the land would crown him in person with a traditional cap, decorated with porcupine quills and *arumtidi*'s feathers – a symbol of declaring someone a village hero.

"Dongruokans," the King interrupted the calm atmosphere created for him to conduct the traditional ceremony for Omollo.

"Eeeeeeeeeee," the crowd responded to the call of their King.

"I know that you are shocked at what has happened today," he said and many people nodded in agreement.

"Yes, I assure you that our ancestors are good," he thundered in a voice of authority, "were they not good, they would not enable me, their servant, to envision this event in advance, and of course, do something to mitigate it," he bragged and his audience chanted their appreciation slogan repeatedly and overlappingly.

"Thank you King, long live the King, long live the King."

"Last week, the spirit of one of our famous ancestors came to me in a dream and told me that something terrible would happen in our village. Realizing how catastrophic the incident would be, I now begged the spirit on your behalf and, of course, later sacrificed something just to spare our village from the tragedy," he testified.

"Thank you, King, long live the King, long live the King," the crowd thundered again.

"Now, they told me that they would send a young man to save the village, and here he is," the King said, pointing at Omollo, who was then seated on a three-legged royal stool in front of the multitude.

"It is this innocent looking youth whom our beloved ancestors chose to use to divert the calamity from our beloved land," the King said and the people cheered for Omollo as enthusiastically as possible,

"This young man is, of course, choked with spirits of restlessness to the brim. Even so, that is not the reason that made him stray away from his parents on a journey to this place: rather, he was brought here by the unseen hands of our ancestors' spirits for a special mission that you have all witnessed," the King lied, and the crowd clapped, fluted and beat drums in excitement – only Omollo was not happy that the king had accused him of being choked with spirits of restlessness to the brim: all the same, he could not correct him since the context did not allow anyone to talk except the King.

To make a long story short, that evening Omollo was presented with a spear, a shield, two he-goats and two cockerels – to use for paying the dowry when his time to marry came. The next day, he was further shown a piece of land on which he was at liberty to build his own home – all being rewards for the courageous act of saving the life of a villager on the verge of death. More still, he was put under the wing of one of the most respectable men in Rabar Village by the name of Elder Mabula Mazinge – a wealthy man who would have been a prime elder of Dongruok had he had a child of his own. A rumour however went around that Elder Mazinge and his wife (Nkamba of Manyanda) did not exchange bodily fluids frequently enough for making a baby. According to the story, throughout their entire working lives, Elder Mazinge had been a gold digger at the village mine, while his wife had been a cereal pounder at the palace. It was said that due to the nature of their jobs, the couple would retire home in the evening so exhausted that all that was on their minds was massaging the paining joints of each other, where after they would fall into a laborious sleep.

In this way, Omollo had finally found a real home, away from home. With all this comfort in Dongruok Village, he temporarily relinquished his search for Bishop Massawe and Wankyo, his lover.

Dongruok, whose name translates as "move forward" was beautiful and progressive. It was one of the first successful socialist villages in Kaya Republic – evidence being that its villagers worked together and were, of course, expected to share the fruits of their labor equally and manage their farms cooperatively, albeit Omollo heard that a 'few rotten bananas' in its leadership would still bite more than the ordinary citizens.

On the shores of the beautiful lake in the village, a new dairy factory was erected to process milk from pastoralists. On the hill behind the village, a cotton mill was built to process farmers' cotton before it was exported to the main textile mill in the capital. The government would also supply subsidized fertilizers to famers, who under the supervision of organic officers, would apply them and harvest most abundantly. For pastoralists, there were veterinary officers on every corner of the village, plus enough cattle dips, which, of course, were also in Omollo's village. The new *Government of the People, by the People, for the People* was also spreading power lines to enable each villager to obtain electricity free of charge.

There were, of course, some problems in Dongruok Village. Unlike in Omollo's village of origin, Dongruokans would queue for hours to access basic goods that were in short supply, such as sugar, clothes, soap and their like. Omollo learnt this was because they depended on local factories that were unfortunately not producing enough of such goods for everyone.

"Why are local factories not producing enough goods?" Omollo asked his host one day.

"Because they are new to us, or rather we are not used to running them," the man answered him confidently.

"And why can't you import goods from other countries like we do in my village," Omollo further asked his host.

"No, we can't do that, we love our own country," the man answered, "and also, unlike your village, we are far away from the border," he added.

"But what has importation of goods from another country to do with hatred of one's own country?" Omollo wanted to know.

"Yes, if we import goods from other countries, our industries will die and our people will become dull," he told Omollo, who in return smiled unconvincingly.

"How does scarcity of goods make your people bright, then?" Omollo asked.

"Hahahaah, have you forgotten that necessity is the mother of invention?" Elder Mazinge asked Omollo back, "because of the scarcity of goods here, the people of this village can even invent a spaceship," Elder Mazinge continued confidently and Omollo now smiled at him naively – as he did not know the meaning of a spaceship; rather took it to be a big ship on Lake Dongruok that he had frequently marveled at.

Omollo's life in Dongruok Socialist Village was very good. Nobody ever harassed him with questions about his past – thanks be to the lying King with all the fictitious stories about his background. Soon, he befriended people from all walks of life in the village and thus did not even feel lonely.

"I had no home, but I have miraculously found one. God is good," he said to himself one day.

A week later, Omollo started cutting poles and plucking grass to build his own hut on his own plot. Most importantly, he arrived in Dongruok Village at the same time as an adult education movement in the village. On the fifteenth day of the month he arrived, all adults who wanted to pursue their educational dreams through adult education were invited to start attending evening classes at Dongruok Village Primary School – all by courtesy of *the Government of the People, by the People, for the People.*

Knowledge of this free higher education at his doorstep now revived Omollo's dormant ambition of acquiring a proper education after he had failed to garner the required marks for joining a public secondary school some five years ago. He was very happy that he now had a chance to pursue his educational dream in that marvelous village. Pursuant to this urge, he became the second candidate to register for the evening adult classes at Dongruok Village.

Soon, a rumour went around Dongruok Village that those enrolled in adult education classes would receive stipends from the government. The following week, villagers from across the spectrum were now scrambling for registration in adult education classes, underlyingly to make money.

On the day of launching the class therefore, the available desks could not accommodate all the senior students who were eager to refute the naysayers' assertion that they were chasing after the wind. Each had a new pen and exercise book and looked so determined to use that rare opportunity to climb the education ladder to its top level.

The first week was orientation week, during which all the students would learn basic skills in one hall, regardless of their different levels of knowledge. Then in the second week, they would take a placement test to determine their appropriate grade level.

Mr. Mulli Mandio in the first class meeting bragged of being the most experienced adult class teacher in the whole of Kaya Republic, adding that he only began teaching adult classes in the independent Kaya after having resigned from teaching similar classes overseas. The assumed wealth of experience of this teacher delighted his students greatly: each counted themselves lucky to be in the class of such a miraculous teacher, who could help them realize their educational dreams even at that late hour of their lives.

Without wasting time, Mr. Mulli Mandio began his class by jogging the memories of his old students on basic mathematical concepts, actually his favourite subject. Right from the start, he fancily defined Mathematics as 'a spoon for eating other subjects' but that marked a sharp turn in attitudes and trust of his students towards him: no sooner had he given this definition than one of the students raised her hand to demand an explanation of the *spoon* she had heard in the definition of mathematics.

"Does the government now want Dongruokans to switch from eating with hands to using spoons?" She asked and the question hit the most experienced adult teacher hard.

Contrary to his expectations, answering the question consumed fifteen minutes of class time and would have taken even longer time if he had not ignored his students' everlasting doubts by blatantly moving on to simple mathematical problems such as:

$7 + x = 11$ – he scribbled on the chalkboard.

"Find x," he told his class, thus opening another can of worms. Soon, the ex-village chairman stood up to offer some advice to their teacher.

"Mr. Mandio, we honestly have no use for x. Money is what each of us needs," he said convincingly, "we would so much appreciate it if you could teach us how to find money, rather than bothering yourself with teaching us what we do not have any use for." The class applauded him appreciatively and for a long time.

At that juncture, confused teacher Mandio reached in his trouser pocket for a handkerchief and wiped away some of the sweat which was inexplicably trickling out of all pores of his body.

Afterwards, he burnt much of his calories in support of an unconvincing motion "that finding x is a gateway to finding money." All in vain: not even Omollo could see a point in learning how to find x instead of learning how to find money. As the problem became critical, Mr. Mandio was forced to invite the head teacher of the village primary school to help him convince the students that finding x was a way to finding money. The students subsequently agreed to start learning how to find x, but allegedly only because they respected the head teacher of their school so much. In any event, the help did not last long. Mr. Mandio complicated matters on the very next day, as he wanted to revise x-equations before embarking on a new math lesson. Thoughtlessly, he again inscribed on the blackboard a similar equation to that of the previous day.

$3 + x = 5$. Find x.

But as soon as he had read out the equation to his students, Nyokelo, who was sitting leisurely at the back of the class with Nyogada, heard him talking about x again and instantly doubted his sanity.

"Finding x again!" She murmured skeptically to her neighbour, Nyogada, "didn't Angula's father find that x yesterday?" She added, making Nyogada want to clarify the issue directly with Mr. Mandio. Accordingly, she raised her hand up higher than everyone else's in the class and Mr. Mandio mistakenly allowed her to ask probably the most confusing question of all.

"Hallo, sir," she started her question in a clearer voice than her age suggested, "does this mean that you did not keep the x which Angula's father found yesterday?" She honestly wanted to know.

Following his previous rough experience, Mr. Mandio was visibly puzzled and chose to solicit help.

"Can somebody assist me with the answering of Elder Nyogada's question, please?" He said.

Fortunately, in contrast to his colleagues, Omollo had undergone the full cycle of primary education and thus had some knowledge of such x equations. In good faith, he now volunteered to help.

"This is a new x, Elder Nyogada; it is not the same as the x which Angula's father found yesterday," he explained, thinking that he would thus have cleared the visible doubts in the minds of many of his colleagues in the class. On the contrary, he had only complicated the matter even more – as the ex-driver of the village tractor immediately wanted to know if the new x had a blood relationship with the previous day's x.

"So, young man," he addressed Omollo using a traditional speech style in Dongruok, "If that is the case, would you tell us if today's x is a brother to yesterday's x?" He asked genuinely, causing a few of his classmates to smile, although the majority applauded the asking of a question whose answer they were also eager to know.

"Sorry, I have not got you correctly my elder," Omollo respectfully replied.

"All right, young man," the ex-driver began clarifying his question, "I mean, yesterday there was x and today there is also x, I can therefore clearly see that the two have a common surname, don't they?" He asked and many people in the class saw his point, which even made Mr. Mandio smile broadly before he intervened to elaborate upon what Omollo had meant by the 'new x'.

"Students!" He called for everybody's attention, "Omollo means that this x is in a different equation from yesterday's x and that is why he calls it the 'new x'. Understood?" He asked his class, only to receive a quick riposte.

But Mr. Mandio, please, why are you saying that that x is in a new equation, when we can all see it is on the chalkboard? Can I march forward and touch it for you?" The ex-driver wondered aloud, "are we learning politics in this class or mathematics? Where is that new equation you claim the x is in?"

As he finished his interjection, the class applauded him at length for his clever question; Mr. Mandio, however, frowned at a reaction he inwardly considered stupid.

"Okay, it is not necessary that we only find x in an equation like this one; we can find y instead," he said in an unfriendly tone, as he aggressively rubbed the x-equation off the chalkboard and quickly replaced it with a y-equation in the same position.

Even then, two women in the left corner of the class remained unhappy with the act.

"So, if that x was not necessary in that 'aquation', I do not know, 'aquarium', then why was he hustling us to find an abbreviated piece of nothing," one of them murmured to a colleague.

A week later, many students no longer showed up for the classes. On the one hand, they would tell Mr. Mandio that they were sick but, on the other hand, they would tell the rest of the villagers that the lessons in that class were not as applicable in a real-life situation as they had supposed, or that Mr. Mandio's knowledge was as shallow as a frying pan.

All the same, Omollo was among the few happy customers of Mr. Mandio. Unlike the majority of his colleagues, he attended the whole orientation week and successfully took the placement test, upon which he was deemed suitable for a class corresponding to level one in an ordinary secondary school. Afterwards, he continued with his studies for three more years – actually, doing very well in many subjects, the best in biology.

Then one day, in unexplainable circumstances, Omollo's biology class presented a topic that unfortunately activated his dormant malignant demons. That day, he learnt about the *human reproductive system* – something, which was very interesting to him since it accounted for some of the experiences he had personally undergone without knowing their scientific explanations. But at the end of that interesting topic, they wrote a test that he discovered, even before the results were out, that he would fail badly.

Now feeling bad about failing in a subject he was known as a master of, he could not get his thoughts off the issue. More unluckily for him, these thoughts lingered in his mind for a long time and eventually metamorphosed into an unforgettable nightmare. The following night he dreamt:

> 'that he and other students were doing the biology test in their class'
>
> 'that one of the test items was to draw and label the female reproductive organs'
>
> 'that Wankyo, his old girlfriend, was one of the students doing the test with him in their class'
>
> 'that Wankyo did not prepare well for the test'
>
> 'that 'Wankyo decided to open up her skirt a bit to observe her own reproductive organ and copy it on the test paper'
>
> 'that a jealous fellow student, called Amisa, noted what Wankyo had been doing and raised her hand up'
>
> 'that the invigilator who was sitting behind the class saw her and allowed her to speak'
>
> 'that Amisa stood up and reported to the teacher, "Wankyo is copying from the original'
>
> 'that the teacher asked, Amisa, "what do you mean?" and that Amisa explained, "Wankyo is cheating in examination by copying her own reproductive organ onto the test paper'
>
> 'that upon hearing that, the whole class booed and jeered his girlfriend, which he did not like'
>
> 'that he got angry with Amisa for humiliating his girlfriend'
>
> 'that he waylaid Amisa outside the school compound and started kicking her in the butt.'

At that juncture, Omollo literally stood up from his bed and started kicking an iron table, which in his crazy dream he considered to be Amisa. Worse still, he kicked the table so hard that when he woke up his big toe was completely dislocated.

To add insult to injury, these thoughts about his past romance with Wankyo translated into a non-stop erection of his magic stick – even to the extent that he had on him a strip sliced out of a bicycle tube for restraining it against his bellybutton whenever it was protesting.

When this queer disease persisted, he visited a psychic at the edge of the village to find out what the hell was happening in his psychology.

And from what I heard, the psychic, prioritizing mysterious images, performed a series of mystifications, at the end of which he announced to Omollo's that his erectile marathon was a function of his star sign – the *Donkey*, to be specific. He then offered to change his star sign from *Donkey* to *Scorpio* or *Leo*, but only if Omollo was willing to bring him three fat rams for the relevant rituals. Unfortunately, Omollo had only tales on him instead of the money that would buy the rams. Worse still, he was too shy about his problem to ask for help with it from his surrogate parents.

Lacking the financial means to employ this expert, Omollo chose to solve the problem by himself. The solution that appeared outstanding in his thinking was to look for Wankyo so that she could personally deal with the disease she had deliberately inflicted on him. Nonetheless, he instantly swept the idea from his mind, allegedly, because it was satanic in nature. All in vain, the sexual fantasies had penetrated deeply into his mind and the non-stop erectional disease had overwhelmed him greatly. In the end, he decided to go and look for Wankyo, once he had the fare to travel to the city.

As luck would have it, there happened to be a gold mine some five kilometers from Dongruok Village. After the departure of the colonialists, who formerly owned it, it fell under the village administration and any Kayan could now mine there and make some money by selling crumbs of gold from their labor to local traders.

Omollo thus joined several others in the mine to raise his fare to Damasawa City, where the cathedral of Bishop Massawe's church was located and thus where he expected to find Wankyo. If that happened, he would scorn the bishop while simultaneously proposing marriage to Wankyo. All the same, he was hardly thinking about how to succeed in his plan, considering that he knew nothing about Damasawa City.

The following week, Omollo started missing classes, as he had to go to the mine to try to earn some money for his planned journey. Luckily enough, he had accumulated the required sum in only his second week of working there.

One morning, he set off for Damasawa City in the mission of finding Wankyo. First, he took a beautiful ride in a modern boat, owned by one of the daughters of Dongruok Village who had recently struck her fortune in mining. As the boat moved, he fixed his eyes on the waves and wondered why they did not get tired of rising and subsiding. Even more, he was dazed by the manner in which the boat climbed them up and down in a systematic, timely manner over and over again. As he had never sailed on a boat before, not to mention in such a broad arm of the lake, he naturally envisaged some sort of calamity. All the same, students from Dongruok Village on the same boat as him relieved his anxieties. The students were returning to their secondary schools in the city (after their holiday break) and, unlike

Omollo, they saw no danger in what for them was a standard journey. As the boat moved, they happily switched from one nationalistic song to another. They would sing about the evils of the past colonial regime, about the perfection of the present government, about the need to stand firm in defending Kayan heritage, about the need to liberate the whole of Gondwana land and about the beautiful Kaya Republic.

"For the two hours we were on the boat, they never repeated a song," Omollo would latter recount. Moreover, their uniform looked neat and they had a style that made them stand out from the crowd on that wooden boat – occasionally code-switching between Linglish and Kilayi, most likely to alert everybody around them to the fact that they were the most learned men and women Dongruok had ever known. Omollo even heard that they were not expected to pay the boat fare from their own pocket: the cost was covered by their village government, an arm of *the Government of the People, by the People, for the People*. He further heard that they would later travel up to Damasawa City with a government warrant. Omollo, of course, envied them, yet consoled himself that he was studying the same things as them in his adult education program.

But even amidst this entertainment and the nature tour he was enjoying, Omollo's could not get stop thinking about how he would make his debut in a city about which he had heard much negative news and considering that his wallet was not that fat, and that he knew nobody in the city.

"It is going to be very tough for a lion to fight a crocodile in water," he thought to himself.

All the same, they were soon on the other side of the lake and he now had to travel some 500 kilometers by bus. Unlike the boat, there were no students on the bus he next took; they had most likely taken a train to the city. The bus sped up and downhills, from one village to another, one forest to another, yet still Damasawa City was not in view. But when all the passengers were tired and hungry, an urban settlement started distinguishing itself from the rural setting: increasingly, more iron-thatched houses started to appear by the roadsides and a growing number of cars and people could be seen dilly-dallying along the roads.

At 3:00 p.m., the bus pulled off the road and the conductor announced that they had reached the terminus. This prompted Omollo to look outside in a more focused manner. As he did so, his eyes caught an enclosure of a chain of stories enclosing a square, actually as full of people as a lunatic's handbag of things.

But while he was still puzzling over his first view of the metropolis, the bus conductor started yelling at the passengers to get off his bus as quickly as possible.

After receiving his heavy suitcase from the bus conductor, he put it on his left shoulder and started squeezing his way through the sea of people in the direction he was facing. Meanwhile, he was very tense and his heart was pumping above average – leave aside the fact that sweat had streamed his body and that draught had engulfed his throat. He maneuvered the crowded city constantly but due to lack of experience in walking in the city, the racing cars more than once missed him by inches – all the same, he did not stop from continuing moving forward with a heavy suitcase on a shoulder (half packed with sweet potatoes).

After a considerable walk, he saw a man grilling goat meat in a kiosk by the road he was walking on – and considered him, judging by his appearance, to be a long-term resident of that city and thus suitable for asking for directions to Bishop Massawe's cathedral. The griller's reaction, however, showed that he mistook Omollo for customer: he rapidly rounded off the washing of dishes he had been doing, wiped his hands dry on his dirty trousers, swiftly scoured this side and that side of his knife blades on a sharpening stone beside the grill and then raised his eyes to look at Omollo.

"How much should I cut for you, customer?" He asked.

Omollo did not answer instantly though.

"I mean 10 or 20 shillings worth, please?" The griller saw the necessity to clarify his question after seeing Omollo puzzled and confused.

At this point, Omollo, who had all the while been trying to hunt for a piece of paper with the address of Bishop Massawe's cathedral in his pockets, greeted the griller diplomatically and apologized for the perceived misunderstanding:

"Good evening, sir," said Omollo nervously, then added in a somewhat persuasive voice "I am sorry, I have not come to buy something from your grill; I would just like to ask you to direct me to Bishop Massawe's cathedral."

Thereafter, the griller, who looked offended by Omollo's revelation stared at him as though he were seeing him drinking a soda made from human shit, and in short order responded in a voice full of withering scorn:

"Young man! Proceed with your journey: you are delaying my business." He said with finality and fell completely silent.

His reaction dumbfounded Omollo for several seconds – a reaction which, of course, stunned the griller himself. Once Omollo's shock had worn off, he hurried off with his heavy suitcase, not saying another word. Deep in his mind though, Omollo wondered how that man could have been so rude to him – a child of God, for that matter.

"Anyway, he does not know what he is doing," concluded Omollo, with reference to a statement by Jesus Christ during his crucifixion.

"After all, he is not the only person in this city," he mused as he moved away fast, "there are so many kind-hearted people out there who will even hold my hand while leading me to the cathedral I am looking for."

All the same, in the assumption that birds of a feather flock together, he played it safe by skipping a dozen or so kiosks near the original griller's kiosk without asking for the directions, supposing that the neighbours of the bad-hearted griller would also be of a similar character as him.

After a long while, he again digressed towards a barber's kiosk – to ask for directions. However, the barber also confused him with a customer, going by the amount of generosity he suddenly emitted towards him: he sprang out of his kiosk and gave Omollo a lovely handshake.

"Come on in, young man, and I will have you shaved to your taste," said the barber charmingly.

Following the bad experience with the griller, such kindness now puzzled Omollo such that he would ask why the man was offering to shave him, had it not been considered very rude in his culture to ask such questions of a kind person such as he took that man to be. Without a proper answer from the man, his inner voice now deceived him that the man was only doing his work: on his way to that barber's kiosk, he had seen city workers busy sweeping roads, mowing the lawn and hacking trees, whereas, nobody would sweep a public road nor trim a wild bush where he came from.

"Perhaps this man is a city worker in charge of cleaning people's heads; everything is really strange in the metropolis," he mused but did not voice his thoughts.

At that juncture, Omollo touched his hair with his left hand and realized that it was bushy and surely deserved a shave. He hence considered it wise to accept the kind offer of a shave from that *man of God* or rather a *city worker*, or whatsoever he was.

To facilitate the process, he carefully downloaded his heavy suitcase and placed it beside the barber's chair. Next, he jumped onto the barber's chair and even enjoyed the privileges of a cape around his upper body and a big mirror in front of him.

The barber, who took Omollo for a customer, quickly fished out a razor blade from its wrapper and started shaving starkly and consistently.

"How do you find it now?" He asked Omollo, as he blew atoms of hair off Omollo's head with his overused kerchief.

"It really looks fine, my countryman, you really know how to do it," Omollo strongly complemented the barber.

"Yes, I am trying my best," the barber, who appeared humble, responded to Omollo's complement in gentlemanly fashion.

Supposing that people who were as kind as him were very few in that part of the world, Omollo chose to exploit the man's hospitability maximally.

"Thank you very much; but I was also wondering if you might, by chance, know Bishop Massawe's cathedral, which is somewhere in this city," Omollo asked him.

"*Aiwa*, Bishop Massawe, whose church was donating clothes?" The barber asked Omollo back.

"Exactly that one," said Omollo hurriedly, though unsurely and that now made the barber smile widely at Omollo and say:

"That man is, of course, known by everyone in this city. Mhh! But what used to be his cathedral is rather a long walk from here, especially with such a heavy-looking suitcase as yours. All the same, you are a young man, and you will manage, I am sure. Just walk straight ahead some seven hundred meters, then turn right into a narrow alley; then descend the road until you come across a place where men are slaughtering goats. Now, turn left onto a road leading to the valley where women are tending gardens, cross a small valley and follow a wide path to your left about two hundred meters. And after that point, mention the name of Bishop Massawe and a mere strolling chicken will show you where his cathedral is. After all, you will easily see it for yourself – a big tile-roofed house. That's it," he concluded.

Omollo, who had been listening to the man carefully, of course, noted something strange in the man's instructions, yet ignored it, as his main concern was then to locate the cathedral. Setting off for the cathedral, he tried to take away his suitcase and leave the kiosk but the barber quickly intercepted him.

"But, young man, you have not paid me my money, Ooooh," the barber politely said, completely unaware that his statement was sending chills down Omollo's spine.

"Which money, *yawa*!" Omollo wondered in his local accent.

"For the shaving, Oooo!" The barber clarified to him by imitating Omollo's rural accent.

"Eeee! Was it for money?" Wondered Omollo, which quite surprised the barber.

"When did you arrive in this town, young man?" Asked the barber in a very composed tune.

"Today," Omollo answered.

"Okeeeeeey, I can see that," the barber said and appeared, by his gaze, to be thinking about something. Then he exploded: "Anyway, pay me my money and quit my kiosk!"

"And it is how much, sir?" Asked Omollo, acknowledging his blunder.

"Ten shillings only," the barber answered sternly.

"Eeeeeeh, ten shillings! For the shaving?" Omollo asked in disbelief, "but I have never spent that kind of money even for my own food for a month," he lamented.

"That is, of course, your own problem, young man, pay me my money and quit," insisted the barber firmly.

"Okeyiiii," Omollo now accepted his fate.

"I'd better pay this money and learn from the incident instead of arguing with a 'fool,'" he thought and now reached in his pocket for some twenty shillings he knew he had on him to pay the man whom he now considered an agent of the dark forces. Even so, his heart was hurting inside for the ugly reality that he would spend half of his treasure for a service that he had not needed in the first place.

He dipped his hands into his left hind pocket but was surprised to discover that the money was not there. He now shifted his hand to the right pocket and again the money was not there – then to his shirt pocket and subsequently anywhere he supposed the twenty shillings bank note might be.

To leave no stone unturned; he poured everything out of his suitcase on the floor and started checking the items in it one after another, but in vain: the twenty shillings bank note was still nowhere to be seen. Next, he separated the potatoes from his clothes and started picking and shaking one piece of cloth after another, still all in vain.

Now it occurred to him that he might have inserted the note in between one of the many pages of the Bible with which he had once been rewarded by Bishop Massawe. Immediately, he started turning the pages of the book, one by one, from Genesis 1:1 to Revelation 22:21. Unfortunately, the note was yet to be seen.

Confused and panicked, he now slowly raised his face up to meet barber's face in great shame. As the barber had been glaring at him angrily from his higher stool at the corner of the kiosk, he did not find it hard to locate the barber's face.

"Countryman, I have lost my money," Omollo broke the news to the barber. Unfortunately, the information that instantly brought the beast out of the barber.

"Boy!" He admonished Omollo, "please, don't even try to make a bad situation worse." He paused for a moment, before cautioning Omollo in a serious tone: "I do not think you would want your sliced body to sink to the bottom of the River Msonge in a sack, would you?"

Upon hearing this, Omollo sat down on the floor of the barber's kiosk and started crying. The barber meanwhile watched him sternly and it seemed a solution to the problem would not come. But then all of a sudden, Omollo thought of something and proposed it to the barber.

"I can pay you with these potatoes, for I can't find my money," Omollo unconfidently proposed to the barber and unbelievably there occurred an instant about-turn in man's tone and gestures.

"Ahhhhaaaa! You should have long told me you wanted a barter trade with me, young man. Take them to that corner please, and feel free to call by again for shaving whenever your hair grows," he said happily, simultaneously patting Omollo on the shoulders as if consoling him after losing a race.

Upon hearing this relief, Omollo instantly grabbed the potatoes with both hands, clinched them against his stomach and ferried them to the corner of the kiosk as instructed. Unbelievably, he was done in just three turns with the task that would usually require six.

Afterwards, he repacked his case quickly and rushed out of the barber's kiosk at the speed of a vomiter to the washbasin. He was, of course, still hurting inside for losing his only money and potatoes, yet he was happy to have got out of that barber's kiosk alive.

"Either a pickpocket at the crowded bus station picked the money from my pocket, or I dropped it when I was hunting for the piece of the paper with Bishop Massawe's address at the griller's place," he thought as he continued moving to nowhere.

Omollo then switched from thinking about his lost money to wondering how Bishop Massawe was going to treat him at his home. In such a miserable situation, fear dominated him such he found himself improvising exchanges between himself and his protagonist at his place.

"Man of God, I have come to repent," he anticipated what he would say upon meeting Bishop Massawe.

"Aahhh, no, he will immediately rubbish this one," he corrected himself.

"For all have sinned and fall short of the glory of God," he said and found it equally unappealing.

"No, this includes him and he will be mad about it," said Omollo and started composing an alternative phrase.

"Man of God, Jesus did not come for the righteous...," he uttered, but corrected himself immediately: "No Man of God, Jesus did not come because of ..."

He could not remember the continuation so he lowered his suitcase from his shoulders to the earth and quickly fished out the Bible from it to find the exact words. Fortunately, it was one of the verses he had considered useful in his spiritual life in the past and thus underlined; therefore, he soon scanned and came across Luke 5:32 and now quoted it correctly; *I have not come to call the righteous but sinners to repentance.*

"Yes," he said after reading the verse twice, and then closed his Bible, put it back in his suitcase and resumed talking to himself audibly.

"What have you come to do here, Satan," he envisioned Bishop Massawe screaming at him upon his arrival at his compound.

"Man of God, in Luke, 5:32," he said, but before finishing reciting the verse, he heard the bell of a bicycle and swayed aside the road to avoid being bumped into by the racing cyclist.

After that near miss, he realized he had been so deep in thought that he had failed to follow the direction he had received earlier on from the barber. Now to find the cathedral, he resumed asking many more people about the location of the cathedral and wondered that whoever he asked about Massawe would first grin conspiratorially and thereafter talk about the bishop strictly in the simple past tense – which was quite puzzling.

"Is he dead? Why do these people always talk about him in the simple past tense?" He at one point asked himself but did not get the answer.

"Or is he not yet back at his cathedral from his long rural evangelism?" He further mused to himself but again no answer was forthcoming

All of a sudden, he was standing before a big blue tile-thatched building that he now supposed was the cathedral. Its main door was locked and nobody was in front of the building. Luckily, he noticed some smoke emerging from the chimney of a tiny building behind the main building so he walked towards it, hoping he would find someone there to ask about Bishop Massawe. Fortuitously, behind the building was the servants' quarter on whose veranda an old man with a hissy voice and probably fading hearing ability was sitting with a dated newspaper in his hands.

"Good evening father," Omollo greeted the man cheerfully – deliberately to conceal his desperation.

"Good evening, son. How are you?" The lip-biting old man replied with a sound as if he had some chewing gum in his mouth

"Fine," Omollo answered.

"Where do you come from?" The old man asked quickly.

"Quite fine, and how is it here?" Omollo escaped answering the actual question.

"Fine, we only experience drought as you can see," the old man responded.

"Excuse me, I am looking for Bishop Massawe's cathedral," Omollo explained himself and the man now stared at Omollo for a while, as if trying to recall his face. Then he stood up from his chair.

"Sit down, young man," he told Omollo while pointing to the chair he himself had previously been occupying.

Responding to the instruction, Omollo lowered the suitcase from his shoulders and took the proffered seat. So far, there were no signs of Bishop Massawe here and he did not know how things would turn out for him with this old man. As he silently mused, the old man went indoors – perhaps to bring out another chair for himself to the veranda so that he could speak with Omollo in detail. Omollo eavesdropped him speaking with someone inside the house, probably his wife.

"Who is he looking for?" The woman was asking.

"The serial wife snatcher," The man answered assuredly.

"Has he eloped with that man's wife as well?" The woman asked.

"I do not know yet; let me listen to him," He responded.

After a while, the man emerged from the house with a collapsible chair and set it in such a way that the two men were now sitting face to face.

As Omollo had assumed as soon as he first caught the glimpse of the cathedral, Bishop Massawe was no longer the bishop of there. The unfolding truth was that he abandoned the cathedral seven years ago after becoming involved in a sex scandal that left even the chatterboxes of Damasawa speechless. Since that incident, ownership of the cathedral had been hotly contested in a court of law between an ex-assistant of Bishop Massawe and Bishop Massawe himself.

"That man kept on exchanging faithful wives like his pants. But as they say in our language, 'nine days for the thief, one day for the owner'," the old man narrated and now cleared his throat before continuing with his narration about Bishop Massawe's deeds, "this last episode was, of course, God's plan to unmask a jackal that had all the time been hiding in sheep's clothing to his faithful sheep," he added, "mmmmh," Omollo nodded and the man continued to tell his moving story.

"One of the choir singers of this cathedral had earlier on pledged a cabinet for the cathedral – to be used for keeping bibles and hymn books among other things. Committed to her pledge, she placed an order for such a magnificent cupboard at her neighbouring carpenter's shop. After a while, the carpenters were done with the making of the cupboard and they took it into the woman's house. Thereafter, the woman informed the cathedral that the cabinet was ready to be collected anytime from her house. Nonetheless, the cathedral delayed in collecting the cabinet – as they lacked a vehicle with which to transport it from the woman's house to the cathedral – actually, three kilometers from here.

But at the beginning of the first week of August of that year, Massawe lied to members of his cathedral that he was going to spread good news to the people who were living far away from highways. We thus donated him a lot of money and prayed for him as he left on a mission that we thought was in the interest of our church. My son, what we did not know was that the man was just heading to his paramour somewhere in this city." He said, cleared his throat and threw away a thick saliva beyond the veranda's edge:

"Unbelievably, his paramour (plan B, as they call them nowadays) was the same woman who had earlier on pledged the cabinet for the cathedral. Coincidently, at the end of that week, the cathedral was celebrating its tenth anniversary and thus invited its members and other dignitaries to the cathedral square." He now pointed to the square in front of the cathedral and Omollo pursued his finger with his eyes.

"And because the bishop was not around, the assistant bishop was in charge of everything on that day deemed it better to exhibit the achievements of the cathedral in the past ten years of its existence, including, among other things, the assets that the cathedral had acquired over the period of its existence." He then paused and scratched the back of his neck with the fingers of his left hand.

"Mmhmm," Omollo encouraged him to continue.

"So he thought, well! The pledged cabinet be on the list of things to display on that eventful day – implying that the cabinet had to be ferried from the woman's house to the cathedral before the event kicked off at noon. Fortunately, one of the church members in the anniversary's organization committee had a pick-up. The assistant bishop now asked him to help the cathedral by fetching the cabinet from the woman's house, which he agreed.

"So, five church members went to the woman's house in the pick-up to Pange Street to collect the cabinet.

"Now it happened that the woman was living in a house with a perimeter wall around it and had only the exterior bathroom (I mean, it was not a self-contained house). I think you know these sort of houses in the city?"

"Of course I do," Omollo affirmed, despite that he did not know those sort of houses even a little.

"The Devil is very crafty, young man! When these visitors knocked at the woman's gate, Massawe, the bishop, was taking a bath in the exterior bathroom at the woman's house. His paramour then heard familiar voices outside and ran like a cheetah to her lover (Bishop Massawe), with an aim of informing him that some of his church members were at her gate and that he had to run and hide inside the house to avoid the unimaginable shame which would befall them if caught."

"Eeehehehe," Omollo wondered audibly.

"So, the shepherd ran in a towel with foam all over his

head and body to dodge being caught with his pants down by his own sheep."

"Mmmhmm," *Omollo was surprised.*

"Yesss, he ran into the house, got into the cabinet, which was in the storeroom, and locked himself inside it so as to be safe and sound. Her lover, knowing that her man had hidden somewhere in the house, now opened the gate for her fellow church members to come in; attributing her delay in opening the gate to misplacement of a gate key by her hypothetical maid. Of course, the church members likewise apologized for their unannounced arrival and for their failure to stay longer in their sister in Christ's house. All was going well up to that point.

"In order to leave the house of their colleagues quickly, they excused themselves that they had to ferry the cabinet to the cathedral as soon as possible – allegedly, to be available at the cathedral for the many other activities pertaining to that day's celebrations. Of course, the donor had no objection to their quick return, for she knew how busy that day would be – she even asserted she would have joined them in the event had it not been that she was not "excessively bleeding on that material day." As she bade her fellow members of the church farewell, she asked them to remember her in their prayers.

"You hear the actions of your father's friend, young man?" The old man checked if Omollo was attentive.

"I hear, father," Omollo answered politely.

"So, the cabinet fetchers took out the heavy cabinet, loaded it on the pick-up, and drove off to the cathedral. As soon as they had left the woman's compound, she started calling her lover to come out of his hideout, declaring that his potential glimpsers were already gone and even teasing him for showing high order of cowardice during the commotion. All the same, Bishop Massawe did not emerge from his supposed hideout despite her calling him repeatedly.

"This got her worried that the bishop might have developed complications with his usual BP. In line with this intuition, she now embarked on searching for him in the house, yet the bishop was nowhere to be seen under the bed, behind the water drum, behind the bedroom door or anywhere else, he should have been in the room. At that juncture, she supposed that the bishop might have jumped over the fence yet the possibility appears to be as slim as the camel's passage through an eye of a needle – the back door was not showing any sign that it had been opened in this century and the bishop's clothes were also still on the hanger."

"MMmmh," Omollo encouraged him to keep on talking.

"What she did not know was that the bishop had hidden in the same cabinet, which she had unthoughtfully given away to fellow church members some minutes ago," he said and moved his hand into his pants, probably for scratching some itchy part in the region.

"Heyyyyyy," Omollo exclaimed as he now precisely imagined the incidents that followed.

"To make a long story short, the time had come to exhibit the assets that the cathedral had acquired in the ten years of its existence, one of the things being the flamboyant cabinet donated to the cathedral by a choir singer.

"Then, the assistant bishop approached the cabinet to display it to the enthusiastic believers, who were all the time appreciating how their wonderful God was blessing his own church under the keen spiritual leadership of Bishop Massawe.

"But no sooner had he opened the cabinet's door than something people concluded to be the Devil was seen curling itself inside the cabinet and coughing as if it had something stuck in its throat Oo yaya!" He exclaimed, "the men and women of God were spooked by it – and if you had seen how they galloped for their dear lives," he said amidst laughter from himself and Omollo, "..you would have believed that life is sweeter than grilled meat," he said and laughed loudly and delightedly at his own words.

"My son, the assistant bishop, who a short while ago had preached about being fearless before the Devil, ran even past his own house in the second street – out of fear of the Devil he believed to have encountered face to face at the cathedral square on that eventful day.

"As the news about the visit of the Devil to the cathedral quickly went around – non-believers in the neighbourhood were soon interested in seeing the Devil. Accordingly, they gathered in a multitude at the cathedral square where the cabinet with assumed Devil inside was resting.

"The police, as well, arrived in numbers to oversee security in that now crowded area.

"Nobody, however, wanted to reopen the cabinet

housing in which Mr. Devil was allegedly resting – save for one drunkard who did not care about anything. This one walked to the cabinet and did not only open it, but also pulled Mr. Devil out of it for the rest to see.

"My son, everybody was shocked to find out that the Devil in the cabinet was none other than Archbishop Massawe.

"Soap foam that had clotted on his uncombed hair and body perfectly rendered him a double of the Bible's Devil. Besides, a tiny towel around his big tummy caused him to appear like a pornography star in front of an assorted audience," said the narrator heartily.

"Heeeeeey, and what did he say?" Omollo exclaimed and chipped in with a clever question.

"Mmh, he said that every incident that happens in a man's life had been long preplanned and predetermined by God," the narrator stated ridiculously and then crushed an ant that was trying to climb onto his foot with his tire sandals before winding up his story in a hurry: "Mmmh! That is the whole account of what your father's friend did, and thereafter, he is usually out of town – and even when in town, he usually hides from sneaky human eyes."

Omollo, who from the beginning had masqueraded as the son of Massawe's old friend, now realized the reality of the situation. He realized that his mission was a total failure. He thus now pretended to the old man that he would move on to his elder sister's home in another part of the town, though in reality he was setting off to an unspecified location. Wisely, he asked the old man to keep his suitcase for him until the next day – lying to him that he was quite worried about carrying such a temptingly beautiful suitcase along at that late hour. And now, free and purposeless as he was, Omollo entered the streets of Damasawa City that evening and began the most turbulent life ever.

<<<CHAPTER SIXTEEN>>>

Living in Damasawa City was as difficult for Omollo as carrying a boar atop a skyscraper. He owned nothing valuable amidst heartless people, who to his thinking, wished him death every single minute of their lives. To delay his death in that hostile environment, he would spend nights at ruins and days at dumpsites.

"There is no doubt about it; the Devil has really caused me to eat maggots for food," he said to himself one day in reference to the last sentence his father hurled at him on the day he had dodged the bullets from his rifle.

Since he alighted at the central bus station of Damasawa City, he had had an assortment of problems – but at least, his magic stick had stopped the lunacy that caused him to leave Dongruok Village.

After two weeks of misery at the dumpsites, Omollo learnt that there existed some petty jobs at the main market for healthy and strong youths of his sort. Consequently, he chose to abandon stinky dumpsites and started looking for casual jobs at the market place. Eventually, he learnt that he could hire a handcart to cart people's luggage to and from the market for money, which he did. The problem, was, however, that most of the people with whom he did this job looked as if they were cursed, a fact that constantly jogged his memories of the spell his own father cast on him a long time ago. At the outset, therefore, he would cry a lot because of his situation but stopped after getting used to his new life.

Now it happened that Omollo heard on a radio owned by one of the shopkeepers at the market hall that the national army of Kaya Republic wanted all youths interested in a driving job to go for an interview at Mbariki Barracks the following morning. As he was very passionate about having a driving job, he was thrilled by the news and hurriedly asked the shopkeeper to direct him to the barracks. Fortunately, he discovered it was just three football fields away from where he currently lived.

That night, Omollo spent most of his time anticipating interview questions and improvising the best answers to them. In an extreme instance, he envisioned himself as having passed the interview and now driving a huge military truck through his village to prove the naysayers wrong. At one point, he woke up from his troubled sleep and vowed loudly:

"I will make sure that I pass this interview tomorrow."

The following morning Omollo put on the best clothes he had – though he wished he could have put on a black suit and a tie, if only he had them. Upon reaching the gates of Mbariki Army Barracks, he was ordered by the soldiers on guard at the entrance to wait by the gate until the time for the interview has come.

"They look deadly but I will soon be their drivers," Omollo thought inwardly.

Gradually many other youths started pouring onto the scene so that by 8:00 a.m. there were about fifty job seekers waiting at the barracks gate for the interview. At around 9:30 a.m., a well-dressed sergeant appeared in front of them and spelt out, in a military tone, the procedure for that day's interview. To Omollo's amazement, there would be no oral interview as he had expected. Rather, the army would employ youths who were physically fit enough to win a marathon. According to the sergeant, all contestants for the fifteen available vacancies would be shown where to start the race and where to finish it. Thereafter, the fifteen winners of the marathon would eventually get the jobs – even if they could not recognize the letter "*a*" in a group of alphabets.

"If this is the nature of the interview, *giniasekao*," Omollo code switched to himself – to mean, *if this is the nature of the interview, I have already have this vacancy.*

Twenty minutes later, Omollo and the rest of the jobseekers were on a military lorry, driven to the point where the marathon was to start – exactly twenty kilometers away from the barracks.

Upon reaching the starting point, a bullet was fired to mark the start of the marathon and every competitor set off. Eager to win the race and get the vacancy, Omollo started strongly from the beginning – though he was not alone in his determination – each of his colleagues equally ran determinedly to win the race and get the job.

After thirty minutes of running though, a natural selection process started manifesting itself. That is, competitors started falling down one by one, at the same time; the military lorry roaming the entire route would take them on board and return them to the entrance of Mbariki Barracks for medical attention. Omollo was, of course, in the same way tired, yet his instinct to win the race was unstoppable.

"I must win this race and quit my filthy job at the market place," he reminded his tired legs that had started to strike.

At 11:00 a.m., the equatorial sun had revealed its true color, causing marathoners' throats to dry up and their bodies to crave for rest rather than work. Even so, Omollo's assessment of the race made him hang on: he was the tenth person in the race, implying that he would get the job; even five more people behind him would still qualify for the promised fifteen vacancies.

With the runners on verge of despair, soldiers in the military vehicle behind the last competitor now fired three bullets to signal that the marathoners had only three kilometers left to the finishing line.

Armed with this hope, Omollo now stretched his tired feet to the fullest and successfully moved from tenth position to eighth.

But in a twist of fate, Omollo and his fellow marathoners saw some youths who had been cooling their bodies under a shade of a mature tamarind by the road they were running on. Unexplainably, these youths, to their amazement, bolted and appended themselves in front of the marathoner who was leading Omollo's group. Their action of course shocked almost exhausted runners, yet Omollo and his colleagues supposed the youths were their fans and thus had just wanted to share their glory at the finishing line.

As these newcomers had fresh energy and cool bodies, they soon created a pronounceable gap between themselves and the original marathoners. Soon, the last bullet was fired and, from a distance, soldiers holding placards labeled 1 to 15 were seen at the entrance of Mbariki Barracks: each had to hold the hand of an arriving competitor in accordance with the sequence of their arrival at the finishing line.

To the astonishment of Omollo and the others in his group, the soldiers were holding the hands of the invaders and leading them to the tent planned for registering the actual winners of the race. As there were twelve of them, only three of the fifteen positions went to the cohort that included Omollo. But upon crossing the finishing line, Omollo and his fellow runners collapsed and fainted through fatigue; thanks must go to the experienced military nurses for saving their lives.

Upon regaining consciousness, Omollo and his group who were in the original race were shocked to realize that they were all losers of the race, except for their three mates who had finished as numbers one, two and three. Infuriated by the obvious nepotism they had just witnessed, Omollo and his colleagues swore to God that they would not let justice be bent before their own eyes to such an extent. Accordingly, they started heckling the soldiers for registering fake competitors at their expense; the soldiers, however, pretended to be blissfully unaware of the trick in the race – a pretence that angered Omollo's group even more. Now in real protest of the injustice, they now lay down around the military lorries at the entrance to stop the vehicles from moving from the location until their conflict with the army officers had been arbitrated by the army's top administration. The aggrieved runners were utterly unaware that their opponent in this saga had long experience in defeating protests of that nature in non-verbal fashion.

As they were still protesting, a jeep full of military police pulled up in the area and its passengers descended upon Omollo's group with whips that stung like the bite of an estranged wife. As the storm at the scene ceased well and truly, the protestors had enough wounds to keep them busy with nursing for no less than two weeks. Worse still, they were given only five minutes to disappear from the place by crawling into the nearby bushes; otherwise, the sound whipping and random kicking would resume instantaneously and constantly.

<<<*CHAPTER SEVENTEEN*>>>

After missing his dream job at Mbariki Barracks in a bruising battle, Omollo resumed his handcart-towing job at the market place. When pressed to talk about the reason for retaking his dissatisfying job, he would say, "One takes what one gets, not what one desires."

Be that as it may, his handcart-towing job was still as difficult as ever. The handcart still had no gears making climbing a hill with it a pain in the neck. And as it had no brake too, descending slopes with it was even riskier. From time to time, the cart would sweep *the Busy Malan* downhill at a speed that would always make people stop what they were doing to stare at him passing: some expected to witness how the device would kill him in a fatal accident; others were trying to decipher the catchy tag on the rear of the handcart, which read, *Observers are worried.*

Unfortunately, neither category of onlookers had much time to view him clearly, as he would have disappeared from their sight in the blink of an eye. To further exacerbate the situation, the cart frequently forced him to pass by people at whom he had been looking for a long time. Notwithstanding, passing by people due to the bully of the cart had never hurt him as much as on the day he passed by a girl called Monica.

Monica was an unexplainably beautiful girl and no wonder she flirted with Omollo's emotions at will. A long time ago, she found Omollo seated on his handcart at the market square, waiting for his clients, and had wanted to use his cart as a bench while waiting for her mother, who would come from a different location. To achieve her objective, she walked directly to Omollo, threw him a fond look and greeted him very warmly.

"How are you, bro?" She said, flashing her beautiful smile at *the Busy Malan.*

"Fine and you?" Answered Omollo timidly and unconfidently.

"Fine," answered Monica and then made a polite request.

"I wonder if I can sit on your handcart, while waiting for someone," she said seductively.

"As long as you wish," Omollo responded involuntarily, and then added jokingly, "not even the Devil can resist the request of a charming angel like you,"

To make a long story short, Monica afterwards sat down beside Omollo on the cart and the two looked as if they were long-time lovers on a park bench by the ocean. And as if the Devil was on a mission, Monica's mother delayed coming to meet her daughter – and that gave Omollo ample time to try to cast his net to catch that tasty-looking fish.

All the same, whenever Omollo sent up his trial balloons to the girl – for instance, by caressing her long hair or fondling her thighs romantically – the girl would from time to time respond by saying: 'Matthew 7 verse 7.'

Reading only a rejection into such a biblical response from the girl, Omollo gave up his advances, supposing that it was a fool's errand to attempt to seduce such a devoted Christian.

"Let alone the religious factor, these beautiful girls are receiving tons of applications into their rift valleys, so many to the extent that rejecting men becomes their part-time job," Omollo inwardly protested but did not show it to the girl.

"One beautiful girl in my village even nicknamed men 'beggars' for allegedly asking access to her genitals day and night," he continued his thoughts and zigzagged his lips in protest.

In spite of everything, the joy that the girl was emitting all the while she and Omollo were sitting together on the handcart confused Omollo a lot: she looked thrilled to bits and even hugged Omollo goodbye with her prickly tits that almost stabbed his chest to death – an act that, of course, imprinted her on Omollo's mind even long after she had dissolved in the sea of people at the market place.

Now with desires for Monica hovering over his heart the whole day long, Omollo went straightaway to his Bible as soon as he got to his house and hurriedly opened it at Matthew 7 verse 7 – to reveal the warning Monica was secreting during their man to woman encounter at the market square.

'Ask and it will be given to you; seek and you will find; knock and the door will be opened to you,' he read the verse aloud and immediately exploded like a madman.

"Heey!" He exclaimed aloud, "stupid me!" He shouted while stumping and throwing his arms asunder.

"Stupidity has denied me a chance to witness the glory of creation today," he lamented and cursed his shallow knowledge of the Bible.

Following this incident though, Omollo vowed to do the needful, if luck would have it that he should run into Monica again. The problem was that the two had not exchanged contact details and the town was terribly big.

From that moment on, Omollo kept looking for Monica everywhere in the big city in order to execute Matthew 7 verse 7 – and in trial and error fashion, he twice ran into wrong ladies, supposing they were Monica, and he was, of course, admonished for acting as stupidly as a policewoman on high heels.

But even when his hope of meeting the girl was fading away, he still kept on narrating about Monica to anyone who cared to listen to him:

"She is hornet figured, smiles like the sunshine, is chocolate complexioned," he one day animatedly exploded his feelings about Monica to his colleague called Jose - yet, Jose appeared to be unmoved by all the complements Omollo was pouring on the girl.

"She is cheerful and can infect even a widow with her laughter," he further eulogized the girl, and now Jose stared at him, as though he were trying to figure out where exactly in his big body such nonsense was emanating.

"And I wish you saw how she pricked my chest with her sharp pointed tits the moment she was hugging me goodbye, Jose." Omollo piled on his praise of the girl - which seemed to annoy Jose.

"Ahha!" Jose now exploded, "you are not serious, *the Peeper*," he asserted in a considerably angry and dismissive tone.

"This is a pure case where a demon is luring a naive innocent villager to the slaughterhouse," Jose added scarily and Omollo was struck hard by the words.

"What have you just said?" Asked, Jose astoundingly.

"Yes! What you supposed to be a girl was, in fact, a *jinni* - an evil spirit in the flesh of human being. Remember that this is Coast Region, *the Peeper*," said Jose with indifference. Omollo now reflected over the statement, but interestingly concluded:

"Even if she is a *jinni*, as Jose claims, I still need her. In fact, I can slay seven Goliaths to get her in my arms," he thought further, but did not voice his thoughts aloud.

So many days passed afterwards without Omollo meeting Monica. Then it happened that he was one day descending a slope with a handcart full of cement bags. As usual, the handcart was then sweeping him down the hill against his wish at a speed of almost sixty kilometers per hour. Then all over a sudden, he heard someone beside the road with a very soothing voice shouting his name.

"*The Peeperrr*, how are you my diaaaaa?"

This mention of his name in such a melodious voice then made him swiftly cast his eyes in the direction of the shouter - just to find that the source was real Monica. Bewildered and confused, he now tried to pull up the cart, but as usual, it blatantly refused to stop, leaving him kicking like a kid being whisked away from his mother by an armed kidnapper.

"Fine, fine, fine, Monica, how are you?" Omollo hurled back a reply as the involuntary downhill run continued. In the middle of the valley, the gravitational force was then content with its impact on the cart, evidence being that the cart stopped. Infuriated as a lion that has been robbed of its cubs, Omollo then vented his frustration and anger by kicking the tires of the cart several times, cursing it and abusing it in all the languages he knew.

He did, of course, consider running back in the direction Monica was heading but his second thought was that any such action would be a fool's errand, considering that Monica had by then plunged on the other side of the hill and, to the best of his experience, would have gotten a hitchhike, something which was a norm for beautiful girls in that town.

Now hurt, frustrated and annoyed, Omollo vowed to find himself a thankful job in honour of Monica. With revived memories of Monica still aplenty in his mind, the cart's destination appeared to be too far, the cargo too heavy and the land unnecessarily undulating. All the same, he bore it all and the load was eventually delivered to its destination.

Fortunately, for his return trip, he got four sacks of maize to cart back to the market square for a separate payment – and he was very pleased then to be able to kill two birds with one stone. After thirty minutes or so, he reached the twin slope that had earlier on collaborated with his cart to seriously wrong him with Monica. As though the sight had catapulted his feelings about the girl, the slope then appeared steeper than he had known it for the past two years. This forced him to stop to assess whether he would descend it safely with such a big load on the cart. Though his inner heart told him that the exercise was dangerous, he relied on his long experience in steering the cart and thus decided to kick off his descent of the slope. For about a quarter of the slope's length, he had the cart under control: that is, he would successfully slow it down whenever it wanted to charge. But halfway down, the cart started to rebel his wish to slow down. To cope with its high speed, Omollo now raised his legs above the ground in such a way that the cart was swaying him like a pendulum.

All the same, he successfully continued to steer the rebellious cart for a considerable distance. Then unanticipatedly, he noticed a blue jeep parked exactly in the middle of the lane he was travelling along. In accordance with the cart pullers' safety protocol, he now hurled abuse at the "reckless driver" from a distance and at the top of his voice – with the aim of making him take his vehicle out of Omollo's rightful lane – but all in vain. Subsequently, he thought of evading the encroaching accident by unlawfully digressing to the opposite lane, but alas: he noticed three ugly-looking trucks roaring along it in the direction he was approaching. So he thought of avoiding the looming accident by using a little pavement to the left of the jeep, but lucklessly, the driver of the blocking jeep, whom Omollo had initially taken for a drunkard, was visible, "lounging" exactly where Omollo and his cart would force their way.

With this realization, the spirit of the Devil advised him to run over the stupid man, whereas, the spirit of God advised him to think of an alternative solution. Now with only four seconds left before the bang, Omollo chose to digress to the bush with his handcart behind him – a choice that, of course, authorized his unkind handcart to use him as a bumper against the shrubs they were then bushwhacking shoulder to shoulder. It was thus rough on Omollo until a merciful igneous rock abruptly bogged down the cart tires and caused Newton's law of motion to eject Omollo almost seven meters into the air, and afterwards into the shrub head down, feet up – eight meters away from the cart.

Eight minutes later, Omollo regained consciousness and now realized his entire body was graced with bruises from sticks and stones. He tried to stand up but felt too weak to move and only wanted to remain in the same position longer; save for safari ants that seriously bit him in revenge for his invasion in their burrow and thus successfully forced him to gather himself up.

Now, cursing the evil driver, his jeep, the cart, the pebbles, the sticks and the ants, he limped his way out of the shrubs to the cart; climbed on it and subsequently broke out into a cry as loud as that of a baby who has been stung by a wild wasp – allegedly, not actually weeping for the physical pain, but for the developments that had landed him in the cart-pulling job.

After half an hour of crying over his life, he tried to pull the cart out from the shrubs but it appeared too heavy to glide on such an uneven surface. Realizing this limitation, he embarked on ferrying the sacks of maize one by one, on his head, from the bush to the road. But as soon as he emerged from the bush with the first sack of maize, he set his eyes on the "empty headed man" who, in his view, had inflicted on him all this misery on purpose, still lounging beside his jeep in the same location.

Anger now possessed him and ordered him to teach that man a lesson he would find fit to hand down to his grandchildren. But as he approached the man for a violent beating, he was astounded to see that the man was unconscious and had vomited all sorts of filth around him. This realization put his attentive body at easy and now he pitied the man; all the same, he forsook him to attend to his salvage operation.

After forty minutes of hard work, Omollo was back on the road with all the maize sacks on his handcart and ready to continue on his fateful trip. But no sooner had he embarked on another crazy acceleration down the slope than he heard the man beside the car, purring like a cat whose head is stuck in a thermos flask. At that juncture, mercy crossed Omollo's mind that the man was dying innocently and that he had to help a fellow human being. In accordance with this feeling, he postponed his descent, approached the man, examined him and concluded he would die if he, Omollo, did not help him out with his critical problem.

As if now in possession of the Holy Spirit, Omollo picked the man up and laid him in the back seat of his own car. In doing this, he noticed the car keys on the steering wheel, which suggested to him that he should drive the man to the hospital instead of leaving him to die at that spot like a hog. Having thought about the idea for a while, he hitched his handcart to the jeep, jumped behind the steering wheel and drove off with the man on the back seat.

At the main hospital, he recorded a statement on the circumstances surrounding the man's unconsciousness, then disentangled his cart from the jeep and pulled it away to the market place, happy to have once more saved someone's life.

A month later, Omollo was with his fellow cart pullers at the market square, waiting for their rare clients to show up. Out of the blue, there appeared a man in a black suit, who Omollo supposed he had seen somewhere before, yet he could not recall where. As his eyes involuntarily followed the man walking directly towards his colleagues, who were parking their carts a few meters away from where he was, he soon noted that his colleagues were pointing the man towards him – which he deciphered as:

'a client had wanted more cart pullers for his many pieces
of luggage somewhere around the market and his colleagues
had chosen him to add to their work force.'

With this premonition, he now rushed forward in his customary fashion to meet the assumed client and, upon reaching him, chanted the cart pullers' usual client-winning slogan.

"Welcome sir, I am quick and trustworthy. Tell me where
your luggage is."

He rapped, yet the man appeared unmoved, "you are Omollo Orwa, right?" The man eventually asked him, meanwhile, looking at him straight in the eye.

The response now caused adrenaline to flood Omollo's blood and his heart to thump violently – for, as far as he could recall, nobody in Damasawa City knew his name of Omollo Orwa unless they were part of the government machinery. That is, he was known in the city as *the Peeper*, which was the short form of a long praise name he inherited from his Uncle Ongoro: *the Peeper of the Peeped, the Destroyer of the Destroyed, the Slinger of the Slung, and the Crumbler of the Crumbled.*

Now that the man had mentioned his home name, his assumption was that the man was a plainclothes police officer, sent to implicate him in an heinous crime by either the Devil-possessed bishop or his non-surrendering father. After musing for a while though, he gathered courage to ask the man a question himself.

"What are you looking him for?" Omollo said scornfully, all the while in escape mode, should his inner voice advise him to flee from the man.

Contrary to expectations, the man smiled widely at him and explained his motive straightforwardly.

"I want to thank him for saving my life a month ago," he said, and Omollo now remembered him.

"Okeeey, so you are the man I picked up sick and took to the hospital, right?" He asked him in astonishment.

To sum up, the earlier accidental encounter that day landed Omollo in a five-star hotel for the first time in his life. Even more, the minister left him with some sparkling bank notes to share with his few friends at the market. But that was not all; the minister continued visiting him at the market square from time to time – and eventually decided to employ him as his driver. Once Omollo had become the driver to the Minister of Natural Resources and Industries of the United Republic of Kaya, punctuality and patience became the most important attributes expected of him. At 4:00 p.m. of his first day at work, he drove his boss, the minister, to Damasawa Girls' Secondary School, where the minister sternly warned the girls about the danger of engaging in love affairs at their tender age. At around 10:00 p.m. of the same day, he drove the minister back to the same school for him to fish out the most beautiful girl there. The minister then picked up the girl who during the official tour had addressed him as *the honorable* and who later that night was ridiculously addressing him as *sugarcane, honey, sweetie, chocolate, the only mosquito in my net* and similar names.

On the following day, Omollo drove the minister to a meeting with a furious President of the Republic, who had heard prior to the meeting that Omollo's boss was conspiring with the "enemies of development" to corrupt local industries. At that meeting, Omollo's boss swore to God before the President that he would be the last person to commit what he was being accused of.

"The enemies of development have set out to discredit my cotton-white reputation," Omollo's boss stated gloomily and broke out into a saddening wail before the President, on the pretext that he was innocent of the accusations being leveled against him. As he was so good at this, the baleful looking President found himself apologizing and literally babying Omollo's boss to stop him crying for the 'uncalled for scorn'.

Afterwards, the two old comrades were reconciled and concluded the matter by bursting out into singing the national anthem of the United Republic of Kaya, which, by chance, the minister happened to master more than the President.

> All humans are equal and Gondwana land is one,
> Bribe is the enemy of righteousness,
> I will neither give it nor receive it,
> I am an instrument chosen by God to save Kaya,
> I am the servant of Kayan men and women,
> Defender of my land and its resources.

Finally, they embraced and the matter was brought to rest for good. Immediately thereafter, the minister ordered Omollo to drive him to a meeting with the most crooked businessman in Damasawa City. The agenda was to buy and hide all products from local industries until the market was very dry, subsequently to sell the hidden goods through the back door at a higher price.

On the next day, he took the minister to a trade fair aimed at promoting local goods – with the slogan *Buy local goods: strengthen our economy*. Here, the minister bought everything, amidst praising how such local products were superior to imported ones. That same night, the minister gave all the goods to Omollo, amidst cursing them as too horrible for a man of his caliber to use.

All the same, Omollo's first real experience of joy and agony of being a driver a politician came on the fifth day when he drove his boss to a rural village north of Damasawa City. There, his boss aimed to mount a show to demonstrate to the common citizens that he had not lost touch with them.

As soon as the minister got out of the car, he hugged a goat butcher at an animal auction, as Omollo stood behind him with his briefcase. Six minutes later, he met a crawling cripple with a piece of a bun in his hand. Animatedly, he asked him for a piece of that sand-choked bun and pretended that it tasted so good.

A few steps further on, he found women who were selling local brews at the local market and proceeded to test each of their brews, meanwhile showering them with praises of how good their drinks were. From there, he ate with miners and danced with traditional healers in the dusty market to prove that, unlike his counterparts, he was not drunk with power, "all these actions are expected to translate into votes, come the next democratic election of the United Republic of Kaya," he later confided in Omollo.

But upon entering his car for the return journey to the city, the minister immediately embarked on what he referred to as corrective measures against all the dangerous behavior he had unwillingly indulged in all day long. Firstly, he substituted the *litungu* cassette that had been playing on his car radio the all the day with blues. Then, upon reaching Damasawa City, the minister went straightaway to the national hospital for what he referred to as 'cleansing', whereby his personal doctor pumped a disinfectant from mouth to anus via his stomach, allegedly, to clear all assumed viruses and bacteria in the contaminated village food he was assumed to have eaten.

At the beginning, Omollo would laugh off such hypocrisies of the minister but after a heavy dosage of reprimands, he learnt to be compliant to his master's wishes – the kind of behavior his boss liked and would reward through gifts.

Now, as an obedient worker of the great man, money was no longer an embargo against whatever his heart wished. He thus switched from taking only strong tea and fried cassava to milk tea and jammed bread for breakfast. Further, moved to a fully furnished apartment in the white men's neighbourhood and thereafter bought a new sports bicycle for himself.

Now so contented with his life, his face, which was naturally dark, started getting browner and his tummy that was originally flat started bulging.

"Who said I am cursed?" He found himself soliloquizing as he gazed at the splendor of his new self-contained room at noon one day.

But three years later, *the Government of the People, by the People, for the People* happened to be tired of wickedness of Omollo's boss – only that he had always been too slippery to catch in any scandal. But as fate would have it, one of this minister's malicious deals hit a snag in the bizzarest fashion that year. In this particular deal, the minister was set to sell live animals from a nearby national park under his portfolio to an Oriental nation. The beasts would be caught at the park and transported onto a jumbo ship at Damasawa Port. If successful, the deal would yield him millions of shillings, with which he would hire mercenaries to topple what he covertly referred to as "the *stupid* government," led by a man who, in his description, used "the strongest terms possible to talk the talk, but the shortest steps possible to walk the talk."

On the third month of the deal, everything was very much on course. A well-bribed team was about to finish the job of trapping wildlife in the park and secretly transporting them in trucks at night to the ship at the dock. In other words, the minister's ark was already teeming with all sorts of animals and would leave the port the following week to the Oriental country in question. But in what looks like a predetermined fate, something happened that week that spoilt the whole show stunningly and completely.

That is, the zoologist hired by the minister to tender the animals in the ark had a seasonal mental disorder, normally rejuvenated by a marijuana cigarette – a condition about which the minister was blissfully ignorant. On the fateful day of the deal, this zoologist happened to smoke a marijuana cigarette, which wonderfully revived his mental ailment to the fullest. Now possessed by a crazy mind, the marijuana suggested to him that the poor animals he had been attending in the ark needed their freedom. Subsequently, he went to the digital dashboard of the ship and started opening animal cages by hitting the relevant keys. He struck key A and a cage of beehives opened; struck key B and it released the hyenas; a further key liberated the cheetahs, then another one left the snakes free to find their way of the minister's ark to the city center.

This foolish act started a catastrophe involving the free and startled beasts straightaway at Damasawa Port. A bee stung a coolie gazing at a pile of sacks. As he ran for cover behind the warehouses, he came face to face with an underfed lion that had just descended from the ark. To exacerbate the problem, the lunatic who had initiated the catastrophe appeared to enjoy the encounter between those beasts and men at the port, judging by the fact that he increased the speed of hitting the keys as time rolled by. Soon every animal that had been on the ark was somewhere in the city.

The result was that, after half an hour or so, the city dwellers of Damasawa would be running away from a giant snake at corner A of the street only to meet a charging buffalo at corner B. Within six hours of rampage, the beasts had revolutionized the lively city of Damasawa into a ghost town: only during the second week after the incident did a few people start re-appearing on the streets, but even then, occasional ambushes by a hyena or a cheetah became a routine. Worse still, in the third week, a man sneezing at the market place was mistaken for the hiss of a rattlesnake and sent the whole market running amok. Besides, three people died in the stampede and one more of fatigue. In the fourth week since the incident, a man jumped down the third floor after his wife had wanted to surprise him, by covering his face from behind with her palms: allegedly, the man mistook his wife's hands for the hug of a python.

By the time things cooled down in the fifth week, the evidence was now screaming that the Minister of Natural Resources and Industries was the mastermind of the menace that had haunted the town so horribly. One daily newspaper even captured his involvement in the saga as bizarrely as, *The minister of wildlife has been working very hard to wipe out wildlife.*

Following the allegations pertaining to this incident, Omollo's boss was arrested and arraigned to a court of law on the second Monday of the fifth week since the incident. Omollo also attended the court, especially, to witness how his life was slowly but surely turning upside due to the accused's actions. Flabbergasted to see his boss in the dock, looking as miserable as a bird whose nest has just been destroyed by naughty boys, Omollo had no idea how to help the important man out. From time to time, he would steal a look at him out of the corner of his right eye, and it appeared as if his boss was fixing his eyes on him, sternly warning him not to spill more beans to the public.

As the judge asked Omollo's boss questions regarding his role in that heinous crime, he mostly pleaded memory loss to a count he was accused of or answered that he was dizzy, – a replies that his instructed him to give to every question."

In the end, the judge described his crime as 'heinous, atrocious, grossly reprehensible and an outrage to public decency' and ordered the minister to pack his bags for ten years in jail – allegedly, "to serve as a deterrent to any other would-be perpetrators of the same crime."

As the judge finished reading his verdict, the families and friends of the defendant who were in the courtyard now broke out into bitter wails, while the relatives and friends of the victims started celebrating and demonstrating, one holding a placard reading, *God does not whip with a stick* and another *God has administered revenge on my behalf.*

Following the verdict, such bitterness possessed Omollo that he found himself cursing his boss audibly for his involvement in an act that he now described as shameful and pathetic.

"Just when I was starting to enjoy the fruits of my labor, this happens and destroys everything!" He said bitterly, "did this man really know that he has workers to pay salaries to before jeopardizing his job?"

"Anyway, he is just a scapegoat!" He corrected his opinion, "I know many more officials who are more corrupt than him in this government, yet they are not in jail," he stated sadly, in reference to many more secrets he was keeping.

"I think the spirits of my ancestors are taking a toll on me now," he thought, "I wish I had gone home and asked for forgiveness from my father or conducted rituals on my father's grave," he further thought, "but can my clansmen forgive me of the abomination I did to them?"

He did not get a straight answer to the question he was asking himself though.

Now after losing his driving job, living in the white men's neighbourhood was like swimming against the current to Omollo. He tried to remain solvent by selling some of the things he happened to have gathered during his short tenure as the driver to the minister; still his expenditure appeared too high for him to afford without a reliable source of income – not to mention the fact that his landlord kept insisting on timely payment for water and electricity without even considering the fact he had lost his job.

He eventually sold all his saleable items at a throwaway price and with the little money he had made, he sought and rented a tiny tin room in the shanty neighbourhood of Malapo.

Now it happened that Omollo's neighbour in this new street was a woman with a hunchback, going by the name of Fauziath Ally. She lived in the last room in the same row as Omollo, or precisely next door to Omollo. To a disinterested looker, Fauziath could pass for a teenager, albeit her own daughter was ripe enough for Omollo 'to harvest' – in fact, her daughter looked older than Fauziath, who was then twenty-six years old.

In all honesty, Fauziath was not a woman whom Omollo would pick in a women's supermarket, if such an establishment existed, for she was neither good-looking nor tidy enough to affect a man's heartbeat. Nevertheless, the environment in which they lived dictated that she and Omollo be more than just friends.

About ninety percent of Omollo's room was occupied by bed. Under it and, of course, in the spaces between it and the wavy wall were two water buckets, a toilet brush, saucepans, a charcoal sack, an old box TV, an old loud speaker, empty bottles, a doorknob, a charcoal stove, a pot cover, a box of dirty clothes and many more valueless things. One of Omollo's friend, of course, nailed it when he said Omollo lived in a storeroom – even though Omollo instantly head-butted him and unfriended him for such honesty. The fact was; the only open space in Omollo's room was the area between his bed and the door, which he correctly used as a recreational area. More specifically, whenever he was resting in that tiny room, he would always sprawl on his back on his tiny bed and send his long legs outside the room through his tight door. As a result, Fauziath would often notice his presence in the room by his protruding legs and would always shower him with warm greetings that he was, of course, starving for. Alternatively, Omollo and Fauziath would frequently meet at the communal tap in front of their residence or outside their rooms whenever each of them had been separately ejected out of their tiny tin rooms by the equatorial heat.

Besides, a similar fate that she and Omollo shared drew them together even more. Fauziath, like Omollo, had run away from her hometown some eleven years ago, after causing what elders of her area described as the abomination of the century. It all started when she was twelve and in standard six at Machobundi Primary School in her village. According to the story, her mathematics teacher introduced her to adults' game bit by bit – and before she knew it, she had loved the game more than food. Unfortunately, however, she defied all precautions her coach gave her (of using protection during the matches to evade injuries pertaining to the game). As it was said, her teacher, who taught her more than just school subjects, regularly recommended a condom during their rumbles, but she had always rubbished him by saying that no kid would enjoy a yummy lollipop in a polythene wrap.

The story went that her belly at some point started ballooning and her body would unnecessarily overreact to even negligible inputs – which worried her a lot. From what I heard, she then shared her new feelings to her confidant who told her without mincing words that she was in the family way. The story added that the revelation struck Fauziath hard – bearing in mind that her father had never thought she would become involved in sexual relationships with men, going by her appearance. Following this development, it is said that Fauziath thought and thought of how to mask the unwelcome pregnancy from her dependable father. Yet whichever excuse for her pregnancy she thought of eventually turned out to be faulty. One justification that is said to have crossed her mind was to tell anybody who was interested:

'that her mathematics teacher asked her to help him with
washing dishes'

'that she accepted and went to his house to help him with
the job'

'that the teacher was then sitting on a three legged stool a
few meters from her and was eating banana'

'that all of a sudden the teacher had a seizure, fell down and
started twitching'

'that she rushed towards him with the aim of giving him
first aid'

'that in this process she slid on a banana peel as she neared
the man'

'that she fell on the man's naughty area with her base'

'that the man's shoulderless snake was upright at that time'

'that it slid into her lidless burrow and spat leaven in it'

'that the accident culminated in her present state.'

Rumour had it that she *mused over the* excuse in all the faculties of
her mind and eventually discredited it for being too ambitious. Upon
this realization, she went back to musing for a better justification for
her situation – and indeed found another promising rationale for her
bulging tummy.

'that she took a bet with her mathematics teacher – on
whether Abdul, a renowned dancer – would win the dance
contest that year or not'

'that she would give her teacher permission to play with her
genitals if he won'

'that Abdul eventually won the contest and she had no
choice but to honor the bet.'

From what I heard, this justification appeared sound at first, but later
appeared stupid – considering the fact that everybody knew Abdul
would win the dance contest for seven consecutive years. It would
therefore be a fool's errand to take a bet on such a prediction. She
thus dismissed this justification and continued to think of a better
rationale for her state.

It is allegedly at this juncture that she found a rationale that
remained faultless, even after her scrutinizing it in all her faculties of
reasoning five times.

"I can use my hunchback to cover up this unwelcome pregnancy,"
she thought aloud.

Now content with the suitability of this latter justification,
Fauziath confronted her father one evening in their backyard, where
he was grazing his sheep, to present her latest excuse for her observably
bulging tummy.

"Father, I can clearly feel that this swelling that has been on my back all these years is now shifting to my stomach," she lied to her father, meanwhile looking at him straight in the eye, actually, as if she was telling the whole truth.

Now her visibly shocked father entered the amazement phase, after which he sighed deeply, thought a little and responded to his daughter in a highly paternal voice.

"Sorry, my child, these people are so determined to kill all of us this year, but I am not going to allow it to happen, I swear by my mother Halima Bakari," he swore in an allusion to his witch doctor's allegations that the hunchback of his daughter was a consequence of a conspiracy of the witches in his clan.

According to the story, Fauziath's father thereafter fell into a two-day depression over the perceived problems facing his family. On the third day, he visited his diviner-priest for a diagnosis, or rather confirmation, of the cause of the new developments in his beloved daughter's stomach. As he had anticipated earlier, the diviner-priest's radar held the old man's brother, Omari, responsible. This was now too much for the old man to stand. In what can only be described as angry frustration, he walked straight from the diviner priest to his younger brother's homestead and challenged him to an ultimate duel. Unfortunately, Fauziath's father was very unlucky in that self-initiated fight: put briefly, he lost a thumb from his brother's crocodile bite and lost all incisors from his brother's crude punch in the mouth.

As expected, the aftermaths of the fight were too devastating to the already struggling family of Ally. That is, the conflict engaged the family in a fresh trouble of treating the main breadwinner, alongside grappling with the broken relationships with the clan members on the same account.

To rub salt into the wound, another strange episode followed just two months later. With regard to this strange incident, Fauziath's father was cooling his aching body on a mat under a tamarind tree beside their house. In this process, the old man fell asleep with his hollow mouth wide open – a hollow that was so large that an astronaut could have seen it from outer space. A passing rat then noticed the mouth and was taken aback with it – I was told, it stopped, rubbed its eyes, stared at it and ultimately uttered quite audibly:

"What am I seeing, my God! Is this something's vulva or a rat's burrow?"

But even before the rat had formed a strong opinion on the nature of that scary burrow on that man's body, a cat that was just strolling around the compound appeared at the scene, causing the staring rat to scamper into the man's mouth as fast as its razor-thin legs could launch it. In this process, however, it almost choked the sleeping man, who only survived after a frantic struggle to clear his throat of the organism.

All the same, its fur stuck to the man's throat, causing him an endless cough thereafter. In consequence of that, he not only grew as thin as a mosquito but also became too weak to perform even his conjugal duties.

All the same, his daughter's ill-fated pregnancy, which should have been concealed by her trick, kept on growing day after day – and now she knew very well that the cat would soon come out of the bag. In such a context, it is said she had no choice but to flee her village without saying goodbye to anybody. Since then therefore, Fauziath had never gone back to her village – not even when she was informed of her father's ultimate demise from the rat-induced disease.

A difficult fourteen years in that hostile city, therefore, saw Fauziath doing all odd jobs to make ends meet. Until then, she had worked as a garbage collector, a shit cleaner, a grave embroider and a manhole drainer – just any job that could put food on her table. One neighbour, who probably hated her a great deal, even gossiped to Omollo that one could, for only 50,000/= shillings, have rain beat Fauziath and sun shine on her for a month long as their gatekeeper or a mannequin at the open market. In a ridiculous piece of gossip, she claimed that Fauziath was seeking money in the same manner an owner of shabby bedroom seeks a poisonous snake that has just flashed across his room.

In one of the regular rounds of small talk with Omollo, Fauziath proposed a partnership in a business of frying chicken for cash. She asserted that she and Omollo could buy chickens at the main market, slaughter them, fry them and sell their meat at the nearby bus station for enough profit. As Omollo was jobless and indeed needed money to survive, he bought her idea instantly.

They subsequently started the business and it looked so promising at the onset. Before long though, parts of fried chicken started going missing from time to time and thus causing a tense blame game between the business partners: Omollo would accuse Fauziath of stealing the pieces, whereas, Fauziath would equally accuse Omollo of the same crime. Fortunately, the truth came out in a manner that left no reasonable doubts about who was responsible for incapacitating the business.

According to the story, the two businesspersons had just come from the market place with the chickens, which they promptly slaughtered and processed for frying. On the day in question, Fauziath was the one in charge of frying the chickens on a charcoal stove in front of her room, while Omollo retired to his tiny room for resting as he had played his role as required by their memorandum of understanding. But now that Omollo was not observing her, Fauziath would take the first piece of chicken to a collection container and the second one to her oral cavity, all the while keeping an eye on Omollo's door, lest he emerge from his room and catch her chewing a piece of chicken without his consent. At one point, she had a piece of meat in her mouth and two more in each hand when she heard Omollo's door creaking. In a premonition of being caught stealing, she dashed behind the building, still in possession of the chicken.

Omollo, having just emerged from his room, wondered why Fauziath, who had been frying the chicken, was nowhere near the frying pan. Her absence also struck Omollo with an uncontrollable urge to eat the tempting pieces of chicken in a container beside the stove. He now looked here and there to be sure that Fauziath was not somewhere near and watching what he was about to do. Overpowered by the aroma of the frying chicken that was pounding his nostrils like a big brass drum and supposing that Fauziath was busy with something in her room, Omollo now picked up two pieces of fried chicken from the dish and quickly galloped behind the house to avoid the wrath of being caught by Fauziath with his pants down. Alas, he was dumbstruck to find Fauziath at the same location, likewise with two big pieces of chicken in her hands, chewing and grappling with shy laughter.

At that point neither of them accused the other of any crime, but rather they kept on chewing their pieces sheepishly, while those on the frying pan continued to burn due to lack of attention.

The business was never the same from that day on, for it became crystal clear that the two were behaving like a hyena working at a butcher's shop. Omollo thus went back to the drawing board on how to survive in that hostile city without any source of income. Given the worsening economic condition he was experiencing, Omollo would now do any odd job, provided that it could put food on his table, be it baby-sitting or milking pigs.

After two days of an indiscriminate job-hunt, he was employed as a fisherman at Capicin Ocean. One day he was under a big tree at the beach, contemplating where his life was heading and how shattered it had all become. Tears spilt out of his eyes on account of the wretched life he was experiencing and he wiped them away with his hand. All of a sudden, a gigantic ship hooted some eight hundred meters out at sea in announcement of its safe arrival at Longo port and, as usual, his fellow fishermen – who were either swimming, mending nets, smoking marijuana cigarette, sprawling on the beach, watching naked swimming women or men repairing boats – cheered for it jubilantly. To Omollo though, the hooting of the ship that day sparked his memories of the old stories his Uncle Ongoro, a seaman by profession, would tell him about ships some eighteen years ago.

"Uncle Ongoro might have worked on one of these big ships," he now thought to himself that evening, "why can't I travel abroad and see other lands just like Uncle Ongoro?"

Irresistible slumber then stole his consciousness and for the next two hours, only his breathing and snoring indicated he was alive. Upon waking, he was amazed to realize that all his fellow fishermen had vanished to their nests in various locations. He thus likewise started walking to his own ghetto that was at the edge of the city.

That night he did not sleep well because of thoughts about going to live abroad. He then thought that he would never get another driving job in Kaya, considering that he did not have any document to prove his driving skills: he had only got his last job through acquaintance with his boss.

Besides, the casual labour with fishnet owners, which he had been doing for the past two weeks, was not generating enough income to meet his house rent and other necessities. Against this backdrop, the idea of stowing away to Laurasia intensified in his mind and appeared to be as promising as a brewery business among the Matovians. All the same, the cocks soon started crowing outside, announcing that it was 4:00 a.m. –time for him to wake up, walk to the beach and catch up with his fellow fishermen for a fishing trip on the high seas.

Now it occurred that they that day got a good catch than the past fourteen days. Later that day, to celebrate their great catch, Omollo and his colleague Abdul went out for a local beer at one of the famous sites in the city. At this meeting, Omollo divulged to Abdul his innermost desire to stow away to Laurasia on one of the many cargo ships docking at the Damasawa Port.

'Nothing goes wrong where there are many people' as the saying goes: something that Omollo had previously envisaged as a formidable task was actually not even a challenge to Abdul. Abdul knew every guard who had been assisting other people to stow away at Damasawa Port and would thus help Omollo to stow away too if he had five thousand shillings for bribing people in charge of the port and ships.

The revelation delighted Omollo despite the fact that he did not have that amount of money for bribery. All the same, the idea of stowing away dwelt in his mind for most of the night. And even in his asleep, he dreamt of himself driving a very long train in Laurasia and getting dollars for his work.

At early dawn of the following day, he woke up and, as usual, set out for his fishing job. As he walked to the beach, he intermittently talked loudly to himself about how to raise five thousand shillings to enable him to escape poverty in the underdeveloped Republic of Kaya.

The following week Omollo sold the suitcase that Prof. Girado bequeathed him and obtained three thousand and two hundred shillings (It could have fetched more money, had he not sold it in a hurry). Next, he sold everything in his one-room ghetto for two thousand eight hundred shillings and now asked Abdul to link him with the stowaway dealers he knew.

On the fifth day of the bribery plan, Omollo met the chief guard and the head of porters to strategize his escape. At this meeting, Omollo was told first to work as a porter at Damasawa Port for not less than four months to acquaint himself with the morphology and practice in the cargo ships before boarding one for Laurasia. The job would also allow him to smuggle his requirements on board, undetected by the ship's crew.

Subsequently, Omollo worked as a porter at Damasawa Port for six months, learning and searching for an appropriate ship on which to stow away to Laurasia. At last, he found one with a suitable structure for his mission. With the help of a bribed forklift operator, he thereafter secured a 4 by 4-square meters room in the middle of the cargo vessel. Equally, the forklift operator created an alley for him under the bottom tiers of the shipping containers that would enable him to exit his engulfed chamber as required.

At the end of the seventh month, Omollo had smuggled all the necessities he needed for his envisaged long voyage (water, polythene sheets for *long call*, jerrycan for *short call*, bread and steamed beans, a watch, a calendar and a life jacket). According to the timetable, the ship would set sail the following day to a country, he was informed was the Maikedona Republic. He would thus now start a countdown of ninety days before jumping off the ship: this had to be a day or two before the ship was docked at its homeport.

<<<*CHAPTER EIGHTEEN*>>>

As usual, one last inspection had to be done on all departing ships to ensure they were free of stowaways, which were a common event on international cargo ships at Damasawa Port. That day, Omollo saw a beam of light directed to his cabin from the alley created for him by the forklift operator for a small bribe. Something was moving towards the cabin through the alley, and that put him on red alert for the worse. In his mind, a crew member had spotted him and was coming to whisk him off before he had even begun to move away from the port. Considering this would not only hamper his longtime dream of a brighter future but also cause him a great loss in his life, he prayed hard while hiding so well among his belongings in the cabin.

Contrary to his anticipation, the movement was by a port guard who knew of his existence on board: it was as if the guard was just looking for him to wave him a farewell or something of the sort. As this guard discovered the point where Omollo was supposed to be, he lighted his omnidirectional torch, making Omollo's cabin as bright as daylight. Even then, he could not still spot Omollo, who was lying low like an envelope among his baggage. Unconvinced that Omollo was nowhere to be seen, the guard carefully surveyed the cabin until eventually his eyes met Omollo's eyes, which were then glowing like those of a wildcat cornered by a kitchen owner. The guard then smiled and addressed Omollo in Kilayi:

"Well done, homeboy. You are going to start your adventure tonight. Good luck."

Profoundly relieved, Omollo now exhaled long and threw a piece of roasted meat at the guard's naive sniffing dog that had become so enthusiastic about his discovery on the ship. The guard and his chewing dog now turned towards the direction they had come from and left Omollo alone in his cabin.

Omollo's cabin was dark, both at night and during the day. He could thus only spot something with the help of his torch, which, in fact, he had been warned not to use at night. So, to play it safe, he only used it during the daytime to track days in his calendar. Apart from that, his cabin was very hot during the day and very cold at night, causing his body to develop rashes and grow hair all over. And when the sea was turbulent, he would have the impression the containers were moving positions to sandwich him in the cabin. On one occasion, the fear of being crushed by the containers dwarfed the fear of being caught by the sailors: and he opted to give himself up to the crew and face any verdict they would pass on him. With this idea in mind, he moved out of his cabin but before he was in open view, he remembered the warning from his trainers about stowing away at Damasawa Port.

"Don't even attempt to emerge from your location when the ship is still in the middle of the sea," the warning rung in his mind, "the crews of these ships are devils in human form. They will throw you in water straightaway in your birthday suit while grinning from ear to ear."

With this memory afresh in his mind, he reluctantly staggered back to his dangerous-looking cabin. Even so, his brief experience of fresh air outside the cabin, promptly notified him that his room was stinking like an unattended public sewer due to the towers of feces in polythene wrappers and the rotten crumbs of beans he called food. Pissed off by the environment, he reverted to the idea of moving out of the cabin into the open space of the ship again. He even turned around and followed the same route as before. But again, before he actually emerged there, his inner voice apologetically counseled him honorably:

"Son of Orwa, bear it, please. A few more weeks of breathing stench will not kill you, but Meek sailors surely will – and very brutally."

Luckily, its wise words appealed to Omollo, who thus retreated reluctantly to his cabin and pretended that the cabin was not so smelly. All he would do – as if he were a crocodile in muddy water – was go regularly to the mouth of the cabin to breathe some fresh air and see the light and blue sky, before retiring to his smelly cabin at night.

It was then three weeks before the time that Omollo would throw himself in the water at night – his trainers had told him not to wait until the ship was at the dock for then it would be almost impossible for him to evade the immigration authorities in the country of his destination without notice. In this light, Omollo became increasingly keen on his countdown alongside regular peeping outside in his quest to identify dry land near the ship. But as if the spirits of his ancestors were still haunting *the Busy Malan*, diarrhea and vomit collaboratively struck him like lightning just in that week of excitement. He purged almost everything out of his stomach through both mouth and anus – working either in shifts or in tandem to empty his stomach. To worsen the situation, both his bread and steamed beans tasted unnecessarily bitter – even more so than wild pepper. He hence became so weak he could no longer care about his cleanliness and accordingly started floating on a pool of shit and vomit all over his cabin.

On the fifth day after this disease had attacked him, he was certain he was dying; he only did not know when. In his death agony therefore, he tried to call the crew to kill him quickly, yet his voice could not carry even an inch. Now without any hope, he repented his sins, both those he knew about and those he did not, and then surrendered his soul to God. Afterwards, he closed his eyes and indeed felt as if his life was slowly but surely ebbing away from him – though, in reality, it was sleep rather than death that was taking his consciousness away.

Six hours later, his senses returned although he was absolutely convinced he was a dead man. Under this assumption, he immediately wanted to know whether he had made it to Heaven or Hell. Preferring Heaven to Hell, he applied his senses to try to locate Jesus Christ, the light, or chain songs associated with Heaven – but all in vain, which depressed his spirit incalculably.

"I am in Hell," he uttered loudly and sighed deeply.

Even so, something was still confusing him. So far, he had not seen any evil people, some of whom he knew by name and had expected to be gnawing their teeth and weeping non-stop here in Hell. Nor did it add up that this hell was dangling in the same way as the ship on which he assumed he had died a few hours ago.

"Was that ship Hell? And is it possible that one can get into Hell alive?" He asked himself a question whose answer he did not have.

But as he tried to turn his neck in search of a comfortable posture, his mouth scooped a cocktail of shit and vomit, which all the while had been diked by his shoulder. It tasted so foul that he started vomiting repeatedly until there was not even air coming from his stomach. The development now made him feel that he had not died properly so far – and he now cursed being alive but that much miserable.

Worse still, everything in his cubicle was already soaked in the stinking syrup that filled his cabin. As his clothes were also wet with vomit and diarrhea, he was now forced to strip, leaving him in his birthday suit. He then opted to escape the filth inside his cubicle for the good air outside it. As he was too weak to move upright, he started only with great effort to crawl away from his successfully messed up cabin. But after taking two paces forward, he remembered he needed water and food to survive at the exit of the cubicle. Again, with great effort, he laid a jerry can of water and a container of steamed beans in front of his head to slide forward as he crawled from the mess. Even so, he would still vomit or purge here, before crawling even a few inches away from the latest repulsive slime.

Fortunately, he felt much better on the following day and thus managed, albeit with difficulty, to eat a considerable quantity of his steamed beans and drink some water from his jerry can without vomiting. The day after that, his condition improved even more.

As the illness had fought him so ruthlessly, he had long since lost track of his calendar; now, of course, he had left both his watch and calendar in his stinking cabin. Considering himself to have risen from the grave, he began living with abandon on the open deck of the ship, for he no longer feared being caught and killed by the ship's crew. One day, he even felt he had seen the ship's captain waving at him from the upper deck.

One evening in the second week after surviving the strange illness, he was lying on his back, with only the upper part of his body slightly raised by his two elbows. In this posture, he was just gazing at the blue container in front of him, trying to figure out what the hell it contained. All of a sudden, he heard a loud bang of something like dynamite, presumably from the cellar of the ship. Then he heard cries of agony from the same direction, and shortly afterwards sirens from the captain's story. Accordingly, he sensed that something was wrong on board and stood upright to find out what exactly was happening. As he looked towards the upper deck, he saw members of the crew hurriedly diving into the sea at the speed of a cheetah. This concerned Omollo greatly and for the moment, he did not know how to react to what was happening before him.

"Perhaps these people are playing a certain game or a certain ritual," he thought; save that something was still not adding up; their diving into the water only suggested danger rather than fun.

As a thousand things rolled through his head, a louder bang occurred and thereafter smoke started emerging from the lower deck of the ship. Upon seeing this, Omollo now confirmed that Mr. Death was on his way to scoop him up like a falcon would a chick. For this reason, adrenaline now started flooding his blood stream, making him climb up the first two rows of the shipping containers as if he were a monkey on a tree. But upon reaching third tier of containers, he felt so exhausted that he wanted to uncoil his fingers and fall freely fifteen meters back to the floor. But as he was still contemplating that move, a dark smoke started to cover the rear of the ship and that made him realize that if he chose to drop to the floor of the ship, he would burn like a dry grass in the harmattan.

In the light of this threat, he climbed up the containers despite his exhaustion, and soon reached the top tier, where he could now clearly see that the story at the back of the ship was caught in an unquenchable fire, and it was spreading to the rest of the ship.

Omollo now mused hard as to whether he should wait for the fire to consume him while he watched or dive into the water and see how things would go there. At that point, he remembered his life jacket in his earlier cabin, yet realized that he had no time to go for it. He in the face of this reality, he chose to dive into the water without a life jacket and try his luck at surviving the wreckage. As a preparation for doing something that looked like committing suicide, he hurriedly recited all the prayers he could remember and thereafter took a steep nosedive of about twenty meters into the sea.

As expected, he sunk about half the sea's depth before re-emerging on the surface of water as if to wave goodbye to the earth. Immediately, he started swimming but it was difficult in the large waves he was not used to swimming in. As he struggled for his very existence, he spotted the crew of the wrecked ship on a raft some meters away from him and now decided to swim towards them with the aim of joining them on the raft.

"The ship we would fight over is already wrecked," he reasoned as he swam towards the crew, "so, what are we going to dispute about now? I hope they will no longer be mad at me."

But contrary to his expectations, as he neared the shipwrecked sailors, they all started growling and gesturing vulgarly. But as Omollo had no other choice than to join them, he continued swimming in their direction, irrespective of all the fuss they were making. But just as he was about to catch hold of the raft, one of the men on it pulled out a penknife from his pocket and threw it at Omollo with all his strength. Omollo saw it flash past his eyes and supposed he must have survived the attack – little did he know that the penknife had stuck in his earlobe and that he only did not feel the pain only because of confusion. Now certain that the men on the raft would go out of their way to ensure he was never part of them, he involuntarily chose to swim away from the raft, despite the fact he was heading to nowhere.

As he struggled to negotiate the giant consecutive waves on that sea, one of the burning containers burst out, flew high off the ship and plunged a few meters from the raft with the "evil crewmen", instigating a storm of high waves that eventually swept seven of the ten men off the raft. Omollo smiled after discovering the catastrophe had left only three "witches" remaining on the raft.

"At least seven Devils have been taken off the earth – very good," he mused inwardly, grinning at how they had already been dispatched to the next world by the flying container.

As he continued cherishing that thrilling moment in his harsh environment, another container flew off the ship and plunged directly on the raft where the three remaining 'witches' were still gathered. This time around though, he did not cherish the death of the men, as he envisaged he would be the next in line for the extrajudicial killing the plunging containers were running among them.

Timid and devoid of hope now, he sped up his swimming just to get as far away from the ship as possible. And as if he were a prophet, soon many hot containers started flying off the ship and plunging into the sea, but Omollo had already gone beyond their radius. Ten minutes later, he witnessed a natural ceasefire of the flying containers as the ship was already in ashes and was slowly but surely sinking.

Fortunately, during this turn of events, some jumpy containers had cracked open and spat floating bales of cotton all over the area. Omollo quickly swam to one of the bales and clung onto its strapping belt. It was at this juncture he discovered that the penknife one of the shipwrecked sailors had earlier thrown at him had actually stuck into his left earlobe – thanks be to God that the salty seawater and the coldness of the sea had stopped too much blood oozing from the wound.

At that point, anger at the penknife's thrower ascended in his throat such he looked around as if on a quest to punish him – forgetting that a natural calamity had already taken revenge for him. Courageously, he uprooted the knife from his earlobe and inserted it into his dreadlock; thereafter, he continued clinging on the strap belt of the bale.

All the same, clinging to something not designed to keep a human afloat for such a long time proved to be very challenging to Omollo. Several times, he tried to sit on its top, yet the round bale would roll and throw him back to water.

Realizing he was just wasting the little energy he badly needed to continue surviving, he eventually stopped trying to mount the object and instead only hang on to it. Six hours later, Omollo sensed that the part of his body, under water, was slowly but surely freezing. He also felt as if some marine creatures had started consuming it, an idea that now jogged memories of a story his Uncle Ongoro once told him about a 'ball-cutter" – a fish in the high seas whose hobby is to chew men's testicles. Now fear penetrated to his bone marrow and he even considered releasing himself to die in the water rather than die between the fangs of the ball-cutter. Fortunately, his mind and body did not cooperate on that decision – leaving with no choice but to continue clinging onto the strap of that restless bale, without a clue as to how long he would remain there.

But at one point, he remembered he had a penknife in his dread, with which he could cut a cushion of the bale into a hanger. Having performed this operation, he inserted his arms into the hook and could then float against the bale with his hands free of any engagement. This was an enormous relief and, in fact, he even fell asleep in that posture for at least seventy minutes.

When he woke up, he opened his eyes wide but could only see endless water and feel pain all over his upper body; it was as if his lower body was missing. After a while though, he recollected all that was happening to him and it greatly depressed him. To deepen his woes, the cotton bale he had all the while been hanging onto had become half-soaked and would definitely sink before long. In other words, he knew he would obviously die in a quarter of an hour or so. In the face of this truth, he chose to untie himself from the bale so as to die freely and instantly.

But as soon as he finished detaching himself from the bale, he dimly saw something like a mangrove clump about ten meters away. In this knowledge, he postponed dying in favour of trying to reach what he had just seen. Using the part of his body that was still living, he now swam with difficulty to the clump he was convinced would save him. However, only six meters away from salvation, he felt too exhausted to move any further and thus gave up and started sinking slowly to the bottom of the sea with both his mouth and eyes closed. Nevertheless, in course of this sad journey to the underworld, a curious fish stung his ankle a bit – and Omollo, who supposed it was a shark, now struggled forcefully until he emerged on the water's surface. To his surprise, the clump was now only three meters away from him. Now with hope and energy inspired by the adrenaline originating from "running from a shark", he peddled himself hard and was soon on the top of a giant waterweed, made up of plants and all sorts of sea garbage, all cemented together into a knot.

He now assessed his body and realized that the part, which had been under water, had turned white, and looked like small fish had tried to feed on it, going by the numerous small fresh wounds it bore.

Being extremely hungry and thirsty, Omollo instantly started eating the healthy vegetation that made up the waterweed – and to him at that moment it tested better than mixed salads in five-star hotels.

On his second day there, Omollo discovered that a fish species living under his waterweed were attracted to blood just like iron to a magnet. As a result, he would henceforth move closer to the edge of the waterweed, prick his finger with a penknife, the one he obtained from the shipwrecked sailors, drop some blood in the water – and the fish would come swarming in multitudes. At that juncture, he would sharply strike one of them with the penknife, eat his catch raw and drink its blood in place of water. But even after the problem of food and drink was solved, the waterweed was still too cold and windy for a human being's body to enjoy. Accordingly, Omollo's body grew long, thick fur, which gave him the appearance of a certain breed of primate in the Ataronian jungle.

Be that as it may, he chose to remain alive and indeed worked on it: catching more fish and eating the vegetation on the clump of waterweed. Then one dawn Omollo was surprised to wake up and see lights in three of his four cardinal directions. His heart as a result leapt with joy in anticipation that he was near a bay somewhere on the planet Earth and somebody would be coming to rescue him. Excited so much, he prayed and sung one of the praise hymns he had learnt a long time ago at Bishop Massawe's church.

At around 7:00 a.m., he confirmed beyond reasonable doubt that he had landed near a bay of a bigger city than Damasawa City – going by the sight of beautiful stories and clusters of residence at the shores of that ocean.

"I have miraculously made it to Laurasia," he thought to himself and grinned in his heart for such a formidable achievement he felt to have miraculously accomplished.

Even so, Omollo's waterweed could no longer move beyond its current location since it had become intertwined with uncountable pieces of other waterweeds, which had already been colonizing the place from time immemorial.

"It is like this is the main destination of all waterweeds in the sea," Omollo said to himself.

At around 11:00 a.m., Omollo saw a sports motorboat passing by, about six hundred meters from his waterweed. This exited him so much that he shouted and waved like mad at those in the boat. Luckily, the two men on board noticed him and started racing towards his waterweed. Their response accelerated his heartbeat even more at the joy of being rescued.

But in a turn of events, the men on the boat, upon moving closer to him, suddenly switched off the engine of their boat and started staring at him unblinkingly, just as if they were seeing a ghost.

Sensing that the men might have been scared by his pathetic look, Omollo made a step further by begging them, using the Linglish language he had long since learnt at his adult secondary school, to pick him up. To his surprise, the spooked men neither replied nor asked anything; instead, they kept on staring at him, speechless. Their indifference, of course, now made Omollo doubt if he was really speaking these men's language.

"Can it be that Mr. Mandio taught us his mother tongue, duping us it was Linglish?" He mused to himself, "why are these men not understanding the Linglish I am talking to them then?"

And indeed, he heard them speaking a language other than Linglish and was in a great shock: as he had assumed that all white men spoke Linglish. He was then amazed even more to see these men start their boat engine and depart without rescuing him.

"Perhaps these haters are going home to collect their rifles for finishing me off," he said to himself. Whatever their intentions were, he had no other choice than to keep calm and see what fate had in store for him.

After two and a half hours of no hope, Omollo suddenly saw a squad of about ten motorboats of different sorts racing crazily towards him. The sight, of course, evoked in him a premonition of a danger – even to the extent he wanted to dive into the water to avoid it but, unfortunately, he felt too weak to escape from a group seemingly so determined to find him.

Realizing the limitations of his context, he remained calm and awaited his fate. But upon reaching a respectable distance from him, all the motor boats switched off their engines and lowered their anchors. Spying on them, Omollo realized, by their uniforms, that they were from different institutions. Next, the commander of each of the boats would take out a pair of binoculars and direct them at Omollo for a considerable time before communicating something to his subordinates, who would jot down what their boss had just said. The commanders would then direct torch-like beams at Omollo and again tell their subordinates to note down what they were saying to them. Alternatively, they would be making long radio calls to people whom Omollo obviously did not know.

"What the hell are these people doing?" Omollo thought to himself.

Bored or rather disinterested, he now screamed at them in Linglish but quickly remembered he had been told by his trainers to play a dumb man – to prevent the government officials of the host country from deporting him.

'If you speak to them, they will know your nationality and send you back or throw you in jail right away. If you do not speak, they will think you are dumb and will thus fail to establish where you come from; hence they will give you clothes and food and even set you free to live your life in Laurasia,' he recalled his coach telling him sternly in his office.

"From now on, I am a dumb man," he mused and swore not to utter any sensible word aloud.

Thereafter, he was astounded to see all the boats zooming in until they were touching each other. Subsequently, all the men who had been observing him with binoculars started discussing something serious, judging by their animated speech. Then, unexpectedly, all the boats left except the one containing the loudest and the shakiest boss in the preceding discussions.

The remaining boss now aimed a unique object in Omollo's direction and fired something out of it that stung Omollo like a rattlesnake. In Omollo's version of events, it was a giant syringe, whose content instantly spewed a sleeping drug into his veins.

When Omollo woke up at around 08:00 p.m., he found himself in a strong iron cage, in the same row as chimpanzees, and gorillas. He quickly surveyed the scene and peculiarly concluded that he was now in Hell.

"Those uakaris killed me," he uttered and sighed deeply.

But upon making a critical observation of his imagined hell, he noted a bunch of bananas and roast meat hanging above his head, a tin of fresh water in one of the corners of his cage and a mysterious source of warmth below his feet. Greedily, he guzzled the food and water; of course, he was too hungry and thirsty to mind whether the things were from Hell or Heaven. Next, he jumped on a strong raised rack in the cage and a deep sleep instantly restrained his senses for fifteen consecutive hours.

Upon waking up, Omollo saw a team consisting of the boss of the boat that he supposed had brought him to that cage and now realized that he was not in Hell. The men were marching towards him with a poster they soon erected in front of his cage before dispersing in different directions. Curious about the poster's contents, Omollo peeped at it from his cage and was rudely shocked by information claiming he was a remainder of *the Extinct Ataronian Aquatic Orangutan.*

While still wondering what had happened to him, he saw the group of the men returning to his cage. Enraged, Omollo yelled at them, to which the leader of the men responded with another syringe of anesthesia. Omollo immediately felt intoxicated and succumbed into a deep sleep. The men then opened the door of his cage, and started attending to or experimenting on him – plucking his hair, transfusing his blood to bottles or collecting a heap of feces he had laid on the box at the corner of his cage.

The following morning more people – who Omollo supposed were journalists – arrived at his cage with pens and cameras. They would photograph him in different positions and write down whatever he said or did. And as if these men were the harbinger of the multitudes, the day after that the zoo was teeming with thousands of locals, all eager to view Omollo as the last remnant of the extinct species.

But whereas the long queue was jubilantly viewing Omollo, Omollo himself was burning with anger inside after realizing that people were queuing to view him in the way they would a dead body before a burial. He even wished he had been reincarnated as a wasp so he could sting and disperse them like pollen. He tried screaming at them but instantly got another shot of anesthesia, which persuaded him henceforth to stop invoking any form of violence in the zoo.

Nine months later, it happened that the Queen of Nanaca Republic, together with her family and friends, were due to visit the zoo to view this remainder of the extinct primate species. Accordingly, the zoo administration found it necessary to modify the zoo so as to seek appreciation from the revered leader of their land.

In this new arrangement, Omollo was moved to a larger cage with more amenities than the old one. Among the facilities was a pool – actually to match the assertion by his chief curator that he was a remnant of Ataronian Water Orangutan.

As the Queen would come along with her friends from Oriental countries – which have always hated nudity in public – each of the primates in the zoo was fitted with padlocked leather pants to impress the queen's guests. Unfortunately, Omollo's pants happened to be so tight, they mapped out his large golf club, quite apart from the fact that they deprived his organs of their usual naked freedom.

A week after all the preparations were done, sounds of sirens were heard from a distance, indicating that the convoy of the Queen and her Oriental companions was approaching the zoo. Consonantly, well-dressed zookeepers paraded to receive their Queen and, of course, outdid themselves in whatever they did on that particular day – all to impress Her Majesty their Queen and her distinguished guests.

Thereafter, the bushy man, who Omollo later learnt was a

professor in charge of the zoo, started guiding and describing creatures in the zoo to the Queen and her friends.

"This is a water orangutan," he started falsely describing Omollo before his own eyes, "as you can see, the species is very close to human beings. It is a great honor that Nanaca Republic has become a custodian of this rare species long thought by scientists to have been extinguished some two million years ago."

At this juncture, he fished out of his old hide-bag an extract from an old newspaper entitled 'Extinct Homo sexuals idaltu,' and started using it to lie further to the Queen and her delegates, sometimes using difficult or rather non-existent vocabularies such as "Paleofoolish Age," "Stupidtoomuch Age," "Mesocheating Age" and so forth. Astonishingly, the Queen also acted as if she was equally conversant with these imaginary archeological terms.

"Of course, I also learnt during my junior high school that most of its kind died during Stupidtoomuch Age," agreed the Queen at one juncture.

"This family of primates, if you have noticed, has pierced earlobes. Kindly observe its earlobes closely and you will see that they are not like yours and mine," he said and pointed to Omollo - whose right earlobe had been mutilated by his father's bullet and his left by the sailor's penknife. This latest fabrication, further irritated Omollo, who now yelled quite audibly in the Queen's own mother tongue he had by then acquired a bit: "A great lie!" - Which, of course, shocked everybody, including the professor. All the same, he professor continued to lie shamelessly about Omollo.

"As I told you, it is an aquatic orangutan whose natural habitat was basically the Ataronian jungle. It can therefore stay underwater for a close to four hours, without rising to the surface to breathe." The professor added another lie, further enraging Omollo, who hissed with disdain to the astonishment of everybody around. Yet the adamant professor persisted with his untruths.

"I almost forgot. It can speak human language crudely," he asserted and this time Omollo giggled at his folly. Again, the professor pretended not to mind him and continued lying.

"Kindly try to greet him now and you will be stunned at how it will respond to your greetings with precision," the professor suggested a test for his guests - little did he know that Omollo was looking for precisely such an opportunity to humiliate him before his guests.

"Good morning, orangutan," the enthusiastic now Queen tried out the test that had been proposed by the professor. Omollo, however, remained indifferent to the input, necessitating the Queen to repeat the test.

"Good morning, creature," the Queen repeated her greeting with an alternative form of address, yet Omollo reacted the same way -

which vividly hit the professor where it hurts.

"Well, it sometimes behaves like that: it sometimes speaks and sometimes does not," he ingeniously tried to mask his disappointments.

"Lieeeee!" Omollo shouted at him, and the Queen and her team almost took to their feet, in shock of how relevant the response of the supposed orangutan was.

This time however, the professor found it wise to take them away from Omollo to avoid further embarrassment from the creature before his guests.

"Let us all move to the next cage to see more of our varieties," he cleverly suggested to the team he was guiding.

Even so, the professor's instruction that they move on was not honored by all members of the team. That is, a section of spectators remained at Omollo's cage to continue viewing him more. Happy to have humiliated his adversary, Omollo next chose to reward those who had lingered with a better view of him by standing upright from the bench where he had been sitting. This new view of him nonetheless gave a three year-old girl an intriguing question that her mother cleverly avoided answering.

"Mother, mother, why has that Gondwanian pooed in his pants?" The girl said in reference to Omollo's extra-large apparatus, which was well mapped by the mini-pants he was wearing. Her mother, of course, played deaf but Omollo, who had also heard her, was both ashamed and impressed.

"At least this naughty girl knows that I am a Gondwanian, whereas that stupid professor only knows masturbation," he thought, simultaneously turning his back in an effort to avoid further embarrassing observations from the kid. However, his back view perplexed the young girl even more.

"And, mother, why does he pooh to the front, not to the back like my father?" She added and her embarrassed mother now ostentatiously dragged her away from Omollo's cage.

Later that evening, the professor came back to Omollo's cage purposely to scold him for behaving badly before the dignitaries. This set Omollo wondering whether the acclaimed professor preached water but drank wine.

"Does this man also know that I am a human being, but just fools everyone that I am an orangutan for some illegal gains?" He inwardly thought but had no way to confirm his theory.

To make a long story short, Omollo saw certain loopholes in that queen-induced cage he could use to escape from the zoo. He observed that the cage had only a single layer of enclosure and was hidden from the eyes of the zookeepers.

While plotting his escape, Omollo started observing the security details of the zoo over and over again. Next, he strengthened his friendship and trust with the zoo attendants – a ruse he had once learnt from small talk with his fellow fisherman called Abdul, who long ago had applied the same trick to break out of jail. Then one day he stole a hammer from a carpenter who was mending his cage – and did not even come under suspicion for primates steal food, not work tools. Now with all the information and a tool he needed in order to escape, Omollo just waited for the perfect day for executing his plan to come.

Now it happened that his traditional cleaner one day entered his pen drunk. As usual, he neither wore a helmet nor locked the gate of the cage, as was required by the protocol of his job. Having noted all the security blunders his cleaner had made, Omollo chose this moment to escape from the zoo. Deceptively, he greeted the cleaner in friendly fashion but secretly reached for the hammer he had been hiding in his cage, waiting for the moment to strike. As the cleaner was busy collecting his excreta, Omollo brought down the hammer at the back of his neck, so hard that the man did not make even a grunt but rather collapsed silently like the Amandoran twin towers, which was exactly what Omollo wanted.

At the speed of light, Omollo undressed the man and put on his gear in a hurry. Thereafter, he took the keys to the man's car from his pocket, ran to the vehicle, which was standing in front of his cage, and jumped behind the steering wheel. He started the engine composedly and drove towards the main gate at a normal speed, praying that the security guards would not discover he was an impersonator. As he approached the gate, the gatekeepers scrambled to open the gate even without identifying who was behind the steering wheel – anyway, nobody had ever thought of the possibility of a zoo animal driving a car. Moved by the courtesy of the security personnel, Omollo drove past their checkpoint and immediately started to speed up as fast as he could, for he knew very well it would not take long before it was discovered he had escaped the zoo in a puzzling way.

After some considerable time, he spotted a long mountain range roofed with a thick-planted forest. The sight thus struck him as a perfect hideout from his tormentors: so he pulled over, abandoned the car and started running towards the trees. Once in the forest, he would climb summits and descend them, over and over again, just to be the farthest away possible from his anticipated pursuers.

All this time though, he was extremely wary of contacting human beings in the forest for fear they would report him to the zookeepers, who, as usual, would net him and return him to the cage under new security measures.

"I would rather come face to face with foxes in this forest than a two-footed creature," he thought as he moved.

Luckily, the forest was full of apples and strawberries to keep his stomach full and springs of fresh water to keep his thirst at bay. At night, he would roost in one of the deer blinds rampant in the area – thanks be to God it was not a hunting season in Nanaca Republic, lest a hunter confuse him with a beast and shoot him dead.

On the third day of strolling through the thick bush though, Omollo felt a strong urge to consume something different from fruits. All the same, he fought off that idea on the pretext that Adam and Eve lived in Eden on fruits and vegetables. But as the days passed by, the itch for a different food catapulted and he now strongly considered surrendering himself to one of the villages he could see down the hill from his elevated position.

On his fifth day in the forest, he started a trial run of surrendering to the village by approaching some joyous boys, who were swimming en masse. As he approached them silently, a thousand things went through his head, especially how similar children's games were everywhere. But even before he was close enough to express his problem, one boy noticed him from a distance, and shouted:

"An ape in uniform!"

"No, a chimpanzee game warder!" Another boy instantly contradicted him.

"A black freak!" Shouted the last one, as all the boys bolted naked towards their village at the speed of an express train.

Their flight however paralyzed Omollo until he realized that the fastest boy was about to reach his village, which meant there could soon be trouble between him and the parents of the fleeing boys, of course for wrong reasons. With this premonition ripe, he now bolted a retreat, bushwhacking the forest like a gazelle. Two hours later, he was sure he was sufficiently far away from his potential pursuers and thus sat down under a giant tree, looking down towards the point he had run from.

Two days later, he decided to retry surrendering to a nearby village, no matter what would happen. He this day walked towards a small church. As he neared the building, the faithful, who were talking outside after the church service, set their eyes on him, and suddenly everything turned into chaos again: the cowardly believers started fleeing, children started crying, men and women wailing audibly and believers' dogs barking competitively. More interestingly, the pastor of the church, who took him for Satan, ran for his riffle at the vestry, and emerged in short order to shoot him dead.

As all this happened, Omollo had wanted to sprint, save for the fact that his inner voice told him not to do so – and indeed two rifles pointing at his chest were eagerly waiting for him to show any signs of impetuous movement. In unexplainable wisdom, he now raised his hands as a sign of peace seeking – an action that baffled his potential assassins and definitely delayed their triggers. Amidst this confusion, a woman, whom Omollo later came to know as Madam Katharina, yelled with all her might:

"Stop it! Stop it! It is a Gondwanian, not a beast!"

Omollo, who had already acquired a bit of Nanacan language, too swiftly complemented what she was saying in his telegraphic language:

"I Gondwanian, not orangutan!"

Thereafter, all the guns that had been pointing at Omollo's chest were lowered, giving these landlocked people a chance to view a Gondwanian at a close range for the first time in their lives. Even so, one woman in this congregation was not yet fully convinced that Omollo was a Gondwanian; or rather, she just wanted to oppose Madam Katharina in public.

Canny as she was, the woman forcefully asked for the opportunity to conduct an experiment that would tell everybody beyond reasonable doubt if Omollo were a primate or a man. Everybody thereafter bought her proposal except for Madam Katharina, who strongly opposed it, but as ever, the majority carried the day.

Each person in the group keenly followed the woman as she pulled out two ripe bananas from her handbag and started dangling them in front of Omollo's face. Omollo contrarily shelved an urge to snatch the banana as the woman 'scientist' had earlier on hypothesized; instead, he kept on smiling at the woman as she insistently floated the bait before his eyes.

But in a strange turn of events, the bananas looked so tempting to chew that the woman's own young daughter is the one who started crying for them loudly and bitterly. In conclusion, the scientist announced her findings to the itching public:

"It is possibly a civilized Gondwanian," she announced, "were it a baboon or a crude Gondwanian, it would have grabbed these bananas in less than no time."

Her supposedly ingenious findings drew applause from the cheerful crowd; Madam Katharina, however, voiced her opposition to the woman's finding loud and clear.

"That should therefore mean that your daughter is a female baboon – if her crying for a banana is anything to go by," she uttered and people cheered as if inciting the scientist to fight with her.

As expected, Madam Katharina's words did not go down well with the rural scientist. She therefore walked to Madam Katharina and punched her – an act she would come to regret for the rest of her life. In no time, the crowd had the pleasure of watching Madam Katharina knocking some sense into that rural scientist: so severe was the beating that nightmares about Madam Katharina thereafter became an integral part of the woman's dreams.

On the following day, news about the emergence of a Gondwanian-cum-gorilla at Zwecke Church was all over other villages in the region.

Tourists and enthusiasts from as far as the tenth village hence began pouring to Zwecke Church Square to see the said queer being. One old man excitingly shoved everybody out of his way for hours and, upon setting his eyes on Omollo, exploded uncontrollably:

"Is this really a Gondwanian? Where is its fur then?"

As constant crowds milled about the church square, the happiness of the pastor of the church was as bare as goat genitals. From time to time, he would seize this rare opportunity to impose his evangelism on non-believers or rather to bully them into paying offerings for his church:

"My God, who does not tell lies, spoke to me last night," he said one day and looked at the crowd in a way that suggested he was chatting with God on a daily basis.

"Last night he told me he will soon change stingy women and men, who are always indifferent when the collection plate hovers around, into sacks of filth!" He thundered and again surveyed the crowd professionally. Indeed they were moved.

"And I told Him that He has my blessing to turn those who do not want to give Him anything into sacks of filth," he said and people who seemingly believed his words exclaimed in chorus.

"Eeeeeeh!"

"Eeeeeh!" He imitated them.

"What did you expect me to answer Him in this light?" He asked the audience that was totally paralyzed by his words. As he probably envisaged, his threat bore fruit: considering even the stingiest Zweckian in the crowd dropped a coin in the collection plate that day.

But on the seventh day after Omollo's arrival in Zwecke Village, news of his presence at Zwecke Church reached the ears of the head of the zoo where he was previously confined. Consequently, the professor, the director of the zoo, hastily arrived in a convoy of four cars at the church compound – allegedly, to recapture Omollo for the zoo.

Luckily, Omollo, who would remain outside during the church services, noticed them from a distance and ran straightaway to the altar, where the pastor of Zwecke Church was serving his congregation. Omollo's act thus triggered uproars of disapproval from one corner of the church to another, with most of the faithful clandestinely criticizing their pastor's decision to tame a beast, which, of course, had to be clueless about what a sacred place was.

"Look at how this creature walks into a chancel as if it is going to the toilet," one man murmured to his neighbor, "but I do not blame it at all. The fool is, of course, its keeper; the thing does not know about holiness," he added sarcastically.

As events transpired, the congregation was flabbergasted to see a group of men with handcuffs and guns in their hands at the entrance of their church. These men were now looking and pointing at Omollo in turns. Their behaviour hence disrupted the ongoing Sunday service, as every believer wanted to know what the game warders were intending to do with Omollo.

Afraid and anxious, the pastor rounded off his ill-fated service to seek an audience with the strangers and ascertain what they were looking for. Subsequently, the congregation duly learnt that the men had come to capture and take Omollo to a zoo – a mission they disapproved. Consequently, every churchgoer now ceased condemning Omollo for entering the sacred place and rather ganged up against his would-be captors, jeering and heckling them until they opted to leave Omollo at the church compound.

Two years later, Omollo was no longer the talk of Zwecke Village, nor its environs. By that time people considered him no more odd than their village chairman, whose armpits smelt he-goat even in mid-winter. To the host pastor and Madam Katharina, he had proved an asset through his noble services as a gardener. His life was thus so stable in that foreign land, and one would think his engagement with the 'true' church of God had eventually freed him of his malevolent ghosts. But alas, the malevolent ghosts later demonstrated they had simply been gathering momentum to strike Omollo even more viciously.

<<<CHAPTER NINETEEN>>>

Madam Katharina was a thick, black-haired resident of Zwecke Village. It was actually this woman's loud slogan of "It is a Gondwanian! It is a Gondwanian!" that had saved Omollo from the guns of her people and made it possible for him to settle in the village. Her eyes were wide and watery, as though Sulphur gas from a sliced onion was entering them all the time. Morphologically, she was slightly bent in her back, making her posture look as if she had a hunchback. In speaking, she preferred imperative sentences to declarative ones – a habit that might, more than anything else, have demonized her among the people of her village. When walking, she took long jumpy paces, as if she were a farmer measuring with footsteps a tract of land she wanted to buy. Idiosyncratically, she had a coarse voice, and always pulled surprises with her vulgar language in public – a style many people claimed did not match her age.

Probably because of these peculiarities, her name was a refrain whenever a parent in Zwecke wanted to threaten their crying baby with a monster. And most likely for wrong reasons, her name was mud among the residents of Zwecke Village and its environs – evidence being that most of her neighbours would gossip about her even to such a strange creature as Omollo was in Zwecke Village. More than once, those neighbours had told Omollo, on condition of anonymity that he was living at the home of a professional witch woman and a magnet of misfortunes. Luckily, the Busy Malan was by nature very lax at buying new ideas on spec.

Madam Katharina had been leading a very solitary life since her husband was sentenced to life imprisonment some fifteen years ago. A soldier by profession, her husband was a great lover of sex and alcohol: passions that eventually landed him in eternal trouble. On his fateful day, he had drunk too much beer and, as usual, could not get enough of the forbidden fruit at the junction of Madam Katharina's hind limbs. Madam Katharina, who had long learnt she could not match that man's demands, allowed him self-service whenever he wanted to enjoy his marital rights – thanks be to God that the man's okra was not crunchy enough to wake her up, if at all she chose to sleep. This arrangement, of course, held their marriage together until that perilous day.

From what I heard, it was at dawn that the drunken man negligently mistook the mouth of his baby girl – with whom they were sharing a bed – for his wife's fur wallet. The story went that he eventually suffocated the little angel to death with his okra – a grotesque tragedy that henceforth turned the life of his family upside-down irreparably. Later the same morning, the government of Nanaca knocked at his door to avenge the brutal homicide of the little girl. According to the story, they dragged the man away by his feet, crying and referring to the death of his baby girl as manslaughter – but all in vain. A court of law subsequently jailed him for life – allegedly, to serve as a deterrent to any other people who love to make love in darkness.

An inconsolable Madam Katharina was thus separated from her husband even before the wedding ring on her finger had stayed long enough to leave a permanent scar of marriage. It is said that her solitary life would later make her so strong she could slaughter a pig without the help of a man. Determined too, she single-handedly raised her son Klaus, until the boy was old enough to join the army like his father.

After Klaus had signed up, Madam Katharina's loneliness doubled (for Klaus would only visit her once or twice in three years). This pressed her to keep a dog, called Gustav, to keep her company. In this light, she also adopted Omollo with the same aim of keeping her company and to help her with mowing the lawn and cleaning her extensive compound.

To facilitate Omollo's stay, she accommodated him in the servant's quarters and would occasionally provide him with raw food to cook for himself. All the same, she sternly warned *the Busy Malan* against getting closer to her main house or getting used to her in anyway whatsoever – a condition by which the humble Malan abode like a pilot to an alcohol prohibition rule.

Thus, until his fourteenth month at the compound, Omollo had never overstepped the bounds which his landlady set, partly because he did not want to incur the disadvantages associated with infringing this woman's rules – normally a food sanction, but largely because he never wanted to annoy his savior.

But in his third year of his stay at her compound, Omollo began to believe that Madam Katharina was as much of a witch as her hateful neighbours purported. This was because, from time to time, she would ululate madly in her house, while intermittently shouting the name of her dog, "Gustav! Gustav!" without any logical explanation for this queer behavior. Omollo came to suppose that during such times she was practicing witchcraft. This supposition nonetheless struck him with an unquenchable urge to watch a white woman's witchcraft; only he did not know how to go about it.

Now it happened that one evening Madam Katharina arrived at her compound from an unspecified location and entered her house with Gustav alongside her. A few minutes later Omollo, who had been lounging on a couch in his room, heard the onset of her usual ululations and chants of Gustav's name. This time, however, his demonic curiosity overwhelmed him and, according to his version of events, walked him without his consent to the prohibited area.

The fact is, Omollo tiptoed, or was tiptoed, to the house of his landlady, allegedly, against his own volition. As the woman's main door was not bolted, he only gently pushed it open: luckily, even the latch did not lament, announcing his presence in the area. In his pursuit of the source of the ululations, he crept through the sitting room to the woman's bedroom, in order to satisfy his itching eyes and ears.

To his amazement, Madam Katharina was naked and was on her knees for Gustav to perform some heinous crime on her. Upon this discovery, Omollo remained speechless for he could not fathom the fact that a serious woman of Madam Katharina's caliber could stoop so low. In his perplexity, he wanted to run away from the sight; even so, the union of his eyes and his 'thing' bogged him down from going anywhere: that is to say, they wanted to experience more of it than the rest of his body wished.

As he was there wondering, Madam Katharina would cuddle Gustav, from time to time, after which she would order the dog to do the 'thing' – notwithstanding Gustav would always fail the woman.

'Sweetheart, here, here,' Madam Katharina would say, yet Gustav would mostly miss the target and become very busy with pounding the atmosphere. Alternatively, Gustav's forelimbs would fail to balance on the back of the woman, or would occasionally slide, leaving Madam Katharina in as desperate a condition as a horny woman can be. Even when he had managed to plug the 'thing' in the 'thing', the dog would still be restless or would prematurely unplug the 'object', reducing Madam Katharina to entreating the dog like God. But if it did manage to connect its urinating organ into Katharina's own, it would still pound at a speed that was not at all meaningful to the yam.

In recalling the incident, Omollo would claim that his pestle was so sorry for the ill-treatment the beast was administering to his kin that it metamorphosed from its cartilaginous state to an iron bar state, complete with its usual thick mucus ooze – all in an attempt to bail the woman out of her agony. Now under the barrel of this fleshy pistol he carried with him, he claimed that he found himself against his will announcing his presence in that prohibited area.

"Madam Katharina," he called her name, "sorry! I wonder if I can help you with holding it to the focal point please."

As this loud but timid utterance broke loose from Omollo's mouth he was in his mind chilling with the fear of not knowing what Madam Katharina's reaction would be – the worst being a yell or a shot from the gun he had heard her husband left her at his departure. To his amazement, Madam Katharina, who was apparently under the strong influence of lust, looked in his direction and responded in her usual rude style.

"Hurry up, Peeping Tom," she ordered him sternly.

In compliance with the order, Omollo opened the door of the

bedroom, and for a while held Gustav in the position as he had earlier on promised. This, of course, pleased Madam Katharina somewhat, though the restless Gustav continued to mess her up even in front of Omollo – an injustice Omollo claimed he could no longer stand.

Disgusted with what he was seeing, Omollo now pushed Gustav aside and plugged his own bulging plug into Katharina's socket, actually without Madam Katharina's permission or knowledge. Wonderfully, Madam Katharina noticed the difference instantly and turned her face to meet the transfigured eyes of Omollo. As expected, the encounter scared Omollo so much he slowed down, as if wanting to stop, unplug his apparatus and run away with it. Madam Katharina, however, quickly read his mind and in timely fashion thwarted his move before he was at a standstill:

"Speed it up a bit, son of Gondwana; that is quite something!" She fired her first ever complement to Omollo.

After that it was back and forth, back and forth, twisting, twisting, back and forth, twisting, twisting, back and forth over and over again – all the while, Madam Katharina was making such loud wails of passion one would have thought a crazy nurse was sinking a rusted injection needle into her eyeball. As Omollo feared that well-wishers would soon respond to the woman's wails by storming into the room, he again tried to stop the exercise but Madam Katharina this time bit his fingers and thereafter behaved to him like a driving instructor.

"Keep left, speed up, drive on the left lane, go now to the right, drive zigzaggedly, remain there young man," she ordered amidst unhampered wails of passion.

The exercise continued in this fashion until the two were bodily and spiritually satisfied. Unfortunately, the hungry duo overdid it: as Omollo could afterwards only move in the fashion of a crawling baby or with the support of the walls; whereas, madam Katharina only crawled to and from the washroom but became too tired to climb even on her bed. Even on the third day, the duo were still quite exhausted from their exercise but content and happy with what they had done – going by the way they would steal a glance at each other from a distance and speak to themselves about the fantasy of the encounter.

"Madam Katharina is like a custard apple," Omollo uttered alone one day, as he stole a quick glance at Madam Katharina from his window and grinned to himself widely, "...catastrophically ugly from outside, yet is quite something when peeled."

Four days later, Omollo was amazed to hear Madam Katharina's knock at his door at around 10 a.m. – thanks be to God that he was no longer scared of the woman since their man-to-woman encounter in her bedroom. He thus quickly opened the door for her and was somewhat surprised that in her left hand she was carrying a presidential breakfast on a blue tray.

"Take this," she ordered Omollo in her usual commanding tone.

"For me?" Omollo wondered as he pointed at his chest in disbelief.

"Not for you, for him," she answered shortly and Omollo was perplexed.

"For who then?" Omollo asked genuinely.

"For the thing," she said while fumbling at Omollo's magic stick.

"Mmh, but why?" Omollo asked jokingly.

"For working in a hard environment," the woman answered kiddingly.

"Which hard environment are you talking about woman?" Omollo joked again.

"In a dark slippery tunnel without a torch," she returned the joke, causing Omollo to smile the widest of smiles.

"And with neither a helmet nor an insurance plan," Omollo added spicily.

After this bizarre incident, Omollo was upgraded from gardener to man of the house. This meant he was transferred from the boys' quarter to the main house; was bought nice clothes and could now eat good food. In terms of their original agreement though, this new relationship would remain known to themselves: but that was only before Madam Katharina destroyed the whole design with her loud ululations during their games of passion.

Before long, Omollo realized that the cat was already out of the bag after a small naughty boy had one day threw a familiar expression at him from a distance, "Du wirst mich vor meiner Zeit töten" – a Nanacan version of, 'You will kill me before my time' – exactly a refrain of Madam Katharina's wail of passion during their love-making sessions.

Three days later, Omollo received further confirmation that their new relationship was an open secret after a hateful neighbour had anonymously hurled annoying information at Madam Katharina at night:

"We are sick and tired of the noise pollution that you and your two pets are making in our neighbourhood."

Hot tempered as she was, such words hit Madam Katharina where it hurts. That night she hissed until dawn and swore to retaliate for such aggression as soon as the sun rose. Indeed, that same morning, she walked to a fine artist and ordered him to paint for her a signboard reading, *Please neighbours, invest in earplugs and pray for my bed. The stone crusher is at the quarry.*

As anticipated, the inscriptions on the signboard rubbed up the already animated neighbours the wrong way; not even her pastor cherished the idea of praying for her bed. The neighbours hence consulted among themselves and unanimously resolved that Madam Katharina must remove the signboard with its irritating message from her gate with immediate effect; also that her orangutan must go. Contrarily, Madam Katharina rejected the demands outright. But after long wrangles with the villagers, she eventually agreed to remove the signboard but swore by God never to send Omollo away from her compound.

"He will only leave my life over my dead body in a wooden coffin," she swore at the last peace talk between herself and the villagers over the issue. What followed in a short order was, of course, a series of dirty games from the neighbours to put asunder their holy union – thanks be to God that the bond between these two lovebirds blatantly defied all such efforts: on the contrary, their love blossomed in equal measure to the neighbours' hatred – something that stunned even the Devil himself.

All the same, Madam Katharina's hateful neighbours successfully assigned the duo sticky epithets that not even a crane could pluck from them. Madam Katharina's epithet became *Love at the First Sight*, while Omollo's was *the Crusher at the Quarry*. As a pair, they became popularly known as *Birds of a Feather*.

<<<CHAPTER TWENTY>>>

Klaus, Madam Katharina's only son, was a lieutenant in Nanaca's army. Malevolent neighbours now wanted to use him to dismiss Omollo, after they had failed in several bouts to scuttle his love relationship with Madam Katharina. In accordance with this mission, they would occasionally send him anonymous letters describing how his mother was keeping a strange creature at his father's compound as her significant other – completely against the advice of every well-wisher of their family. The bizarrest of all such letters was one entitled, "save our village" in which the anonymous author was warning Klaus that his mother could possibly give birth to a bouncing baby dinosaur – purportedly if by chance her offspring happened to blend her ugliness with that of Omollo. The letter further speculated that the newly born baby dinosaur would subsequently grow up to devour all beings in their village and its neighbourhood – just like in the movies. In conclusion, the writer strongly urged Klaus to prevent this foreseeable calamity hitting the people of his village – specifically by kicking Omollo out of their community before it was too late to save the situation:

'God will bless you abundantly for this humane act of life,'
one section of the letter read.

To make a long story short, such seditious letters, from the 'witches' of his village, hurt the son of Katharina to the extent that he would sometimes lose sleep over the issue. He considered described episodes in his father's compound an abomination and would regularly write to his mother, asking her to kick Omollo out – claiming that he could not stand the thought of her sharing the compound with Omollo even for a single minute. All the same, Madam Katharina constantly defied taking orders from her own product, which caused the tussle to continue. In Klaus' last letter to his mother, he vowed he would come in person to the compound to eliminate the nuisance for the sake of keeping his lineage sacred. As usual, Madam Katharina did not take him seriously and hence did not warn Omollo of the impending danger to his life.

On the fateful day, Klaus arrived at their compound when darkness was seizing the Earth and hid behind the servant's quarter – actually the house in which Omollo had previously lived. Omollo and his lover were then in the main house: happily eating potatoes and rice at the dining table in preparation for the adults' match that night. In due course though, they heard a squeak at the back door, but which they took for the retired Gustav playing with the door – only to realize shortly afterwards that the suspect dog was lying comfortably under their table right at their feet. In this knowledge, the duo moved to check the back door but found it locked, as usual. In the end, they did not discover anything significant and thus gave what they supposed to have heard the benefit of the doubt. Meanwhile, Klaus was hiding in the storeroom, just waiting for the right time to execute his evil mission.

Before long, Omollo parted with Madam Katharina to take a shower before going to bed. But no sooner had he opened the door of the toilet than he felt something very cold on the back of his neck; and it was the barrel of Klaus's pistol.

Klaus, who was actually afraid of the giant that Omollo was, did not even wait for an interrogation session between them; rather, he fired his pistol immediately and a bullet hit Omollo directly in the back of his neck, sending him to the ground like a sack full of stones. Content with his performance, Klaus opened the back door and disappeared into the darkness without Madam Katharina knowing he was the executor of the tragedy.

Simultaneously, Madam Katharina heard Omollo's wails of agony and hurried to the scene to find her sweetheart in a cesspool of blood, twitching like a chicken that has just been beheaded. In great desperation and pain, she thereafter howled at the top of her voice, which caused her malevolent neighbours to start pouring into the compound with lanterns and torches in their hands. Outwardly, they expressed their sympathies to Madam Katharina but inwardly they were grinning from ear to ear at what was happening to their antagonist.

Once everything had settled down in the compound, it was crystal clear that somebody had shot Omollo in the neck, necessitating the church elders hypocritically to rush him to a hospital that was about five kilometers from Zwecke Village – thanks be to God that Omollo did not die but rather developed a severe mental illness.

<<<CHAPTER TWENTY-ONE>>>

The bullet that logged in Omollo's neck disfigured a key nerve to his forebrain. The doctors who attended him claimed that recovery of his sanity was not possible and recommended he be confined in a lunatic asylum for the rest of his life. All the same, Madam Katharina rubbished their observation by unauthorizedly taking him from the hospital to her home. A week later, however, Madam Katharina finally came to terms with the fact that Omollo was not the same man she had known before the tragedy and now approved that he be taken to a lunatic asylum about a hundred and fifty kilometers away from Zwecke Village.

That day, Madam Katharina energetically waved Omollo goodbye as a slow moving car took him out of her life slowly and probably forever. Deep in her mind, she was overwhelmed by her thoughts and stricken with grief that another great man was leaving her life indeterminately and that she would have to resort to the underperforming Gustav, her dog, for a serious relationship. Omollo for his part could not wave her back simply because his mind was lost, which only added to Madam Katharina's pain.

Omollo thereafter remained in a zombie-like state for twenty good years at the lunatic asylum where he was confined. During all this time, he could not even remember his own name. Then one day, unexplainably, Omollo recovered his mind in a way that baffled even professional medical doctors. On the very day, he dreamt:

> 'that he was a striker for his village's soccer team in the World Cup'
> 'that one of his teammates crossed a ball that found him just before the opponent's goal'
> 'that he headed the ball into the net with all his strength and might.'

In acting out this dream, as was his habit, Omollo somersaulted on his bed so hard that he forced his head between the bars of his headboard. The resulting bump instantly blew the unfeasible dream away and Omollo now wanted to stand up but was bogged down by his trapped head. As an irrational man, he started struggling to stand up and move, blissfully unaware that his head was struck in the headboard. Fortuitously, in this course of his struggles, he massaged the back of his neck in some miraculous manner, which instantly corrected the disfigured nerve that all this time had been responsible for his mental disorder. Gradually nervous electricity started flowing into his brain and after so many years, he slowly started regaining his awareness of the world around him.

Once Omollo's memory had been restored, it was so dark in his room he could not even see his own stomach. In that total blackness, he tried to move his body but realized that his head was stuck between iron bars, which, however, he could not figure out to be the headboard.

"I am dead again," he thought in reference to earlier events in his life.

"This time for real I suppose," he continued thinking while struggling unsuccessfully to free his head from the pair of bars.

Nonetheless, after several bouts of fruitless struggle for most of the night, he calmed down and accepted that fate should take its own course. His last recollection was then of being in a pool of blood after a gunshot from an unknown shooter at Madam Katharina's place – little did he suspect that the incident he had in mind actually occurred twenty years ago.

"I am dead," he repeated aloud to himself. I now believe the assertions of the neighbours that Madam Katharina is a magnet of misfortunes and an embodiment of pain."

"But why would God try to kill me again by hanging if I am already dead by a bullet from an unknown shooter?" He questioned himself with reference to his stuck neck.

"How long will God keep me in this noose – and why?" He reflected and felt so sad for his life.

Now in quest to know where he was, his revolving ears picked up the sounds of some men and women snoring, singing or shouting in all his cardinal directions, which further confirmed him that he had made it to Hell.

As a result, a thousand things about suffering in Hell now rolled through his head, until the darkness started changing shifts with daylight. Around eight o'clock, he was astonished to see a man dressed like an astronaut opening a door of the little room he was in. The man looked at him and smiled widely – most likely after discovering his head was trapped between the headboard's iron bars. After that he left the room without saying a word and Omollo did not say anything either. Shortly afterwards, the same man re-appeared with a hacksaw and an injection gun in his hand, and fired an injection missile to Omollo who, because of fatigue, did not show any resistance. Omollo thus fell asleep for at least an hour. Upon waking up, he marveled that his head was completely free of the iron trap and quickly stood up to celebrate his freedom. As he peeped through the small window to see what was happening outside, what he saw instantly reverted his thoughts back to the destination Hell. Small raindrops were falling and in them two fat women, wearing only fishnet dresses, were shielding themselves from the elements using mere walking sticks.

"This place is definitely Hell," Omollo mused to himself, but quickly erased the thought.

"Or rather it is a prison," he thought again.

"But how come they have imprisoned the shot instead of the shooter?" He reasoned logically but failed to find a rational answer.

Now tired of fearing the unknown, Omollo played it calm and gave his eyes an opportunity to survey the room in which he was locked. His eyes duly reported back to his mind that everything in that room was so strange – strangest of all being inscriptions on the walls of his room and apparently on all clothes there too, reading, *Beware, the dude sometimes bites.* Struck by this input about a biting dude in his room, he quickly scanned around for the dude in question but saw nothing. So he relaxed and waited for his destiny.

At exactly 10:00 a.m., all the lunatics in the asylum had to go to the dining hall for breakfast. Some of them could walk on their own but others had to be dragged like goats resisting walking to Nyanagoku Goat Market.

As Omollo entered the hall, one potentially dangerous woman was standing half-naked on the table and reading the riot act to an inattentive crowd. With a hot bowl of soup in her hand, she now went as far as declaring that the gathering in that hall was illegal. Acting as a police chief, she ordered everyone to disperse within five minutes or else she would be forced to fire tear gas on them – supposedly, the bowl of hot soup she was holding. Following this announcement, the apparent workers in the hall tried hard to contain her but the woman continued to defy every technique they applied to appease her: until one ingenious worker appeared in a real Nanaca police uniform, posing as the chief police officer in that region, and ordered her to climb down – which, she amazingly did without any resistance.

A few meters from the woman, a dangerous looking man, holding a fork and a mallet in his hands was acting like a crazy dentist, judging by the way he was eager to pluck out every tooth he happened to spot. Workers of the facility asked everyone to conceal their teeth, an instruction that, unfortunately, only Omollo and one innocent looking young man tried to heed. Mad as he was, the would-be dentist would sprint towards whoever exposed their teeth from time to time, though the workers would always stand between him and the person in question, clearly to avert the looming tragedy. As if that was not enough, a young girl, who had supposedly gone mad by watching porn, would from time to time, sprint forward to sag the trousers of one of the inmates in the room – allegedly, to view what she called the "package" they were blessed with in their pants.

At a washbasin at the left corner of the hall, a blonde woman was busy washing foam off a bar of soap and growing ridiculously angrier with time, as despite all her efforts to clean it clean, the foam kept appearing on the soap. A few meters beside her, a man was riding a saucepan for a taxi, raving and hooting at people in front of his makeshift vehicle in the manner of a bus driver in a crowded street.

At one old table near the toilet of the hall, a strange-looking man was desperately trying to smoke a carrot and showed no signs of stopping, despite several bouts of failure to light it with a box of matches he had earlier on stolen from the kitchen. Simultaneously, one bizarre woman at the southern entrance of the hall was wearing underpants on her neck and a bra on her butt, trying to walk like a beauty contestant, though no eyes were on her except Omollo's and those of his like-minded colleague. At the left side of the hall, a man was painting the wall red with ketchup, while another man was parking sandals in a deep freezer. Through the glass window, Omollo could see, three old men on a basketball court, competing to see who could shoot the highest urine jet.

After breakfast, Omollo immediately went back to his assigned room. As he entered his bathroom, what he saw in a big mirror beside the door suggested an older double of himself was standing behind him. In a reflex response, or rather fear, he quickly turned around to see his ageing doppelgänger but was dazzled to discover that there was no one there. While trying to figure out this mystery, he went back to the mirror – and again saw the image of a wrinkled faced and gray-headed man whom he did not consider himself.

"Is this my image or am I imagining things?" He now thought to himself, "how come I have become this old overnight? Maybe, as transgender people hold, I am trapped in a wrong body."

Blissfully ignorant of his absentmindedness for the twenty-year period he had spent in the lunatic asylum, many hypotheses now crossed Omollo's mind as to how he might have assumed that strange-looking body; however, none seemed more logical to him that evening than the Kabumba-Namazizi Hypothesis.

His Uncle Ongoro, in explaining the genesis of homosexuality on the planet Earth, had once narrated him the story of a man called Kabumba and a woman called Namazizi, which Omollo now considered applicable in his own case. According to his late uncle, Kabumba had an accident that destroyed his brain but spared the rest of his body. On the very same day, Namazizi also had an accident that mutilated other parts of her body but spared her brain. According to his uncle, some medical students in internship secretly swapped the brain of Namazizi into Kabumba's head to see what would happen.

The story went that when the anesthesia had worn off, Namazizi found herself in the body of Kabumba, yet she could not explain how that had happened. Namazizi subsequently returned to her home in Kabumba's body, only to discover that she had just been buried at the compound. According to his late uncle's story, the woman later persuaded her kin that she was indeed Namazizi but all her persuasions fell on deaf ears. Eventually, Namazizi (in the body of Kabumba) took the matter before the court of the elders, whereat Namazizi's husband asked Namazizi (in the body of Kabumba) to justify her ridiculous claims that she was his dead wife:

"You have east bended manhood, deny it," Namazizi (in the body of Kabumba) put to her husband, who almost took to his feet, upon hearing the assertion.

"Longer left ball, right?" Namazizi (Kabumba's body) continued.

"Out-popping O-ring, dark spotted butt, bald pubic area," she rapped until the elders asked her to stop and walk away with her husband.

The story is, of course, very long, but that is basically the gist of it. Omollo was quite convinced that his case was of the same nature.

"Luckily, my brain was transferred to this old man's body in time," He concluded his digressed thought.

Two weeks since regaining his mind, Omollo realized he was in a lunatic asylum. Immediately, he started pleading with his keepers that he was a rational man, but all in vain: the more he pleaded he was sane, the madder he was considered to be – or rather, his claims that he was in another person's body even rated him very high on the scale of lunacy.

"Psychiatrists who tested me after this claim reported that my lunacy had risen from 65%, to 85% in those two weeks," he would later joke.

After some time, Omollo now learnt that declaring his normality could not bear fruit at that place, considering that whatever anyone said in that asylum was viewed in a prism of lunacy. He thus learnt that the lunatics' caretakers relied on vision, not hearing in determining the mental states of their clients. Consequently, he started demonstrating sanity instead of declaring it and, indeed, his new strategy worked wonders – going by the fact that he was recategorized from the group of foolish lunatics to bright lunatics after only three weeks. He now hoped that his doctor would one day declare him a sensible man and set him free – but all in vain: whenever they checked his lunacy, they would always report a range between 55 and 60%, which justified his further confinement.

In the third year of his awareness, Omollo now thought of escaping from the asylum in the same manner he had once escaped from the zoo imprisonment. All the same, the security in that asylum appeared so tight that he could not succeed without a proper plan. On several occasions, fellow inmates who had attempted to escape the camp were netted and brought back to the asylum under tighter security measures than before. Nonetheless, after two months of studying his environment, Omollo had some ideas about how to cross the three consecutive walls encircling his asylum without capture. Specifically, he had observed that there were three big dumpsters behind their wards that would be emptied by garbage trucks on a weekly basis. Here he saw a likelihood of getting out of the asylum in the form of garbage. Consonant with this thought, therefore, he set out to track precisely the day and the time the dumpsters were emptied.

Two months later, Omollo ascertained that the dumpsters would be emptied every Friday at exactly 10:15 a.m. Even so, the surveillance cameras and unblinking warders were still a mountain to climb before his plan could succeed.

The day Omollo escaped was an unpleasant winter morning to the extent that whoever was outdoors was in proper winter clothes, boots, caps and scarfs. No snow was, of course, falling, yet a thick mist was blurring both vision and concentration.

A wardress of Omollo's ward would, as usual, pass by around 09:10 a.m. to lead her charges to the dining hall for breakfast. On this particular day, Omollo clearly heard her from distance yelling at every lunatic to put on their winter gear and prepare for action. As Omollo was then living on the bright lunatics' ward, the wardress would rather peep in the door of the lunatic in question and simply yell at them to put on their gear; she would not physically help these lunatics to get dressed, as was the case on the stupid lunatics' ward.

Nonetheless, it was part of Omollo's plan to allure the wardress into his room and, of course, he had long since worked out how best to achieve his aim. As he heard her approaching his room, he scattered bank notes previously stolen from the manager's office all over his room and patiently laid in wait to see how she would react to the sight.

As anticipated, upon reaching his cell, the wardress was amazed at what she saw: bank notes all over the floor of a lunatic, who, in her assessment, did not even know what the notes were for – little did she know the plan Omollo was brewing for her. No sooner had she bent to gather the notes on the floor than Omollo swiftly gagged her mouth with a pillow to stop her screams from resounding throughout the camp. Next, he pulled an injector gun from her shoulders and quickly injected her several times. As expected, she immediately fell asleep, providing Omollo with the chance to execute his escape plan.

Omollo next collected all the bank notes he used as bait, undressed the wardress, pushed her naked body under his bed and quickly put on her uniform. Afterwards, he completed the job the warder had been doing with the rest of the cells so as to suspend immediate suspicion from other warders, who he knew were as alert as gazelles in a lion infested jungle – thanks be to the woman's clothes, which disguised him even to his fellow lunatics. As there were now only four minutes left before the arrival of the garbage truck, Omollo ran behind his cell and jumped into one of the huge dumpsters erected at the location.

On the sixth minute, the truck arrived. Its turnboy jumped out, pushed the giant wheeled dumpster with Omollo inside up to the truck, fixed it onto an automatic loader and pushed a switch button for the uploading. The loader subsequently lifted the dumpster threw its contents, including Omollo, into the truck compartment. During this process though, the turnboy noted some human-like garbage dashing in the flash of lightning from the dumpster to the truck compartment. The turnboy thus growled something but Omollo, who heard his growling, quickly dug himself into a pile of garbage in the truck so that when the turnboy peeped inside the compartment, he could not see anything unusual. To remove all doubts though, he consulted the driver and advised him that they search through the garbage for some strange garbage he thought he had seen. The driver, however, swiftly slammed his suggestion.

"This is ridiculous. Is your work to research the anatomy of garbage or to upload dumpsters onto the truck? I mean, you now aspire to know the make-up of each refuse in a dumpster and its scientific names! Oh, my God!" Commented the arrogant driver, leaving the turnboy dumbfounded.

Annoyed to the brim, the turnboy did not join the driver in his cab, but instead chose to cling to the back of the truck as they left for the next station in their collection of garbage. After a while, Omollo could no longer remain underneath the heap of garbage for he would soon have suffocated to death from its stench. Hence, he surfaced to the top of a heap like a ghost, and now his eyes met those of the turnboy, whose eyes had, of course, been on the pile all along.

"Eeehheeee! So, you are one of the pieces of waste we have collected today! I knew it – and I told Jest, but he ignored me as usual," he complained, while gazing at Omollo furiously and unblinkingly.

"Of course, Jest will have to answer for this," he lamented, "I alerted him and all he could do was to pour cold water on my alert."

Omollo did not offer a word of feedback to these repeated complaints.

"And youuu," he next said, while pointing at the face of Omollo with his pointing finger from above, "you have pretended to be garbage right? Thinking that you are as clever as the devil. I nonetheless hope you will not change your mind upon reaching the mouth of a garbage crusher." He glared at Omollo long enough to make his point clear but, again, Omollo did not respond even to this new threat. This led the man to question Omollo's hearing ability.

"Are the ears of this baboon really working properly?" The turnboy asked himself but did not utter his thought.

The truck continued moving through the wilderness as the rogue turnboy simultaneously kept on reviling Omollo with every nasty word he knew, whereas, Omollo remained speechless but vividly imagining how his bones would be ground bit by bit by the garbage crusher.

"I would rather remain in Egypt than die in this wilderness," he inwardly mused about his wandering life in allusion to a biblical verse in the story of Israelite exodus from Egypt.

But amidst these thoughts, the truck stopped, heightening Omollo's fear to the extent that he found himself asking his foe a question:

"Where are we now?" He asked the turnboy.

"Not, 'we'! I am not one of your kinds. Anyway, *you* are a few meters from the garbage crusher if you really want to know where we are," he replied in a voice full of revulsion and disgust.

This response made Omollo choose to jump out of the lorry before he was on a feeder of a garbage crusher – thanks be to God that the angry turnboy did not inform his driver that he had noticed a man in the lorry's back compartment – probably because he did not want to be bullied further, or rather he just wanted to get rid of Omollo once and for all and spare himself the nuances of police interrogation.

As the truck stopped, the turnboy alighted and went aside to stack more garbage dumpsters for the loader of the truck to dump. Unexpectedly, Omollo now climbed on the walls of the cubicle to the front, jumped on the roof of the driver's cab, then down to the lorry's bonnet and lastly onto the tarmac road. At this juncture, the driver, spotted him and, shouted loudly to the turnboy:

"Hey! Who is this?"

"Garbage," the turnboy, who visibly had a grudge against the driver, gave a disgusted answer.

"Chase him now!" The driver ordered.

"I do not chase trash off the truck; I load trash onto the truck," the turnboy said awkwardly as Omollo dissolved in the streets of Samburg at the speed of a gazelle that has just broken loose from the zoo.

Nonetheless, Omollo's triumph of escaping from the lunatic asylum was only short-lived. Soon the ugly reality that he was the only Homo sapiens floating on that chilly road that morning started mocking him. Worse still, he was not even sure how long he could remain on that road without food, warmth and water. All the same, he kept moving in the direction he was facing – bizarrely in the fashion of someone who is running late for a very important appointment. From time to time though, he would stop and stand still to admire the surrounding skyscrapers, probably in an attempt to discover the truth in the hearsay accounts his Uncle Ongoro would "peddle" when Omollo was still very young.

'Whenever, I go to Laurasia, I sleep in a hotel as high as a kite,' Omollo now recalled what his uncle would say about the skyscrapers and how everybody would laugh uncontrollably at how bold a liar they supposed he had become.

"Nobody believed that a man can live in a house in the atmosphere. We genuinely believed that Uncle had just perfected the art of lying," he thought further, "but here I am, son of Orwa, proving what my uncle asserted back then and we could not believe."

"I wish I had a camera to photograph this building and take the picture to my countrymen; then they would believe these things, I suppose," he reflected, while watching a magnificent skyscraper adjacent to where he was standing.

"And look at how clean this city is – and it would be even cleaner if smokers did not soil it with cigarette filters and broken bottles every three footsteps apart."

This last thought he uttered aloud – actually, as if he were talking with an imaginary friend. Then, seemingly in a sudden diversion of attention from skyscrapers, he wondered about the reason why most of the billboards in this city showed either a beautiful and prosperous white woman or a wretched black child.

"These pictures of destitute black children most likely come from villages other than Dongruok or Rabar, I bet," he said to himself.

"If these people enjoy hanging up pictures of rural Gondwanian children, why don't they go and photograph healthy children of Dongruok Village then?" He asked himself, yet did not find any answer.

After four hours of strolling, Omollo was now tired and badly in need of warmth, food and water. His mind thus advised him to seek refuge at a church, in the belief that church followers would pretend to love him in daylight as a brother in Christ, a piece of hypocrisy that would however enable him to get food and shelter, the things he seriously required to postpone his death. As a result, he started asking people he met to direct him to a nearby church in the town: the exercise that nonetheless proved harder than he had envisaged:

'I have no idea,' was the response of many people he asked.

"I am a retired information officer; go and ask information officers who are still at work," one old man told him and rendered him speechless – but just because he did not know that the man was indeed a retired information officer from Berlinda International Airport.

Others, rather than directing him to a church as he wished, would point him out to shops that sold maps. Then, all of a sudden, he noticed a black woman crossing a road and highly anticipated he would get his long sought solution from this person, his near kin. He hence ran towards her as a prodigal child runs towards a long-lost father – unfortunately, only to be disappointed that the black woman, like white women, just gave him a contemptuous look and sprinted ahead in the fashion of a startled rat.

Perplexed and stressed by now, Omollo turned to taxi drivers for directions to a church, but they also snubbed him as soon as they noticed that he was not talking business.

"That is not part of my job," one such taxi driver said.

Finally, *the Busy Malan* met a generous woman who could have given him the right directions: unluckily, she was funny in the head.

"Young man!" She addressed Omollo, while making a gesture indicating pity, "unless you are destined to metamorphose into a sheep, the true church is up there," she said, pointing to the sky, "here on Earth you will stroll a lot trying to locate one, and I bet you will find none," she added as she moved away, causing Omollo to grin, irrespective of his miseries.

Omollo later walked and eventually noticed a building with a big tower. Anticipating that it was a church, his heart pumped hard as he moved towards it in hurry. Contrary to his expectations, the church was dead silent: which means there were neither church members to help him with his troubles, nor benevolent angels to protect him from the vengeance of natural impulses. Upon this realization, Omollo threw himself heavily on the stairs leading to the church as an entire array of thoughts, unable to pursue their full cycle, flashed across his mind like a torrent. After a considerably long while though, he stood up and resumed moving in the direction he was facing. But after a few steps, his heart suggested him that he try knocking at people's doors to ask them for help. Having mused over the idea for a while, he saw it as quite a practical solution to his problem and instantly launched his knocking exercise at the black gate of one magnificent house by the road. Nobody inside answered him, but of course because they did not hear him: he did not know he had to press a doorbell at such big houses, rather than banging gates.

A disappointed Omollo then moved to the next house and was about to get the same results, had a well-bred kid not been passing: seeing him suffering in the cold. She considered him a naive guest of the house whose gate he was knocking at and thus advised him to press the doorbell. This he did but then heard a croaky voice on the other end of the line, asking him to say who he was and what he wanted.

"I am Omollo, son of Orwa," a Samburgan sentence curiously rolled off his tongue and confused the owner of the house even more.

"Where are you from, and who do you want?" The tenant now asked Omollo in a different tone altogether.

"I am from Gondwana and I am seeking some help," he poorly argued his case.

"Excuse me, please, I am not a philanthropist. Please go to a charity instead," the man replied shortly and with finality – indicating that Omollo had lost his bid again.

Thereafter, Omollo repeatedly rang at nearby gates, yet would all the time get rejections, which forced him to conclude he was in a street of bad-hearted people. With this in mind, he ingeniously decided to cross a dozen or so streets before resuming his ringing exercise at the gates of strangers. By chance, he found the gate of the third house in the new street wide open and walked into its compound easily,

assuming that the luck was now on his side. But alas, a landlord who
had been following him all the way from his second floor window
soon started screaming shrilly once he realized Omollo had digressed
towards his door.

"You spook, stop it!" He yelled.

Omollo heard him shouting but did not immediately realize that
he was the spook in question; rather he had supposed that the man was
trying to save him from an attack from a fierce dog in the compound.
Insulin thus poured into his body as he braced himself for self-defence
against canine. However, his revolving eyes spotted no such creature;
and the fact that the man still continued screaming now ticked his
consciousness to realize that he himself was the spook.

"Ok, if you are deaf, then wait for me to come and blow off your
head right away," the man concluded angrily and Omollo, who had so
far sensed the danger, fled the compound as quickly as his tired hind
limbs could allow.

"My father really knew how to curse a child," he thought, as a
light sweat that had defied even the winter weather rolled down his
armpits.

At this juncture, he fumbled in the left pocket of his stolen clothes
and reached the bank notes he had previously dangled at the wardress.
And as if impressed with what he had touched, he fumbled in the right
pocket and discovered that the wallet of the wardress was there with
more bank notes in it.

"I think I can buy something with this money," he said and kept
on moving speedily to nowhere.

Around 5:00 p.m., winter darkness was then engulfing the
earth and this accelerated Omollo's mind to work extra hard since he
was keen to postpone his death to a future date. During his daylong
wandering in the city, he remembered having seen some houses, which
looked like they were the abandoned ones: based on his experience
of living in similar houses before in Damasawa City: weeds and grass
often colonized roads leading to them, their compounds would all the
time be as bushy as the beards of he-goat and they knew neither light
nor smoke. Omollo regretted not occupying one of those properties
during the daytime.

"Maybe one of those houses without lights is abandoned," he
thought but corrected himself in a brace of shakes, "what if their owners
have not lighted them because they are still at work or on holiday?"

He kept on marching to nowhere, his feet now feeling as if they
were freezing. All of a sudden, he saw a chain of buildings that looked
like a factory. As he moved closer, he spotted a big poster announcing
that the premises were an energy plant. This information triggered the
knowledge of his form two physics that energy plants have to do with
heat; thus, he strongly anticipated the heat would be somewhere in

that facility and he had only to locate exactly where. After a careful observation, he saw a big furnace at the far end of the facility with a long wide chimney churning white smoke into the atmosphere. His heart hence leapt with joy at the prospect that the smoke he had seen was coming from fire. Without even thinking of the plausible dangers in the compound, he now jumped over its wire fence and jogged towards the furnace as if he were one of the workers at the facility.

As he had predicted, the roughly fifteen meters diameter around the furnace was as hot as the hinges of Hell; he even stopped moving closer to it, as beyond that point was hotter than human flesh and blood could stand. Instead, he made his way to a go-down near the furnace and hid behind a water tank by its side.

Having found such a hot place at the moment when he was on the verge of freezing to death, his heart rejoiced and he thanked his ancestors for giving him fire in the middle of nowhere.

Around 5:00 am the following morning, Omollo set off for fear that the guards of the facility might notice him and arrest him for trespassing; absurdly, two more people who looked to him like fellow homeless were also fast asleep in the same zone. This morning, he was heading straightaway for one of the abandoned buildings he had seen in the wake of the previous day. Fortunately, there were many such buildings in the town. As soon as he climbed over the gate of the energy plant, he started identifying target houses, although he did not walk to the first ones he saw: he wanted privacy, which meant looking for a more secluded location. At around 11.00 a.m., he noticed a deserted house he deemed suitable for his living – specifically, a mansion whose ownership was not immediately evident. As he imagined he might be infringing the privacy of some naughty ghosts, his heart was then pounding hard and fast.

"Who abandoned this house?" He wondered but retracted the question as soon as he had asked it, "am I a historian to start working out the past human experiences? All I want is somewhere to lay my head."

With an artificial confidence, he wagged through the thicket colonizing the compound of the once magnificent villa until he was touching its walls. There he surveyed the house and discovered that its doors were locked, so he would have to make his entrance through one of its broken windows.

"Maybe it is the habitat of a jumbo snake," his fears heightened, but being out of options, he eventually plunged inside the house.

To his amazement, the house, though looking magnificent from outside, was no better than the abandoned houses in Damasawa City: no water, no electricity, no furniture or sewage system. Fortunately, some of its doors and windows were still intact.

"I will occupy one of the rooms with an intact door and windows and I will have cut the cold by 50 percent," he contemplated.

After having secured a habitat, Omollo's next mountain to climb was how to appease his extreme hunger and thirst. His inner voice told him to jet off from his new home in search of food and water – and, as usual, he listened to it.

While moving away from "his house", he marked the route to ensure that he would definitely return to the same address, with or without food. After a while though, he noted a big river blocking his progress in that direction – and now with the prospect that he would drink from the river, thanked God for creating the river. After this blessing, he anticipated that his only remaining problem would be hunger and cold.

Consequently, Omollo descended into the river, cupped his hands to drink water, but wondered that the water could not go down his throat as he had predicted – simply the water demanded that the protocol of entering someone's stomach be strictly followed: food first, then water after some time. In this sad knowledge, Omollo heavily sighed and looked at the heavens, probably in the hope of catching manna tossed to him by the benevolent angels singing up there. Unfortunately, nothing of the sort happened.

Amidst this desperation though, Omollo noted that some fifty meters away from him, was a man feeding bread to ducks, while his son was having fun of running a dog for a reward of dry meat every round. Under the auspices of hunger, he now rushed towards these men to ask for the food they were in his view, "playing with", supposing that kinfolk would value him ahead of the animals they were feeding just for the joy of it. But quite the contrary: no sooner had Omollo neared the men than they started growling in the fashion of a wild cat that has sensed the encroachment of a dog. Omollo, of course, smelt danger in the men's reactions, yet he kept on begging for food simply because hunger does not require civility. All the same, the combined team of father and son eventually dispatched him empty-handed like an unsuccessful thief.

"Are these creatures really human?" He now reflected in protest at what had just happened to him.

"How can they value wildlife more than their kin?"

At the end of the day, Omollo reluctantly retreated in an unfavorable direction, finding himself back on the streets, complete with his cold, hunger and thirst. Worse still, he still had no idea where to find food in this hostile city.

After three hours of aimless roaming, he came across a kiosk that smelt of food from afar. Hungry as a wolf, he literally ran to it in the fashion a child runs towards a mother who is returning home from a long journey. As he knew the money he had on him would buy him food, he, without a word, fished out three bank notes and dangled them in front of the seller at the kiosk, while pointing at food in the pot. The trick worked quite perfectly – she quickly gave Omollo some food and a jug of water for a note, which, of course, was worth more than her food. Nevertheless, Omollo at least had his first decent meal since he had left Madam Katharina's place some twenty-seven years ago.

Then Omollo ate and drank water to his capacity and could breathe normally again. Nevertheless, as his senses returned, he remembered he needed a box of matches for making fire to warm his extremely cold house that night. Now full and happy, he asked the food vendor to show him where he could get a box of matches and she was more than happy to show Omollo a nearby supermarket.

Unfortunately, Omollo had never been to a supermarket before and thus had no idea how it operated. He hence reached the entrance of the supermarket and just stood there, expecting a shopkeeper to take his order, as was the case with the kiosk in his native village. Yet none of the numerous "shopkeepers" in the supermarket approached him, which he found puzzling. After a while, he noticed that other people would just pass by him, enter the shop and leave with purchases. He thus also decided to follow their example. Once inside the building, he selected some bananas and started chewing them as he calmly admired the many goods in the shop, at the same time searching for the box of matches he badly needed that evening. But all of a sudden, he saw two men in uniform charging towards him like agitated buffaloes. To his amazement, these men then accused him of stealing the bananas, which he denied vehemently as long as he was willing to pay for the bananas.

"Why should you guys arrest me while everybody else is picking whatever they like and going out with them unrestrained," Omollo defended himself, but was unfortunately greeted with peals of ridicule. Thereafter, the men invaded his pockets, fished out his wallet, took out more money than the cost of the bananas, opened their handcuffs, and ordered him to get lost.

Now with no hope of getting a box of matches, the cold was so bad he felt as if his ears were bleeding from inside. While thinking hard how to solve his critical problem, he luckily spotted a pair of women smoking cigarettes at a bus stop and quickly ran to them for asking help.

"Would you help me with a box of matches?" He hurled a request in his Malan tone.

In response, one of the women looked at him contemptuously and thereafter fired a jet of saliva that almost hit him in the face. Her racist colleague, however, fired at him the box of matches she was holding on her right hand - reportedly, because she had nothing to hand with which to beat him.

"Go away, nigga. We know no peace in Nanaca since you chimps started owning passports," she growled, "why are you roaming around every day like city buses? Don't you people have a home to go to?"

Conversely, Omollo did not care about her slurs at all or rather that his need for warmth dwarfed his need for dignity. At the speed of a missile, he picked up the box of matches hurled towards him and bolted in the direction of 'his house' without a word – as was expected of him anyway.

The fire he made, added to the food he had eaten, kept him warm and now he allowed his mind to wander as far back to his friends at the lunatic asylum.

"They were lunatics, yes, but wonderfully friendlier than those who are calling themselves sane white men, but who only see skin color in mankind. I wish someone would blind them all to bring to an end this obsession about the color of the primates," he uttered and then allowed sleep to steal his consciousness away.

The two years Omollo lived in Samburg City were very hard on him. In the first few days, he relied on the money he had stolen from the woman in the asylum but before long, he got through it, or rather was ripped off in various fashions. Subsequently, he lived by scavenging, though soon realized that the activity was not rewarding in a city whose residents were so stingy they would always fence off their dumpsters precisely to prevent individuals like Omollo from picking through them.

All the while, Omollo tried looking for different kinds of jobs but employers always turned him away on the grounds that he lacked papers to prove his nationality, profession or age. Some went as far as claiming it was against the law of Nanaca Republic to hire a retired person, which they thought Omollo was.

But one day, Omollo did meet a man who would employ men without documents. Unfortunately, that man was a conman. He gave Omollo, along with some other poor men, the job of moving blocks on a construction site. Omollo and his colleagues thus worked diligently for fourteen consecutive days in the hope of being paid on the fifteenth – little did they know that their corrupt boss had staged a rip-off plan on the very day payment was due.

At around 2:00 p.m. the construction site was teeming with individuals referred to as illegal immigrants. All of a sudden, their foreman pretended to have noticed four people in police uniforms encroaching on the site. Acting as if wishing well to his subordinates, he shouted a false alarm that every illegal worker flee away from anticipated immigration police – evidently to avoid arrest. As expected, the alarm threw the site into turbulence.

Omollo, who was on the other side of the building, of course, did not hear the foreman's fake warning himself; nonetheless, seeing everybody fleeing, he did the same, anticipating that maybe some dynamite was about to go off at the construction site or something of the kind. The grueling race subsequently took the group through thickets and alleys and only ended after twenty minutes had elapsed, or rather when not every runner could continue in their flight. On the following day, Omollo and his colleagues returned to the construction site, only to find a new administration there, which bizarrely told them that they were the new company: allegedly, hired after all the executives of the former company had been arrested for hiring illegal aliens.

Pissed off by developments, Omollo resorted to begging in the streets of Samburg City as a substitute for unfruitful job seeking exercise. And since he had all that it took to be a successful beggar in Samburg City – right skin-color, old age, and poor health – *the Busy Malan* would not go home with less than 20 euros for his efforts a day. This success nonetheless, irritated the local beggars, who teamed up with the local police to ensure that Omollo would not beg in the streets – frequent arrest for begging, allegedly, without a license.

Now tired of being persecuted by the police, Omollo resorted to helping blind men to maneuver their way around the city for a small payment at the end of the service. This was indeed a well-thought-out activity, considering that the blind men did not know he was a black man and thus treated him like a fellow human being, albeit one with a peculiar accent. Soon, however, wicked police officers noticed his new job and again started arresting him for every wrong reason they could find – on one occasion for running instead of walking in the street: the arresting officer claimed in court that he saw him running in the street in the manner of a black man rushing to an ATM after having stolen his white wife's credit card. Omollo, of course, told the court that he did not have any wife; but even then, he was locked up in a cell for four more days – allegedly, to give investigative unit a room to carry out a background check on him. On the fifth day, however, he was released unconditionally, thanks be to the big tattoo on his back that read "Property of Samburg Zoo". From what I heard, the state prosecutor dropped the case after realizing that the government would have to compensate Omollo for torture if his case reached the ears of those fame addicts otherwise known as human rights activists.

Omollo's next job in Samburg was collecting and returning plastic bottles to supermarkets for cash. Again, only a few people threw away their deposit bottles in the first place or rather they threw them in their padlocked dumpsters, which bottle pickers could not access. To further exacerbate his miserable plight, Omollo walked alone, ate alone, slept alone, and even danced alone on rare occasions that alcohol clouded his memory.

"The people of Samburg normally pretend to be busy, but I do not believe them anymore," he one day vented his anger at the lack of a friend despite all his efforts to make one, "if busy, how do they always find time to walk dogs and bask in any sun they happen to see? They pretend to be reading even at amusement parks. Mmhhh!" He twisted his mouth in protest.

"Everybody will tell you that they mostly read fake stories in novels. So why can't they befriend me and hear the real story of a man who has seen everything?"

Three months later, Omollo was, as usual, peeping through the mouths of dustbins at a petrol station in search of empty bottles. All of a sudden, somebody shouted 'chairman', which had actually been his nickname at the lunatic asylum. Moved by the utterance of the word in that unique tone, he now looked around and realized that the source was a young man standing by a posh car beside a petrol pump. Now each of the men thought they must have seen their opposite number somewhere but neither was sure where.

"Chairman, isn't that you, I am Günter Müller," the man cut short the mystification session between them.

Upon hearing this, Omollo dropped his sack of bottles or rather it fell off him, and galloped towards the man as a stray horse would to a human being. Upon contact, the two embraced each other tightly, laughed heartily and cried like lunatics.

Günter had been Omollo's fellow inmate at the lunatic asylum for a long time. They initially did not know each other, principally because Omollo was in his zombie-like state. But no sooner had Omollo regained his memory than he knew Günter Müller by name and deed. They subsequently remained friends at the asylum for the next seven years.

Despite being born into a very wealthy Nanacan family, Günter's life had been joyless. His mother died of labor-related complications when he was only three weeks old. Twelve years later, his materialistic father was killed by a rain of falling debris as he tried to catch his newly finished three-story building that was then falling under the bullying force of an earthquake.

After his father's death, Günter was forced to remain in the custody of his bad-hearted aunt called Gisela. Three year later Aunt Gisela conspiratorially had him locked up in a lunatic asylum to deprive him of his father's massive wealth, which is how he came to meet Omollo. Being the only sensible men in the asylum, Muller and Omollo became best friends, and most importantly, vowed to help each other in the future, even at that time when the future to them was a big joke.

"So, you have also escaped maaan!" Omollo wondered aloud after their sensational moment had elapsed.

"Not at all. My wicked aunt died of a heroin overdose," Günter answered and shed a tear at the memories of his nightmare.

"What good news! I now have proof that God does not whip with a stick," Omollo commented cheerfully.

"Right! So, in her absence, there was nobody to bribe the psychiatrists to keep lying that I am 90% crazy," Günter said and laughed long this time.

"So, how many percent of craziness did you retain after your aunt's death?" Omollo asked jokingly.

"Hahahahahahaah! Well, the last doctor found that I was just 48% crazy, only ten percent lower than the Nanaca chancellor," he said and the two burst into more long joyful laughter together.

Günter was living in Berlinda, the capital of Nanaca. After the death of his wicked aunt, he had no other relatives with whom to share either his father's wealth or his house. Five months before meeting Omollo, he had broken his leg and greatly needed someone to help him with getting into and out of a taxi whenever he had to attend a clinic. In the end, he was forced to hire a home moving company for this job. Seeing Omollo thus delighted his heart that finally he would get a trustworthy person to share his sorrowful life with. For this reason, he unreservedly asked Omollo to go and live with him in Berlinda.

To Omollo, this was the best news he had heard since storming into Laurasia some thirty-seven years ago. He thus asked Günter to give him a few minutes to return the bottles he had collected to the supermarket, which Günter did very gladly. About seventeen minutes later, Omollo jumped into Günter's posh car for a trip to Berlinda City for deceptively a new chapter in his life.

Omollo and Günter's next project was suing the Government of Nanaca for locking them up in the wrong facilities for wrong reasons: Omollo would sue the government for locking him up in the zoo and lunatic asylum undeservedly for a total of thirty years; Günter, for his part, would sue the same government for confining him equally undeservedly in the same institution for fifteen years. From the evidence they had, they foresaw their plans leading to a juicy settlement at the end of their cases.

"We will become the wealthiest guys in Berlinda and subsequently travel the whole world with big cameras hanging on our chests – just like the Amandoran tourists in Sasana Beach," Günter joked one day and the two laughed joyously at their image on tour.

Indeed, preparation for suing the Government of Nanaca was so far on course. Günter was solicitously helping Omollo with collecting documents about his miseries in the country. These items included a book that eventually convinced Omollo just how long he had been confined in the lunatic asylum.

"I have now believed that I was truly locked away for twenty years," he said to himself, as he stretched to feel the scar on his back he got from falling from a mango tree in his youth. It was as fresh as if it had healed only yesterday, which assured him after a long time of speculation that he really was in his own body.

"Yes, I was locked away for twenty good years in the asylum; this is definitely my own body," he concluded.

And from the clues in the book he was holding, Omollo determined he was then around seventy years old, a realization that now made him think he would soon die without a child to perpetuate his lineage.

"My father was a professional curser," he now uttered to himself at the scary thought to a Malan of "sinking without trace."

"Fifty years of roaming about like a stray dog without a single result to show. I should now marry quickly and sire children before dying," he contemplated.

Overwhelmed by the premonition of dying without a child, Omollo faced his best friend that evening and divulged to him his last wish in his supposedly a short remaining life. Günter, as usual, took Omollo's wish seriously. Instantly, he proposed that Omollo search for his better half on the internet – arguing that a search on the ground was not suitable for a man of his age, that the internet would easily help find a similarly stranded partner to himself.

To facilitate the online search, Günter next lent Omollo his laptop and trained him for three hours on how to go about the exercise. On the second day, Omollo was still so fascinated by the whole concept that he found himself thinking about it aloud.

"Finding women starving for men on a stall and choosing them like a cloth in a second hand shop?" He uttered when he was making his bed.

"Laurasia has real wonders," he said to himself when he was mopping the kitchen.

"SRM means single and ready to mingle," Omollo reminded himself of the online partner-searching acronym while in the bathroom.

"MBA means married but available. CD means a chain divorcee. Mmh, my memory is still good," he flattered himself as water showered sparsely on his back.

"TP means a temporarily divorced woman, SSC is a single and self-contained woman, isn't it?" He asked, as if he was unaware that he was alone in the bathroom.

"Yes, a woman with everything in the house, including children, of course; and I think this sort even suits me best. Haahahhaha!" He now laughed to himself.

"OW means occasional widow," he stated, "these sorts are potentially dangerous. If their husbands rarely live long, what about me at my age? They can kill me in a week's time I suppose. Hahahahaah!"

"SR means serious relationship. What does this one mean," he asked himself, "did Günter said it means no smiling or joking after marriage? I will ask him to remind me what 'serious' means in this context. Hahahaha, it is the only acronym that I do not remember," he said.

"POD means partner on demand. Haaahahaha – my head is still fresh at seventy," Omollo boasted and grinned widely in the bathroom.

On the seventh day after launching his internet partner search, however, Omollo's enthusiasm stated ebbing away. Three days before, he had settled on an image of a woman he wanted to meet physically and declare his unquestionable love to – only to discover that she was 1000 kilometers away. That dampened his heart but Günter kept him going with more advice.

"In internet relationships, you should be moving your goal posts from time to time, man," Günter said amidst shaky laughter.

On the sixth day, he liked another beautiful and looking responsive woman, but soon learnt her interest on the internet was to make love with men over the phone – unfortunately, something Omollo found not only stupid but also disgusting.

"How can I sire a child with a woman on the phone then?" He mused and even smiled in spite of his desperation.

"That is how it works, brother. You should try harder and harder, have as many as possible," Günter advised him when Omollo reported his latest disappointment.

"This is funny, brother. So how many fiancées do you have on the internet yourself?" Omollo asked, intending perhaps to emulate Günter's online dating experience.

"Seventy-two so far," Günter replied and laughed long.

"Then how come that none of these sisters-in-law showed up to look after you when you broke your leg," Omollo asked jokingly and Günter could not restrain his laughter.

The search continued and at some point Omollo was close to catching "a big fish", had something accidental not transpired. Omollo had been chatting with a certain woman for a while and the two had reached the stage of exchanging iconic smileys, which, unfortunately, Omollo was very poor at. On the fateful day of their love, Omollo's would-be fiancée had sent him an iconic smiley denoting, *I'll love you until I freeze.* Quite moved by that good-looking gift, Omollo reciprocated the gesture by also sending her a good-looking iconic smiley from the gallery of his chat window – little did he know that his return smiley actually denoted, *You are the most evil woman ever born on the planet Earth.*

Waiting for the reaction to the receipt of his gift, Omollo rather received racial slurs that would haunt him for the rest of his life –

blissfully unaware that he was paying the price for bartering honey with poison. After this episode though, Omollo forsook searching for a partner online, or rather accepted his everlasting bachelorhood.

"By the way, bachelorhood is a proven way of preventing heart disease," he comforted himself.

Now it happened that Günter was very busy the following week – even to the extent that he could neither tweet nor upload his photos on a book of faces. Fortunately, he was done with whatever business it was at the end of that week though, and hence chose to celebrate the completion of his tasks by inviting Omollo for drinks and small talk on his magnificent balcony.

That evening, showers were trickling one by one to the ground, creating a perfect atmosphere for strong liquor they were sipping on Günter's heated balcony. All of a sudden, Omollo saw lightning, followed in short order by a powerful thunder, the like of which he only remembered having heard in his youth. It then scared him so much he closed his eyes to let it pass by in peace. However, when he opened his eyes to resume his talk and drink, he discovered that Günter had fallen off the balcony and was now lying below in the rain and the part of the house where he was now sitting was on fire.

As if completely sober, he dashed across the balcony to turn off the main switch in the sitting room. Next, he reached for the landline and informed the fire brigade of what was transpiring at their home. Thereafter, he galloped down the stairs to attend to Günter; unfortunately, by the time Omollo reached him, he was already dead.

Involuntarily, Omollo picked Günter up, laid him around the back of his neck and started off with him in the direction of the gate at the speed of a falcon to a pray. But as soon as he crossed the gate with Günter on his shoulder, the fire brigade and the police arrived at the scene in their usual noise-making cars. The police then leapt out of the cars with guns pointing at Omollo's chest and yelled at him at the top of their voices to raise his hands. Reluctantly, Omollo laid Günter on the ground, and thereafter obeyed the official order so as to calm down this pack of trigger-happy men and women who were eager to shoot him dead.

Subsequently, some police officers put Günter's dead body into an ambulance and disappeared with it to an unknown location, while the remaining ones threw Omollo into a different vehicle and drove him to a police station – where he would stay for three months under accusation that he was the one who had murdered Günter and thereafter blamed lightning for his death.

As Omollo would later narrate, that was his worst experience in Nanaca.

"I was physically tortured and treated as a terrorist," he explained, "and I received much more vicious racial slurs from the investigators than those common citizens would hurl at me in the streets."

He would later offer a mind-blowing account concerning a big scar from a cut on his forehead.

"An interrogator asked if my people still lived in trees when I set out from my country to Nanaca Republic, to which I ironically replied: 'They had moved to anthills, sir. The only person who still clung to living in trees was the ambassador of your country to my country, sir,'" he would start saying with laughter but quickly resume a gloomy face, "he then took offense at the answer and retaliated by subjecting me to a series of electric shocks for what he referred to as trimming down my lunacy."

After the expiry of his remand period, Omollo wandered the streets of Belinda like a stray dog in his struggle to exist. All the same, police officers continued to harass him, while the homeless of Berlinda, whenever they spotted him, would shout at him like a serpent that has just creeped into a Christian congregation.

To exacerbate the problem, the homeless ganged up on Omollo (for allegedly taking away their job of picking up empty bottles in the streets) just on his sixth day of his freedom from the cell. Fortunately, however, Omollo sensed their malice in advance and thus tried to call the police to thwart his foes' plan. Unluckily though, Omollo had not yet mastered the mobile phone, despite having owned it by then for nine months: in the past, he had often wrongly dialed the police and subsequently denied having done so.

"Maybe my phone called you by itself," he would reply to an angry police officer inquiring after the reason for his call.

Unbelievably, on this critical occasion, Omollo dialed another wrong number when he really did want the police. As a result, instead of a man of the law, he contacted a renowned jokester of the city.

Thrilled at such a rare opportunity to have fun, the jokester merrily impersonated a police officer, without Omollo's knowledge of who was on the other end of the line.

"Some people are planning to follow me," Omollo announced.

"Are they real people or animated?" The jokester responded.

"Ahaha! What is wrong with you, officer? Can people call police officers for ghosts? These are real men and women!" Omollo roared.

"Okeee, will they follow you on Twita or on a roadway?" The jokester asked back.

"On the road now! Are you really a police officer?" Omollo began to have some doubts.

"Okee! Okee! Are they armed?" The joker asked.

"Yes, of course," Omollo answered.

"With biological or chemical weapons?"

"I do not know what you mean, but I can see that they are carrying sticks with them," Omollo replied.

"Okeeee, USB or walking sticks?" The joker asked.

"Walking sticks now, are you mad?" Omollo thundered.

"Where are you?"

"Near Central Magaran Church. Hurry up!" Omollo insisted.

"Could you tell me the exact GPS of your location to avoid confusion, please?"

"I do not know what you are talking about, I have told you about the danger I am facing; I am actually not interested in any other irrelevant stories at this point, do you hear me?" Omollo screamed.

"Don't you have a mobile phone with you?" The jokester asked.

"So, you think I am calling you from a key holder, Eee?" Omollo asked him angrily.

"Is your phone not a smart phone?"

"I am sick and tired of your questions, if you can't help me out, then leave me alone and I will know how to redeem myself!" Omollo roared.

"By the way, does your insurance cover you for any injuries?" The jokester asked and Omollo could no longer stand him.

As he ended the call, the madding crowd was now only a few meters away from him with every lynching gadget in their hands. Sensing obvious danger now, he ran and stood on the streetcar tracks for a face-off. Strategically, there was a sea of stones at the point, which he turned into missiles against that disorganized group. Given his background as a bird hunter, and his old games of taking aim with stones at Rabar Hill, he would pick a stone and pelt it at a man, then pick another and pelt it at a woman. On his fifth turn of picking and throwing stones, he now realized that all his adversaries had melted away like butter on a frying pan. Consequently, he sighed deeply for that meant he would live more to tell the tale of the day.

All the same, Omollo continued to struggle to exist on the streets of Berlinda for about three years without a clue as to when his miseries would end. He would sleep in a sleeping sack in parks during summer and in public places and ATM booths during winter.

Then, in a change of fate, it happened that the Minister of Natural Resources and Industries of Kaya acquired a mansion on the richest street of Berlinda City. The minister would visit this home abroad at least quarterly. During her stays, she would often invite her friends and business partners for festivities that came to be known as *bunga bunga* or celebrations for refrigerating hot heads.

On this particular visit, she had come to celebrate her thirty-sixth birthday, allegedly, "away from uncultured Kayan journalists who find it natural to poke their noses in everybody's affairs." For this visit, she brought along a team of a hundred people in a government plane, which her father's friend, Mr. President, had lent her for a week to use as she wished. Most of this team consisted of beautifiers, entertainers, friends, and bodyguards.

All the same, racist neighbours of this woman hated her with both their feet and hands – allegedly, for her ostentatious signaling of economic might through her regular throwing of parties and parading posh cars. More than once, those hateful neighbours had tried to eject her from their neighbourhood but had always failed totally: the woman owned her house legally and had earned respect in government circles, due to the fact that her chain of hotels employed more than three thousand citizens of Nanaca Republic. Further, the woman had so far earned three national awards of Nanaca Republic and was expecting to get a fourth one at the end of that year. Apart from that, she had the personal mobile number of the head of state, whereas, her jealous neighbours could only call the local police.

The story went that most of her hateful neighbours had already swallowed their pride, yet a few original 'witches' in the neighbourhood were still persisting with their terrorist attacks and during that particular holiday they planned a big terrorist attack nicknamed the 'mammoth humiliation of a female baboon"– little did Omollo know that he was a planned gadget for use in this attack.

The day it happened, Omollo had planned to spend the night at an underground train station and wake up at dawn to collect bottles dropped in the area before the arrival of his rival Berlinda bottle collectors. All of a sudden, a beautiful-looking woman came to the station and sat on one of the benches there, as if waiting for a train. Next, she fished out food and drink from a brown paper bag she had with her and started consuming them. Omollo spied on her from a respectable distance to see if she would throw any leftovers into the dustbin for him to pick out and finish off – actually, in the same manner that vultures lie in wait for lions to abandon their meals at the animal park.

Sooner than expected, Omollo saw the woman moving away, leaving behind her bottle of wine and a complete hamburger on the bench she was seating on. He now rushed to the remnants just like a vomiter does to a washbasin – actually, without inkling that the food and the drink were meant to trap him for a conspiracy plan that the jealous neighbours of the minister had staged for their protagonist.

The drugged hamburger and wine of course made Omollo sleep like a log, or rather transformed him into a perfect gadget for humiliating the female baboon. Once Omollo was unconscious, the conspirators of the mission parked him in the huge box of a refrigerator they had brought with them. Then, they supported him with package pads to position him straight in the box, irrespective of the fact that he was fast asleep because of the drugs. Next, the gang placed a saucepan of stinky sewage on his head – well covered by a polythene paper to stop the stench oozing from it before the set time.

At around 10:00 p.m. friends, relatives, and business partners were giving the minister from Kaya birthday gifts. Considering that she was travelling by jumbo government plane, she, of course, accepted even sacks of apples, rabbit meat, or portable toilets.

At around 11:00 p.m., four unfamiliar youths arrived at the ceremony hall with what ostensibly looked like an expensive brand of refrigerator, claiming it was a birthday gift from their father to the minister. They then placed their present near the high table where the minister and other dignitaries were seated – and I wish you could have seen how the minister was then grinning like a lunatic at the market square at the sight of the tallest and the biggest gift she had so far received on that particular day.

"My father does not feel well enough to attend your birthday party tonight; even so, he has sent us to bring you a small token of goodwill on your birthday," one of the young men murmured in her left ear.

"Tell your father that I am very grateful to him," she replied in a fake Nanacan accent.

"Tell him that from what he has done to me today, I will reciprocate by waiving all taxes for his businesses in my country," she added, though without actually ascertaining who the gift sender was. Of course, she had many evil deals with the 'white demons' of Nanaca, and one such devil could have tried to seduce her through such gifts into selling them a part of her rich country.

After the youths had exited the stage in style, both international and local guests were now seated in a hall holding five hundred people, all of them closely following the series of events at the birthday of the honorable minister. Most of the time, the professional emcee hired to immortalize the event played classic music but, occasionally, a guest would stand up and exaggeratedly wish the honorable minister a long life in serving her young nation – their version of "a long life to serve their egos."

Yet amidst all this entertainment, people at the high table had the impression that the refrigerator in the box beside them was like scratching. This obviously frightened them, and they would have fled like a man chased by a lion, save for the emcee of the event who assured them that in today's world of technology, some refrigerators could actually sing, flute or dance.

As the drug dried up in Omollo's veins, he felt as if a Burmese python had just swallowed him but he was still alive in its stomach. To save his life before it was too late therefore, he started struggling to eat his way out of the imagined serpent's stomach: struggles which as a consequence disentangled the box in which he was packed, whereupon Omollo fell with it horizontally and raucously. In the series of events that ensued, the fall changed the box's position so that a saucepan of sewage, which had been skillfully planted on Omollo's head, spewed out its contents at the minister and colleagues, exactly as had been masterminded. The pungent stench now threw the hall into tumult – worse still, Omollo started banging the refrigerator like a man locked up in a train toilet.

Soon security officers, police force and fire brigade arrived at the scene, yet they could not see what to fight – only an accompanying journalist got a highly sought after image of a minister and her friends covered in sewage.

Two hours later, the standard bureau and the special police force of Nanaca Republic had established beyond reasonable doubt that the refrigerator was not a biological weapon, as it was previously suggested by eye witnesses, but rather a cage for a man known as Omollo Orwa, an ill-fated human being the enemies of the minister had decided to use as a tool to humiliate her.

After a thorough interrogation, the government of Nanaca established beyond reasonable doubt that Omollo had not committed the offense of defacing the image of Nanaca – as originally claimed by the press. However, for the sake of preventing a repeat of his being misused by terrorists for a similar mission, the Government of Nanaca Republic asked him to declare his nationality for deportation. Fortunately, Omollo, this time around, fully cooperated, considering that he himself was now fed up with his shameful life in Nanaca Republic. Readily than expected, he announced to the authorities that he was a Kayan and ready to go back home the soonest possible. Coincidently, he was of the same nationality as the now furious Minister of Natural Resources and Industries of Kaya.

<<<*CHAPTER TWENTY-TWO*>>>

In the third month of that year, Omollo boarded a jet for the first and, of course, last time in his life. The episode rang a bell concerning his first car-ride to Arwing a long time ago. He wondered at how a pipe dream of people of his class had turned to be true in his life: there he was in a Dreamliner, rubbing shoulders with dignitaries. What's more, the finest feather he was wearing aligned with his naturally huge body so well one would have thought he was the CEO of a multinational company. Deep in his mind though, Omollo was very much worried, especially that he would vomit in the plane – as had, of course, happened to him during his first car ride to Arwing City.

Luckily, sitting beside him was a young man who, by chance, was also a national of his country. Unlike Omollo, whose meals had depended on how much Laurasians threw away, this flight neighbour looked like one of the few black men who slept and ate well in Laurasia: his skin was sparkling like that of a cobra and not only were his fingers fat, but also his earlobes. As Omollo would later narrate: "If he had a problem, then it was something as well hidden as a wife's nagging."

Omollo gathered that the young man was also travelling back to Kaya for what he described as a business trip. Like many Kayans, the man talked as if he had just swallowed a brand new radio and was therefore both informative and off-putting in equal measure.

His good side was that he saved Omollo from swallowing a hot towel: *the Busy Malan* had internalized that airhostesses distributed food and thus mistook a hand towel they gave him to sterilize his hands for a special kind of food only served on board an airplane.

This young man told Omollo he was living in Berlinda and would only travel back home once every five years, allegedly, on business missions. By chance, he was on such a business trip on the very day Omollo encountered him. Omollo later learnt that he dealt in what translates into Linglish as 'financing bulldozing of voters.' Specifically, he would go to Kaya during national elections to lend money to contestants of different seats. Successful parliamentary candidates would later pay him back four times the amount within two years after their election. This, of course, shocked Omollo.

"And what happens if a borrower loses an election?" Omollo asked, and the man giggled for a long time at such a degree of naivety.

"They actually do not lose elections," he ultimately said through his laughter, "anyway; they give their houses, land or cars as pledges. So, I eventually confiscate these in situations where a borrower dies or stupidly loses an election. After all, most of them are from the party, with seventy years' experience in propaganda and rigging elections. Without exaggerating, two days before an election, I will know the number of oppositional supporters who have been paid not to vote; the number of electoral supervisors who have been tamed; the number of police officers who have been tasked to intimidate voters; the number of electoral commissioners who have been compromised, and the number of fake polling stations that have been established to add fake votes." He said and at this stage surrendered to his persistent laughter.

"I will also know the amount of terror poured over coward citizens concerning what would happen to them if they vote unwanted candidates," he continued and laughed like a lunatic, while Omollo remained open-mouthed at what he was hearing.

"I will also know the number of revered figures in the society, often pastors and imams, who have been paid to lie to their congregations that my client is the choice of God, and his opponent the choice of the Devil," the man went on and laughed as if he would never stop, "I will also know the organizations paid to publish fake opinion polls."

"But didn't my late friend tell me of some modern technology? I remember something like the BVR system – that makes it completely impossible to rig an election. Aren't those gadgets used in Kaya elections?" Omollo asked honestly.

"Hahahahahaha!" Laughed the young man, "they are used in the elections, of course. The problem, however, is that powermongers assign one company to supply the technology as a ploy to the public, but simultaneously hire another company to frustrate the technology for their advantage."

He laughed even longer and was still laughing when he continued: "If business gets tough, the whole opposition is bought to fix an election."

Then he switched to what he considered a serious piece of advice: "So, my elder, engage in this business too, it is paying handsomely." Evidently, he assumed Omollo was one of those rich pastoralists in Kaya Republic who kept their money in pots and buried them in the ground.

"Currently doctors, university lecturers, bankers and so forth, have all forsaken their professions to become a counselor or a member of the rubber-stamp parliament. It is really a paying industry," he added and laughed hysterically.

"I will think about the proposal," Omollo lied, while thinking contrarily: "How can an educated man talk about his own country in this sickening manner?"

He now went as far as remembering his estranged father's view of the white men's education on the black men:

"My father was quite right that a white man's education can never make a black man productive to his own people," he further recollected.

"Beside me here is a learned black man whose thoughts and desires are to sabotage his motherland," he mused, "how can what this man is saying be happening in a country I once left trying hard to build democracy and transparency? Is this man really speaking about the same country as mine? Aren't we speaking about different countries altogether? Anyway, I am on my way home and I will find out by myself what my country has become."

Omollo now closed his eyes and fell into a deep slumber. He did not even realize the plane had landed at Damasawa International Airport. Luckily, as everybody else was leaving the plane, the disgusting young man beside him woke him up.

"Countryman," he called Omollo, "wake up now and disembark. We have landed in the Bewitched Republic of Kaya."

"Hey no! Where! But I was going to Kaya Republic, which country is this? Why have we landed this early?" The disoriented Omollo asked a chain of questions, actually out of confusion and ignorance.

"You are such a joker, my countryman," the young man commented, "so does that mean you do not know the nickname of your country?" He asked.

"Which country are you talking about, young man? Kaya Republic?" Omollo asked the man scoldingly.

"Yes, Kaya Republic. You mean you do not know its nickname of the Bewitched Republic?" The young man was astonished.

"Anyway, thank you," Omollo answered him summarily and pulled his suitcase from a luggage compartment, before starting to follow the disembarking passengers.

"Why doesn't this airport look like the Damasawa Airport I had been to several times in the past?" He thought, but quickly corrected his thought, "forty years is, of course, long enough for me to forget how this place looked. But no, why don't I see even the fifteen meters high statue of the founder of the nation that used to be at the entrance of the airport?

"Maybe they built another airport in Damasawa," he continued reasoning alone, then instantly reviewed his latest theory, "can this place really be Damasawa Airport? How come the number of white men exceeds the number of black men here then? Have colonialists reoccupied this country?"

Omollo continued musing over these issues as he queued to check out. Amidst his thoughts though, he caught sight of a portrait of the first president of Kaya Republic on one of the walls of the airport building and now believed he had landed at the right airport.

"How male are you?" One of the immigration officer at the counter cut short his thoughts with a silly question he could not answer.

"Why are you looking like a terrorist?" He further asked after reading annoyance on Omollo's face.

"Are you breathing?' He changed the question. This time Omollo reluctantly answered him and was allowed to move on to the queue before the next desk.

"What is the government doing about this scorching heat? What is the distance from one air conditioner to another in your national parks?" Omollo overheard a white tourist in front of him asking an immigration officer silly questions and anger almost tore off his chest.

"How come this officer is taking silly questions from a white man, whereas, his colleague is asking silly questions of a black man?" He thought and wrinkled his face.

As soon as Omollo passed through into a reception area, insulin spilled into his blood at the sight of uncountable black men hugging arriving white men like girlfriends.

"They do not know how these guys treat us in their countries," he now uttered aloud and felt like jumping on the roof of a nearby kiosk and ordering every black hugger of a white person to spare him an embarrassment.

"Anyway, I still have so many mountains of my own to climb," he appeased his anger and silently walked out of the hall.

Unluckily for Omollo, all the passengers he had been trailing jumped into cars like monkeys to a tree and left him staring blindly at the car park in front of the airport. With no clear idea of where to go to next, he stood still for a moment to think and shortly afterwards silently followed a path that many local pedestrians seemed to be following out of the airport.

Ten minutes later, he reached the verge of the airport perimeter wall and again did not know where to continue. While considering his next move, he sat on a small stone under a huge tree beside the road and his mind wandered to what he had seen so far.

"Why do most of women I have seen look whiter; have extra baggage behind and more bulging tits in front? Did the women really look like this when I left this country?" He thought, "have they undergone Darwin's evolution or are my eyes playing tricks on me?"

"Why are they competing in dressing scantily? What has happened in this country?" He further pondered, but his mind quickly shifted to locating Mwanayama, where he had left one of his famous homeboys before leaving for Laurasia.

"Ochola might be dead now but his grandsons are likely alive," he thought, "I will introduce myself to them and thereafter beg to spend a few days with them before I set off for Rabar Village."

Now in scanning his environment, he noticed a bus stop with crowds of people just on the other side of the highway bounding the airport. Whenever a bus stopped there, the mass would invade it and start struggling to board it - rather like mongooses trying to get into a burrow to escape the wrath of an angry hunter whose maize they have stolen.

"If I still remembered the way to Mwanayama, I would not try to board any of these buses; I would better go on foot. This is crazy," Omollo thought.

After gazing for some while at the commotion at that bus stop, Omollo crossed the highway and a big trench containing filthy black sewage showered him with its disgusting stench as a welcome to the real Bewitched Republic. Even as he wrinkled his nose against the appalling odour, rogue youths were urinating in it from time to time or throwing all sorts of rubbish into it, actually, as if their aim was to reinforce the smell. Meanwhile, the crowd around the place talked so loudly one would have thought they were competing to talk, or rather that whoever was the loudest in their culture was also the rightest. Whenever a bus drew up, the crowd would run to it en masse, pushing and shoving each other out of its narrow door like crazy. Absurdly, the bus conductors would make the doors of their vehicles even narrower by standing in the center of the entrance for no apparent reason. In this context, tougher guys would enter either two sides of the conductors, while the toughest of all would jump through their windows or hang on the rear bumpers for a free ride.

As these scrambles to board the buses continued, a pickpocket would stamp on a passenger's foot or hit them with an elbow, head or teeth to divert their attention for a fellow gang member to rob the same confused passenger from the other side. Accordingly, a woman or a man would break out into an idiosyncratic wail after their wallets or mobile phones had been pickpocketed. Thereafter, the crowd at the bus stop would abandon their wait for the bus to get some news for their itching ears from the horse's mouth. Impersonating police or journalists, they would flock around the weeping person with questions that no one knew why the victims were answering.

"What was in your purse? How was it taken away from you? What were you going to do with the money?" They would ask – and would mostly round off their questioning session with 'pole' or sorry in Linglish.

"God will give you a better phone than that one," they would tell someone whose mobile phone had disappeared. Sometimes, touched by the story of the victim, they would donate them the fare to enable them to finish their unlucky journey. Interestingly, nobody called the police for such incidents.

Apart from the stealing, some youths at the bus stand acted as promoters of the buses. They would shout out the destinations and intermediate stops of the buses in voices resembling frogs. As the buses started pulling away, they would now run alongside them and the bus conductors would push a coin or two into their palms; otherwise the boys would throw terrible insults at them.

Omollo watched all this activity at the bus stop in disbelief. He clenched his suitcase tightly – supposing that one of the hooligans roaming the place might snatch it from him and run away with it. Deep down, he badly wanted to ask someone how to escape from that place quickly, yet he imagined that everyone there must be a mobster.

After pausing in perplexity for a considerably long time, Omollo discovered that every bus stopping there had a board in the windscreen displaying its destinations; however, none of the boards was showing Mwanayama. The realization catapulted his urge to ask someone a question, so he approached a middle-aged woman who, in his assessment, looked like an original Kayan woman, judging by her unmodified hair, skirt beyond the knees, and abstinence from the habit of intermittently tossing her head like a white woman who is clearing long hair from her face.

"Could you show me a bus heading to Mwanayama?" Omollo asked the woman, who in turn scanned him suspiciously from head to heels before responding with a question.

"Which place did you ask me about?"

"Mwanayama," Omollo now repeated the name of the place distinctively, yet the woman appeared never to have heard of the place and turned to her colleague, sitting on a stone about seven meters away, for help.

"Angeli!" She shouted, then continued in a sonorous voice, "I wonder if, by chance, you know of a place called Mwanayama in this city?"

"MMh! Did you say Mwanayama?" Angeli also wanted to confirm what she had heard but then continued even before anyone had answered her question: "There is no such place in Damasawa." She said and this forced Omollo, to move closer to her and clarify the place he had in mind.

"Where Damasawa Regional Hospital and Damasawa Tobacco Factory are located," he elaborated.

"Okeeey!" Angeli now recalled the place.

"He is talking about the buried street," she updated her colleague and this knowledge caused both women to survey Omollo afresh.

"If I may know, when was your last time to be in this city, old man?" Angeli now asked him, "for it is like you are talking about the buried street," she clarified after noticing that Omollo was speechless.

"Sorry! Did you say 'the buried street'? What do you mean by the buried street?" Omollo snapped back.

Before she could reply though, there arrived a bus to the destination where the two women wanted to go and, as usual, commotion recommenced at the stop with the two good women in the middle of the act.

Out of ideas, Omollo remained staring at them with many more questions pouring into his mind but no answers. Later through observation, he learnt that all the buses were heading to the Central Bus Station of Damasawa City, where he assumed he could get a connection to Mwanayama Street.

At around three o'clock, therefore, Omollo painfully squeezed his way onto one of the buses. As he stood with his heavy suitcase on just the second step of the bus (due to the congestion aboard), a nauseating odor, likely of a rotten fish, intruded his senses so much that he tried turn back and alight; however, being so tightly sandwiched, he could not even turn his neck. Feeling like a trapped rat, he swiveled his eyes and saw how all the passenger were soaked in sweat. It was also as if they were competing to make as much noise as possible. One passenger, for instance, apparently the loudest one, was on the phone, instructing her new housemaid on how to cook *mnafu* vegetable with little oil. The second loudest one was also on the phone lying to his wife that he was in another town and could not make it to Damasawa City on that very day. As if that was not enough, the bus driver was playing squeaky music on his car radio, while his conductor was peeping outside and shouting to everyone beside the road to come aboard. Soon afterwards, the conductor asked the driver to turn down the volume of the radio, after which he began to announce the conditions of travel.

'If you are a standing passenger, lower your hands from the upper hand rails at your own risk," he announced.

"If somebody laments that they have been pickpocketed, we will ruthlessly deal with the standing passenger whose hands are out of my sight!" He stressed and puzzled the likes of Omollo, who were new to that mode of transport.

"More importantly, do not try to masturbate in this bus, not even if someone rubs you the wrong way!" He added and now a light laughter spread through the bus – save for Omollo, who was at a complete loss over what the man was talking about.

As this transpired, the bumpy bus could hardly move in the congested streets of Damasawa City. At one stage, it stood still in a traffic jam for twenty minutes, forcing the driver to digress from the main highway into dirty potholed alleys, at the cost of the packed passengers knocking their heads against one another like fighting rams. But amidst all these catastrophes, Omollo was distracted from his suffering by the sight of a man carrying a young woman on his lap like a baby. Immediately, he supposed they were newly-weds on their way from a honeymoon, yet what he then overheard them saying refuted his initial supposition.

"Are you an office secretary?" He overheard the man ask.

"How did you guess my work so precisely?" The woman responded in amazement.

"I can feel the texture of your palms; they are not the palms of a land tiller," The man replied gently, simultaneously squeezing her soft palms and eyeing her with apparent lust.

"And you are a mechanic, right?" The woman now took her turn to baffle the man.

"Amazing!" Exclaimed the man, "how did you yourself guess my occupation so exactly?" He asked in vivid bewilderment, while the woman took her time giggling before spilling the beans.

"Well, I can feel how you are professionally jerking my base," she said and the funniness of her statement now forced Omollo to focus his attention elsewhere in order to conceal his laughter and avoid the embarrassment of the two finding out he had all the while been eaves-dropping on their private conversation.

Meanwhile, cars hooted uncoordinatedly, their drivers stretching their necks outside their vehicles to throw one or two items of lethal abuse at fellow drivers of whose behavior they occasionally disapproved. So timely were the venomous remarks, and delivered with such great ease, one would have thought abusing others was a compulsory course at their driving schools.

Even worse, vehicles were stuck in a jam for about forty-five minutes at one road junction, to make way for a presidential motorcade. This was not good news to Omollo, who had a thirty-kilogram suitcase on his shoulders. After an exhausting wait, the pilot cars eventually flashed along the traffic-free road, followed shortly afterwards by the motorcade of the President, who was nicknamed Vasiko da Ghama on account of his bushy beards, style of hat and frequency of travelling overseas. Simultaneously, a thick dust now enveloped the whole area; people responded to its toxicity with coughs, sneezes and eye closing. Seven minutes later though, the dust started subsiding and all mobile objects in the area could now resume their movements.

"The man who has just passed by was exceptional from birth," one old man now started narrating to a younger man with whom he was sharing a double seat, in reference to the President who had just flashed past like lightening.

"Is it because he is President?" Asked his colleague, somewhat contemptuously.

"Not really; it is because he was born with a watermelon for a head, yet he grew up to became the best president in the history of Kaya Republic," asserted the man.

"Be serious, papa," the other man said scornfully.

"Ask everyone here," the old man said confidently (and looked around for support that did not come).

"He had a watermelon for a head at birth," he continued after seeing that everybody else was unresponsive, "his parents consulted so many magicians to transform his melon into a proper head."

"Don't tell me you are telling the truth?" The listener now wanted to confirm.

"Of course," the old man responded confidently, "they consulted uncountable magicians to change the boy's exceptional head into a human-like head – all in vain. And at one point they accepted the reality about the form of their son's head."

"So, you mean that your president's head is melon?" The listener asked the narrator in amazement.

"No, no, no. The history of the boy, changed completely when he turned eight. It happened that he was then travelling with his parents from this town to their village of origin by bus," he said and picked his nose before continuing, "as usual, the bus was so full of passengers that everyone was sweaty, thirsty, and hungry – just like now."

"Ehehhe," the young man encouraged the older one to keep speaking.

"At that juncture, a three-year old girl who was on her mother's lap a few meters from the boy genuinely confused the boy's head with a watermelon," he said and now stared at his old watch before resuming his intriguing story, "to quench her extreme thirst, the young girl asked her parents to buy her a piece of the melon she claimed the vendor was carrying on his head."

"Ehehhehehe."

"Even so, her ashamed parents turned a deaf ear to her request; as they did not know how to tell her that she was asking for someone's head. Reading neglect in her parents' unresponsiveness to her request, the girl burst out into a loud cry that attracted the attention of all Samaritans in the bus."

"Ehehhe."

"One of the Samaritans then passed her parents a knife to use for cutting her a piece of the said melon just to quiet the crying girl, even pledging to pay for the piece."

"Ehehhe"

"Realizing the ignorance of the girl and the Samaritans, the melon-headed boy's parents now intervened with clarification and temporarily put the matter to rest," he said, "nonetheless, this episode not only embarrassed the boy's parents but also warned them that their sons head could be eaten in the near future, if they did not do something about it."

"Ehehehe."

"So they resumed their search for a magician who could change the boy's head into a human-like head. In this mission, they travelled from one magician to another and from one country to another. Notwithstanding, most of those they consulted did nothing other than ripping them off," he said and now paused to swallow the saliva gathering in his mouth.

"But because a will always find a way, they eventually met a man who could fix their son's head," he continued.

"Ehehehe."

"That day, they pulled up to ask one man for the way to a magician they had been referred to by someone – little did they know that they were talking with a real magician about the problem that had been troubling them all the while."

"Ehehehe," the listener called for more of the story.

"It was said they opened up to the old man who eventually smiled and told them that their problem was over, though they did not believe him – considering that they had been travelling for almost two years non-stop and many of the self-aggrandizing doctors they met had simply ripped them off. And judging by how he looked, this old man appeared far from possessing such powers as he claimed. So they ignored him and were about to start off again," he said and sighed with tiredness, "but out of intuition, the melon-headed boy himself asked his parents: 'If you have given everybody else a chance to experiment on me, why should you deny this papa a chance?' He asked."

"Ehehehehe."

"It was said that, after the boy's suggestion, his parents then recalled the man and gave him an opportunity to show his magic – of course, pledging to pay him anything he wanted if he should succeed. The man then pulled out his belt and harshly whipped the boy's head with it and uttered: 'From melon to head!'"

"Ehehehe."

"Then he told the man and his wife to take their child and go on their way with him without talking to anyone.

Amazingly, upon reaching home, the boy's head became what it is today."

"Ehehehe."

"The bewildered parents instantly rushed back to where they had met the magician, yet the magician was nowhere to be seen. They thereafter asked numerous people, yet they failed to establish his identity," he said, and was interrupted by his listener.

"So, you mean they do not know him unto this day?"

"Wait I complete the story," the old man said, "the man re-appeared after ten years, but unfortunately they messed him up instead of rewarding him."

"MMh, how could they afford to maltreat such a noble man and why?" The visibly annoyed listener asked the narrator.

"MMh, human beings have evil hearts," he said.

"The boy's father had then become Principal Secretary of the Ministry of Land and Settlement. As a boss, he instructed his personal secretary to bar people who did not matter from entering his office."

"Eehehehe," the listener gestured for more.

"So when the magician wanted to meet her boss, she malevolently tossed him from one department to another until the old man became totally pissed off. And do you know what he did next?" Asked the narrator.

"Not really," the listener replied.

"He repeatedly slapped the woman hard on her face until she was now hugging him tightly to prevent more slaps."

"Ahahahahhhhah!" Laughed the narrator.

"The commotion, of course, brought her boss out of his office just to find an old man knocking some sense into his secretary. This surprised him and after inquiry, he now learnt the man was fighting like this just in order to meet him. Probably afraid himself of beatings from the man, he now asked him to channel his problem through the same woman he had just been beating. Unexpectedly, the old man had no any problem with following this instruction.

'Tell your boss that I have come to claim my ten million shillings for treating his son ten years ago,' the old man ordered the now disciplined secretary, who immediately ran like the wind to deliver the message.

"Ehhehheheeh," the listener encouraged the narrator to

tell more.

"But mamamamama! The boss's stomach protested as soon as he received the bill from the man whom he now well remembered: 'For which service should I pay him all this money?' He grumbled: 'Should whipping and chanting some unintelligible words cost so much? Even international hospitals do not charge this amount of money.' He lamented and thereafter ordered his secretary: 'Go back and tell that man to write me a detailed breakdown of his bill so I know what cost what.'"

"Eeeeyyyyyyiii," the listener wondered, then further encouraged the narrator: "Eeeeee.".

"Yaaa," the old man continued, "the magician had no problem with giving the breakdown of his claim either. He wrote it down thus:

1: *Knowing where to whip* = 5,000,000/=
2: *Whipping* = 5,000,000/=
3: *Chanting magic words* = *discounted.*"

"Hahahahahahaha!" The listener, Omollo and many more people laughed and encouraged the speaker to continue telling the story.

"Yesss, when this breakdown was taken to the boss, he again exploded into unjustifiable anger and went as far as abusing the magician for greed. Eventually, he only gave the secretary 5, 000,000/= to take to the magician – in other words, just half the amount the magician claimed."

"So, what followed next?" The key listener wanted to know.

"Mmhhh, the magician accepted the money happily but emitted a warning alert to the boss via his secretary: 'Tell your boss to count me out in turning his son's head from just a head shape into a real head,' he said with finality and left for an unknown destination."

"Hahahahahah! Are you saying that this was the same boy who is now your president?" The listener wanted to confirm.

"Of course, yes, the same once melon-headed boy," the narrator affirmed and laughed at length.

"How did he become the President then?" The listener asked.

"That boy, as I told you, was exceptional from birth. He used to sing and dance so well even in kindergarten and he grew up to become a chief entertainer of the ruling party, which in turn, rewarded his good work by making him their candidate for president in the national election," the narrator said.

"But why was he not defeated in the election by contestants with real heads?" The listener asked again.

"Hahahahahahahahah, hahahah," The narrator laughed vibratingly.

"Don't forget that he is a member of the ruling party, which has perfected the art of winning elections in their seventy years of monopolizing power. How could he then be defeated?" The narrator responded in astonishment.

"By the way, do you know their slogan?" He asked the young man, and then laughed loudly again.

"How could I know? Do you forget that I am not a citizen of this country?" The listener responded.

"Their slogan is, 'The way to the voters' hearts is through their stomachs. Famish them, show them food and utter your wish,'" he said and shook with laughter.

"Anyway, as I told you, the man was miraculous from birth – and thus, nobody can describe him well," he said, paused a bit and then continued: "His leadership says it all. Soon after ascending to power, he sold the old city to a foreign company after it was discovered that the city was sprawling over an oil reserve." He now coughed intermittently, cleared his throat and continued with his monologue:

"The people started, OOooo, aaaaaaa, and some started demonstrating in the streets in protest at his decision, but mmmmmmm! His army gave them 'the beating of the male thief.' Hahahahahahah!" Here he succumbed to a shorter bout of laughter before resuming his story:

"And those who clung to the city were, of course, buried alive by bulldozers leveling the city for an oil field."

"Does that mean he doesn't fear a revolution from his citizens for such unpopular decisions?" The listener wondered.

"Hahahahahaha! Who can dream about toppling a man whose statue alone has four bodyguards with AK 47s?" The narrator said and again laughed hilariously.

"One army commander, of course, once tried to topple him, but his execution broke the record of Jesus Christ's execution." The old man paused, removed a kerchief from his dirty trouser pocket and used it to absorb a stream of sweat rolling down his cheek, "he was killed by skinning, buried naked and then a public latrine was built on his tomb. Hahahahaha! Even as we are speaking now, people are urinating and excreting on the remains of that man." He further narrated that despite the naive blame that people cast at their president, he had achieved development in every part of the country.

"Look now," he said and paused for dramatic effect, "we have been sitting in this traffic jam for over a half an hour simply because of the economy booming under the leadership of a man whom many people hate as much as the death that killed their mothers. Everybody has a car, some even have helicopters," he added and laughed hysterically.

"But why don't you tell him the reason he is called Mr. Ten Percent," a woman, who appeared to have become frustrated by the old man's narrative cut in.

"Hahahahaahahaha, hahahahahahah, haha!" The old man laughed loud and long, "that of course is a slur by the opposition, which is too jealous of our man," he said amidst ambushing waves of laughter.

"It is not a slur, it is the truth," said the woman confidently, "he is called Mr. Ten Percent because that is his price for each corrupt activity in which he engages."

"Don't tell me!" The usual listener wondered in his local dialect.

"No, no, no, that is a blatant lie," said the old man.

"Not a lie," objected the woman in a serious tone.

"If you have enough money," the woman proposed to the listener, "write to that man today that you want to buy a state house and he will agree to sell it to you provided that ten percent of the price goes into his bank account."

"You are singing the same tune with the opposition parties; you are likely a member," blasted the old man.

"It is ideas like this old man's that make us immobile in this sea of poverty," said the woman, "imagine: his daughter died and he was ..." she began, but the listener interrupted her.

"Whose daughter?" He asked.

"The president's daughter ooooO!" Said the woman in her local dialect.

"Eheheheheh," encouraged the listener.

"He was sleep-talking – and do you know what his wife heard him saying?" She asked.

"No," replied the listener.

"'When will you pay me that ten percent of the funeral cost if I allow you to bury her in my homestead','" said the woman and many people in the bus who overheard the woman now laughed heartily.

"Nzzzhhhhhhhh!" Hissed the old man disdainfully, "you are talking about his ex-wife, in whose head there is a big caterpillar walking, aren't you?" He asked in a fury.

"No caterpillar is even creeping in her head: she is entirely human in her nature, which is why she divorced your monster," said the woman harshly.

"But did her divorce bar the strong man from marrying miss beauty the following year?" Asked the old man contemptuously, "her divorcing him was obviously a blessing in disguise, of course."

Briefly, Omollo had become so absorbed in the animated political bickering in that bus that he even forgot about his sufferings aboard that crazy bus. He now related the stories of the passengers to those he heard earlier on and concluded that something was very wrong in Kaya. Nonetheless, the bus safely reached the terminus and a swarm of passengers engulfed it, forcing Omollo and the other passengers to launch a new struggle to squeeze their way off the bus.

Thus at 5:15 p.m., Omollo found himself at the Central Bus Station of Damasawa City. Not knowing where to go next, he remained stranded with his suitcase on the pavement. At this moment, he was no longer thinking about his search for Mwanayama Street, but rather how to remain alive in that strange city – because the information he had gathered so far indicated that Mwanayama Street had long since been turned into an oil field.

As he stood gazing at everything on that pavement, old cars roared aggressively on the potholed roads in the surrounding area, everybody around was speaking at the top of their voices and loud music boomed out from two separate music shops in the area. As if that was not enough, banging and clanging, most likely of local smiths hammering at something, emanated from the back of the buildings encircling the station. Occasionally, boys stacked with poisons against rats, bugs, cockroaches and fleas all over their bodies would flash across the street with a digital horn speaker that boringly reproduced the same blaring advertisement of the products over and over again.

On the eastern side of the station, a crowd was discussing something at the top of their voices, while a woman was weeping in a pitch that defied all the odds of noise in that area. In Omollo's experience of bewailment, only a white woman who has lost her virginity in a rape incident would make a sound like that one he was hearing. He thus considered rape a possibility for the commotion, yet something in his line of thinking was not adding up:

"Who might have raped the wailing woman amidst this sea of people," he wondered but could not work out his doubt. Now, as if overpowered by the intensity of his curiosity, he found himself asking two girls standing beside him if, by chance, they knew why the woman was moaning so sadly.

"I am not sure, but she sounds to me like a woman whose smart phone has been snatched away by a thief," the first girl suggested, actually in a serious tone.

"No, she sounds to me like a primary school teacher whose salary has been pickpocketed," the second girl offered an alternative hypothesis, which made Omollo break out into a short delirious laughter.

"Perhaps, my suitcase is the next target for snatching," he shortly mused in reference to the concept *snatch* that featured in the suppositions of the girls about the origin of the woman's wail. In response to his inner voice therefore, he clung tightly to his suitcase. But still feeling quite unsafe where he was, he quickly scanned the area and identified a humble bar about a hundred meters away from where he was standing as a potential safe haven.

As he crossed the threshold of the bar, he spotted an empty chair at one corner of the bar and proceeded to occupy it. A few minutes later, a peculiar woman came directly to his table, warmly welcomed him in her bar and recited him a long menu he could not follow.

"Give me a bottle of cold beer," he cut her short to avoid complications; after all, his primary inner motive was simply to pass the time and think.

As the woman walked away from his table though, his eyes were more baffled that the face of the woman resembled a Miss Universe, whereas, both her left buttock and breast were larger than their right counterparts.

At this point, a middle-aged man drinking beer adjacent to him tracked his eye movement and grasped the opportunity to strike up a conversation.

"Songimani, if you covet this Kayan woman, tell me to make things work for you. Eat the real fish, man, not its picture," said the man brightly.

Omollo, of course, noted that the man had assigned him a wrong nationality, but ignored it for the want of just talking with someone.

"Not really liking her, I just wonder how unfair God can sometimes be," he murmured in reply.

"What do you mean?" Asked the man who appeared to have been thrust in the clouds by the many bottles of beer he had consumed.

"How could he have put the look of an angel on the face of this woman but a look of a monster on her butt and breasts?" Omollo commented in a low voice.

Upon hearing this, the man, who was having a sip of beer at the time, nearly choked before bursting out into loud long laughter that caused everyone at the bar to turn their necks towards him and Omollo. After a long struggle with his hysterical laughter, he eventually told Omollo something that Omollo could not easily take onboard.

"Songimani, you seem to know very little about the Bewitched Republic of Kaya, I see," he said amidst suppressed laughter:

"Nobody knows how it started, but somewhere along the line, it was decided that a beautiful Kayan woman must be white, possess chemically straightened hair, and have enough package at the back," he said cheerfully and laughed bouncily.

"That is when the Zhangians saw an opportunity to make and sell Kayan women drugs for ballooning their butt," he added, but this time in a sad voice:

"Now what you are seeing is a case where a Zhangian butt drug has botched, my brother. This country is under the bully of an animal called liberalization."

"Is that a new species?" A confused Omollo asked for clarification and the man, who was already well tanked, laughed inconsiderately loudly.

"Songimani, liberalization means keeping mum even when they are throwing shit into your food," he said laughingly.

"It appears that my forty years in Laurasia have witnessed a revolution that my small head cannot comprehend," Omollo unconsciously divulged his place of departure amidst crackly laughter.

"So, you have been in Laurasia for forty years, man," the man picked him up on what he had just said.

"Somewhat," answered Omollo obscurely.

"Then I must warn you to watch your BP, man. You have not even started seeing the wonders of this country yet," said he told Omollo and resumed laughing:

"This is actually the only place in the world where stories' collapsibility is not an earthquake or bombshell, rather the fatigue of standing on one foot for so long," he added and laughed sheepishly and long again.

Omollo thus spent a long time with the man, and almost forgot that he had nowhere to sleep. All of a sudden though, the bar owner apologized to them that she had to close her business for security reasons.

That announcement now threw Omollo into panic, but he quickly remembered a Kilayi proverb that translates into Linglish as, *He who conceals his genitals does not beget a child.* In other words, he found himself obliged to divulge his homelessness to this mysterious friend – thanks be to the alcohol that made this task very easy for him.

And contrary to his anticipation, that his request would take long time to process, the man gladly said "yes", and more strangely, without even a 'baby' condition. Immediately, the two took a bus, which was fortunately then not as congested as during the daytime.

Omollo's host was Dr. Makunja – a man who had been crowned twice by the President of Kaya Republic for genius, but upon whom now even a street sweeper of Damasawa City looked down without any feeling of guilt. The story was told that Dr. Makunja and the President had studied together from kindergarten to university. He and the president-to-be would sit at the same desk during tests and examinations in the spirit of 'you scratch my back and I'll scratch yours.' It was said that Dr. Makunja was endowed with the gift of knowing all the answers for test questions, whereas, his friend was endowed with the gift of importing test answers from all his neighbours – of course, for a handsome payment after receipt of the goods. Allegedly, Dr. Makunja, for the sake of good neighbourly relations, would always open his borders by means of a generous body posture for his neighbour to import per his capacity.

Mr. President did not forget his friend when he made it to the promised land: evidence being that he appointed him his Minister of Internal Affairs – and would even have appointed him Prime Minister, had he not privatized his mind to alcohol. Even as a minister, people who knew him said that alcohol-induced misbehaviors were as natural to Dr. Makunja as walking. Even so, Mr. President would always come to his defence in whatsoever (The President consistently argued that he was so patient as he could not distinguish between when the words emanating from his friend's mouth were initiated by the man himself, and when they were the result of beer).

One day nonetheless, he got on the nerves of his friend, and was sacked from his ministerial position once and for all. According to the story, he, on the very day, attended a cabinet meeting under the strong influence of demon drink, which, as usual, inspired him to say things unexpected of someone in his position. It was said that the then prime minister of the United Republic of Kaya had directed all ministers, including Dr. Makunja, to outsource some money from the institutions under their portfolios for reinforcing the perimeter wall of the leaders' mausoleum. After issuing the directive though, the 'democratic' prime minister invited cabinet ministers to ask questions or offer comments regarding the implementation of his directive. According to the story, Dr. Makunja then raised both his hands and asked:

"Has any corpse of a leader escaped from the mausoleum before?" He asked, causing the meeting room to go dead silent: his colleagues thinking that something must have got into his head. But after waiting for an answer for far too long, he realized he was not understood and hence expounded his question.

"And if not, why should we outsource the money to reinforce the perimeter wall of a graveyard? Or do you guys mean that this is another avenue to squander taxpayers' money? Why can't we reinforce the walls of maximum security prisons with such money – if at all we are possessed with spirits of reinforcing walls?" He hissed, "even corrupting the nation needs some intellect, my brothers!" He concluded his contribution and now reinforced his colleagues' speechlessness.

The story added that the challenge was reported to the president, who would as usual forgive him. Nonetheless, Dr. Makunja made a bad situation worse by confiding his intriguing question at the cabinet meeting to international journalists – who, as usual, scooped the news up as a falcon would a chick, spiced it up considerably and started sharing it with the rest of the world. This latest transgression now infuriated Mr. President and forced him to fire Dr. Makunja from both his cabinet and advisory team for good.

From what I heard, Dr. Makunja subsequently protested his demotion by running for Parliament on the ticket of the opposition party. An intriguing story had it that many people turned up to his campaign launch, which made him grin widely in his heart, actually in the belief that he was their definitive choice – little did he know that many of the attendees of that meeting were merely paid goons.

When he first went on stage to addressing the audience, the crowd would relentlessly cheer, while also intermittently pointing at him. In Dr. Makunja's thinking, they were thrilled at the Aristotelian and Lutheran ideas he was emitting on the stage like mad that day – but alas, everybody came to learn that he had forgotten to zip up his trousers and the crowds were so jubilant over nothing other than his rolling balls as he moved from one angle of the stage to another.

That, however, was not the reason that stopped him from attending political rallies afterwards. The story added that a crowd engulfed him at the end of the meeting and carried him above their heads – as if to show that they were very moved by his redemption speeches. Dr. Makunja too foolishly let himself be carried by his assumed enthusiasts – little suspecting that the group had been paid by his opponent to teach him a lesson he would never forget. As soon as this crowd lifted him up and carried him on their shoulders, they started pinching him, some even using pliers they had brought along for this specific purpose. I heard he cried piteously, but the hooligans outsmarted him by singing and cheering in voices that dwarfed all his persistent calls for help. Reportedly, this torture continued for over two kilometers, after which they laid him in his car, soft and crying like a wounded animal. One barely credible claim is that the journalists around him later reported he had been crying with the joy of seeing how his citizens loved him. Rumour had it that this episode was so traumatic that a small drop of diarrhea would always escape him whenever someone in his vicinity mentioned, "political rally."

As a result of this incident, plus his habit of boozing, it was said his life become so pathetic that he could not even feed his family. I heard that, at this juncture, his friend, the President, again ordered that he be hired as a lecturer of political science at Damasawa University – a position he held when he met Omollo that evening.

At the time of their encounter, Dr. Makunja was living alone in a big unfurnished staff house at Damasawa University after separating from his wife, the true reason for which was known only to themselves. Whereas, Dr. Makunja claimed his wife took offence after he had protested against her loud prayers, that God should paralyze his mouth and endowment at the sight of beer and other women's vertical smiles; Dr. Makunja's ever-gossiping neighbours confided in Omollo, on condition of anonymity, that the learned man's wife and children fled from the house ten years ago to escape dying from a concoction of hunger and shame.

As if to prove that her wife's prayers were really working wonders, as soon as they were separated, Dr. Makunja tripled his extramarital engagements and beer intake. Since then, friends and relatives had frequently tried to plead with him to take control of his life; nonetheless, he would always stalk out in anger whenever someone insinuated that he was self-destructing. From what I heard, he only cherished whoever teamed up with him in thinking that his woes stemmed from malpractices of the ruling party and, of course, the impacts of colonialism in Gondwana. The story added that Dr. Makunja genuinely believed that his problems would end on the very day his opposition party won the election. At the same time, a joke went around that he himself had not voted in the past three elections, allegedly, because the elections were held on Sundays – a day when, unfortunately, he would be too drunk to walk to a polling station.

When Omollo entered the house, it had neither electric power nor tap water: such amenities have long been disconnected by the service providers because of insurmountable bills. Further, Dr. Makunja did not even have bedsheets, allegedly, because thieves would always steal them from him. The irony, however, was that he had numerous umbrellas, notepads and pens to take along with him whenever he was too broke to afford a bottle of beer.

'You never know these days. Because of environmental degradation, it may rain even without warning," he would say whenever someone asked him the reason for carrying an umbrella in the midst of the dry season.

As for the pens and notepads he never used, he would give ever-satisfying answer: "These are the work tools of a learned person, such as I am."

The following day, the duo woke up at around 9:00 a.m. with a mild hangover after the large amount of alcohol they had consumed the previous day. Dr. Makunja then asked Omollo to accompany him to a bar, for that is where he usually took his breakfast. To Omollo's amazement, Dr. Makunja collected two helmets from his spacious storeroom and handed one to him before they started off. Omollo naturally assumed they would be going to the said bar by motorcycle. But then, after following Dr. Makunja for a considerably long distance without reaching the supposed parking spot, he was prompted to ask a question in order to dispel his doubts.

"Where is your motorbike, doctor?"

"I do not have one," Dr. Makunja promptly answered him, which stunned Omollo.

"Am I not dealing with a mad person here?" He silently questioned the sanity of Dr. Makunja.

"Then why are we cooking our heads with helmets in this scorching equatorial sun?" He asked incredulously, but Dr. Makunja only smiled widely and pointed to the signboards hanging every twenty meters by the road they were following.

"Read that," Dr. Makunja said and Omollo looked at one of the boards that read, Beware of students throwing deadly stones.

"I do not understand," Omollo declared and Dr. Makunja laughed for a long time before replying.

"Mmh! Songimani, this is a university and students are always rioting here," he eventually explained.

"But why are they rioting?" Omollo asked eagerly.

"Fighting for their rights, of course," Dr. Makunja answered, as the two continued walking across the campus.

"So, does that mean people who work here wear helmets every day?" Omollo asked.

"Depending on how much they care about their safety, but today many people will be wearing helmets for there is a high likelihood of a riot," Dr. Makunja answered seriously.

"Why do you think so?" Omollo asked him.

"I actually heard on the radio that students would riot against the grand misuse of the national income today," Dr. Makunja answered.

"What do you really mean by the misuse of national income, sir?" Omollo now asked him politely.

"Hahahahahahah, haahahahahha!" Dr. Makunja laughed joyously, "you know our president recently married an illiterate girl just because she has a protruding butt and a romantic look, right?"

"Not really," answered Omollo.

"Yaah! He is married to this low-life girl and the high life of the state house has gone to her head," said Dr. Makunja.

"What do you really mean?" Asked Omollo for clarification.

"Listen, the president went to one village in the south and coveted one of the girls who were dancing a traditional drum in his honour," said Dr. Makunja, "what he next did was to marry the girl a few days later, even against my own advice."

"Ehehehe!" Omollo encouraged him to go on narrating.

"Then in this girl's sixth month at the state house, she happened to see sewer trucks draining sewage at the state house, which is how she thought of the possibility of having an excretion machine for the contents of her bowels," he said amid derisive laughter.

"What is an excretion machine?" Asked Omollo in amazement.

"A machine that could enable her to push dung outside her soft belly without using her own energy, imagine!" Said Dr. Makunja and they laughed at the idea together.

"Eheehhehehe," Omollo wanted to hear more of it.

"Yes, she told her 'tamed husband' that she badly wanted the machine – and the story went around that the two 'sheep' subsequently travelled to Dagai in a government plane to look for such a device," he said amidst joyous laughter, "the 'sheep' subsequently roamed all over Dagai in an attempt to find an excretion machine," he added and grinned widely, "and every shopkeeper whom they asked would almost laugh at the incredulity upon hearing about what they were looking for."

"Ehehheeee," Omollo encouraged him to speak.

"All in all, one unscrupulous shopkeeper, or rather a clever one, took advantage of their folly to become rich."

"Ehehehehe," encouraged Omollo.

"He told them that he knew a designer who would tailor make the machine they were searching for them in just a few days – and, according to what I heard, the two dummies were as happy as two ducks in the rain, imagine," he said amidst laughter, "but do you know what it cost?"

"I don't know, sir," answered Omollo honestly.

"One tenth of the national budget," he said and paused as if to allow Omollo a moment to reflect on the cost.

"That corruption is exactly what the students are protesting against today," Dr. Makunja added and fell silent. Omollo too felt silent, as he mostly could not follow Dr. Makunja's talk.

"Likely my understanding and this man's understanding of things seem to be as far apart as the sky and the earth," Omollo thought inwardly but did not say so aloud.

In an effort to reduce the discomfort on his head, Omollo switched to surveying the glory of the university whose campus they were strolling across. In a little while, he noticed the presence of iron bars in almost every window and door of the university and was prompted to resume his questions to Dr. Makunja.

"Sorry, doctor," Omollo said out of the blue and produced a canny question:

"Was this university a prison in the past?"

"I have not read that, why would you ask such a thing?" Asked Dr. Makunja.

"I am just wondering that every of its door or window is iron-barred," Omollo said, sending Dr. Makunja into insuppressible laughter.

"Songimani, this is the Bewitched Republic of Kaya, remember! You actually have not seen all of its wonders. Thieves of this country can even steal your golden teeth if you sleep with your mouth open," said Dr. Makunja through his laughter, "what do you expect in a context where a university graduate cannot find even a manhole emptying job after graduation! What!"

As the two continued walking past the main administration block of the university, Omollo's eyes again caught sight of an inscription yellowed with age; *The mission of the university is to become a reputable world-class university in research, science and technology.* This prompted Omollo to ask Dr. Makunja another question.

"So, is your university doing so well in technology?"

Dr. Makunja, unexpectedly, exploded into such laughter that he sat down by the road until his fit of mirth subsided.

"Which technology are you talking about, Songimani? You will kill me with laughter this year! Oohhh!" He eventually lamented after a long battle with his uncontrollable laughter.

Now embarrassed, Omollo did not speak, instead pointed out the mission statement he had read, whereupon, Dr. Makunja burst out laughing all over again.

"Well, notwithstanding the university ranked ninety thousandth in last year's world rankings, its conscience is seemingly clear that it aspires to be a leader in science and technology," joked Dr. Makunja. Then, realizing that the joke had fallen flat, he briefly elaborated his statement.

"There's no science and technology in this country, or even their babies, my brother. We import even brooms and toothpicks from the People's Republic of Zhang in this country." Dr. Makunja again laughed twitchingly.

"So what do science students in this country study?" Asked Omollo seriously.

"Well, they do the histories of how everything was made, and that, as you see, is a lot of work," answered Dr. Makunja sarcastically and laughed as joyously as before.

Thereafter, the two men continued walking quietly across the expansive campus as Omollo was now engrossed in his own thoughts.

"How can Dr. Makunja talk about the lack of technology in a

country where fifty years ago Elder Mazinge claimed was capable of making a spaceship locally?" He wondered.

All of a sudden though, Omollo noticed a story on the opposite hill to the main campus, which looked modern and more elegant than the rest of the rotting buildings on the campus.

"Is that building also part of the university?" He wondered aloud.

"Of course, yes," answered Dr. Makunja.

"But why is it shining more than the rest of the buildings?"

"Yes, that is the School of Theatre," said Dr. Makunja briefly, as if his statement was a matter of common knowledge to everyone but then expanded: "It is where the children of the leaders of this country study," he elaborated after sensing he was vague.

"What do you mean, doctor? Do children of the leaders only study theatre in this country?" Asked Omollo in astonishment.

"Of course, yes," said Dr. Makunja, "they are training to take up the mantle from their parents," he stated vaguely again.

"And what has taking up the mantle from their parents got to do with studying theatre?" Asked Omollo, inadvertently triggering Dr. Makunja's hysterical laughter again.

"Songimani, you thrill me a lot my friend," said Dr. Makunja and sighed deeply before resuming talking.

"To lead this country, one must be a very good actor: learn how to cry so that citizens can believe you are merciful; learn how to fake seriousness against corruption so that they can believe you are a liberator; learn how to lie without the blink of an eye to woo voters to vote for you; and learn how to project the truth told about you as a political tactic by the opposition to pull you down," he said and stopped for a moment to allow Omollo to ponder what he had just said.

"You cannot perform all these core roles without a degree in theatre, my friend. In other words, you can't rule this county even for a day without these skills, I tell you," he concluded and a studious silence followed: Omollo tagged along behind Dr. Makunja, while contemplating how survival for existence had brought him together with this strange fellow.

Then, all of a sudden, Dr. Makunja bolted back in the direction they had just come from, actually in the fashion of a donkey that has sensed the encroachment of a tsetse fly. Omollo also bolted behind him, supposing that Dr. Makunja had noticed a hive of infuriated bees in the forest reserve they were now walking through.

Soon though, Omollo realized that they would have emerged at a battlefield: that a crowd of students was preparing to throw stones at a crowd of armed police officers on their left side, while the police officers were preparing to respond with tear gas and rubber bullets towards the students on the right.

"Yaap, we have survived it," said Dr. Makunja happily after they had reached a mini supermarket near the university administration block.

"So, why were we running, if we are not a party to the conflict?" Asked Omollo innocently.

"Hahahahahaha!" Laughed Dr. Makunja, "if stones and tear gas know peoples' identities, then you can say that! Any moment you are caught up in such riots in this country, run like a cheetah," he added and laughed his typical long laugh.

"If the police catch you, you will get a thorough beating and it will cost you a fortune to see the sun again," he said and continued laughing, "but even if students catch you, they will christen you a spy, and the bad name might cost you your life."

At this juncture, Omollo felt a headache and walked to a pharmacy near the supermarket with an aim of buying some aspirin. Dr. Makunja followed him.

"How much do two aspirins cost?" Omollo asked the pharmacist, but Dr. Makunja quickly intervened.

"Why two aspirins?" He asked in surprise.

"I have a headache, and I think two is the dose," Omollo explained and Dr. Makunja exploded with laughter.

"Give him four aspirins, please," he instructed the pharmacist, thus surprising Omollo even more.

"Why are you ordering four aspirins, for God's sake? Do you also want to take some yourself?" Asked Omollo in a serious tone.

"Not at all, I am quite fine. All are for you," said Dr. Makunja, "everything in this country is counterfeit, remember! Therefore, at least four counterfeit aspirins should do the trick." Omollo just grinned.

Two weeks later, Omollo was fed up with Dr. Makunja's habit of begging him for money. He was further frustrated at how he would blame the ruling party and colonialism even for the smell of a brewery emanating from his armpits. To regain his freedom, therefore, Omollo sought a tiny tin room in the city suburbs and moved there instantly. Thereafter, he started looking for any job that could put food on his table. Fortunately, it was then raining cats and dogs in Damasawa City, so that many roads in the city center had, as usual, turned into streams or swamps. In this context, Omollo now joined other jacks-of-all-trades of the city in lining up stepping stones at strategic swampy pedestrian crossings for the small fee of 100 shillings for each stone ones steps on. He would thus pick up more than 10,000 shillings a day and was indeed very happy with his new enterprise; unfortunately, before long, the rain stopped and pushed him back to square one.

After a long period of joblessness, Omollo heard of a company at Manyata Beach, which would employ everyone willing to work. As quickly as he could, he walked to the location, where he found a multitude of people sprawling along the whole beach like crocodiles basking in the morning sun. In trying to make sense of what was happening there, he noticed two smart looking men under the shade of an ancient mango tree. The men were sitting on collapsible chairs under a big banner reading as; *Crowd for Hire International Company Limited (CHICL)*. Intuitively, Omollo approached them and discovered that they were indeed the directors of the company he had in mind.

This Crowd for Hire International Company Limited would receive orders from people who needed the services of a crowd for an activity. Many of its clients were shopkeepers who needed a crowd to loot their competitors' shops; politicians who needed a crowd to cheer for them or, alternatively, heckle their opponents at political rallies; pastors who needed a crowd to lure sheep into their churches; wives who needed a crowd to harass their disgusting co-wives; or rich men who needed a crowd to moan for their dead relatives.

After receiving such orders, the directors of CHICL would blow a whistle and all job seekers on the entire beach would queue in front of their mango tree. Subsequently, the directors would count those willing and decide what to pay them in relation to the nature of the assignment at hand and the amount received from the client. After all these factors had been considered, the directors would address the crowd on the nature of the assignment and the available payment for each participant. Each participant would normally get between 1000 to 10,000 shillings per assignment.

When Omollo informed the men he was looking for job, they did not even bother to know his name: simply told him to join the others sprawling on the beach and wait for the job to come. And indeed, after a short while, a famous politician in town needed a crowd to pull down a house on a prime plot he was contesting against a prominent local businessman. According to the normal procedure of the company, a 6,000 shillings advance landed in Omollo's hand.

A few minutes later, a crowd of about one hundred and fifty weird people started marching to the site of the assignment. As it would have been prophesied even by a sinner, no sooner had they started demolishing the house than police cars arrived on the scene, as usual, with their blaring sirens and rocket launchers. Put briefly, the commotion that followed stopped Omollo from returning to CHICL for a job offer – rather, *the Busy Malan* resumed his futile efforts at searching for a job and was unsuccessful over and over again.

Luckily though, he one day came across a con artist masquerading as a pastor – a man who would give him simple assignments for a fee. Omollo's first assignment in this arrangement was to attend the con artist's church the following Sunday and pose as a dumb man – an assignment he accepted without reservation.

At the agreed time, therefore, Omollo followed the given directions until his eyes caught sight of a big hall with brilliant inscriptions reading as; *Shortcut to Paradise Church of the Holiest (SPCH)*. Even so, he was still not sure if this church was Pastor Msuke's church: since he could not remember the name of the church that Pastor Msuke had mentioned him. Accordingly, he hovered his eyes around the area in search of anything that might confirm the church he was seeing was the right one. Fortunately, his eyes caught the church's slogan, which had Pastor Msuke's name at its end:

> 'Choose you this day what ye will be upon dying; a biofuel or
> a superstar, but as for me and my house, we will be superstars
> – Joshua Msuke, 2008.'

As he walked through the door of that church that day, Pastor Msuke acted as if the Holy Spirit had descended upon him and told him secrets about Omollo in advance. As part of the pretense, he led Omollo onstage straightaway and tried to ask him questions, which Omollo could not answer as long as he was acting dumb. As masterminded, Pastor Msuke then declared out aloud and every faithful churchgoer believed him:

"God is showing me that this man has been dumb from birth."

Next, he mobilized the whole congregation to pray for Omollo as dedicatedly as possible – so that he would speak. Nonetheless, in accordance with the original scenario, Omollo did not speak, whereupon, Pastor Msuke posited that God would answer prayers at a time of His own choosing. From what I heard, Pastor Msuke thereafter met Omollo secretly and congratulated him greatly for playing his role on that particular day beyond expectations. He therefore asked Omollo to return to his church two weeks later – this time around as a dumb man who had been cured by Jehovah Shammah.

On the day in question, Omollo set off as planned for the *Shortcut to Paradise Church of the Holiest (SPCH)*. In preparation for the big occasion, he first walked into a nearby bar where he took three cold bottles of beer, allegedly, for boosting his confidence and his Linglish. Thereafter, he ate four bananas, allegedly, to suppress the overpowering smell of the counterfeit beer he had consumed. Now, he confidently walked into the church, where the congregation was then deeply praying to God – to keep the Zhangians healthy all year round – lest they fall sick, fail to manufacture affordable GM seeds and cause every common Kayan to die of hunger. Given the gravity of the issue at hand therefore, each of the "sheep" was kneeling down with a portrait of the founding father of the People's Republic of Zhang against their chests and were so absorbed in their weighty prayers that they did not even notice Omollo's arrival in the hall.

Pastor Msuke however, noticed him, most likely because he had been expecting him at that hour. As Omollo entered the hall, he and

Pastor Msuke, who was kneeling on the altar facing the entrance, now exchanged secret codes skillfully, after which Omollo occupied an eye-satisfying angle – deliberately to feast his eyes on the sparkling female congregants who were filling that church to the brim.

As usual, the following session was dominated with singing spiritedly and shouting madly in the name of praising Jehovah Nissi. This, however, did not prevent *the Busy Malan* from falling into a deep sleep – actually, so deep that collection plates passed him by several times without him reacting to them as Pastor Msuke had expected. This, of course, burnt the pastor inside but he managed with great effort to conceal his frustration.

At some point though, the self-aggrandizing founder of the church took to the altar: whereupon, the "sheep" made a deafening noise to welcome their shepherd. By chance, the turmoil awakened Omollo and convinced him that the time he had been waiting for had come. Consequently, he braced up for performing his assignment as soon as Pastor Msuke summoned him.

"Hallleluyaah!" Pastor Msuke now bellowed in a tone and a pitch he deemed fit for the holiest servant of God he was impersonating.

"Ameeeeen!" Replied the congregation.

"Alleluyaah!"

"Ameeeeen!"

"Do you remember the old man from Songi?" He asked the congregation, who initially appeared to be clueless as to what he was talking about.

"The one who two weeks ago came here as a dumb man," Pastor Msuke described Omollo and the congregation's memory was now jogged.

"Yessss," they answered in a lengthy chorus.

"God is telling me that He has healed him so that the doubting Thomases can see with their own eyes what our God is capable of doing," he said bouncily and paused long enough to give way for the faithful to crane their necks to search for Omollo among the congregation. All in vain, Omollo was perfectly camoflauged by the fine feathers he had borrowed from Pastor Msuke for the occasion; hence, no one else other than Pastor Msuke could therefore identify him.

"This man, who was dumb from birth, has been completely cured by Jehovah-jireh and above all can now speak the Queen's Linglish without a hint of hesitation, halleluhiiaaa!" Added Pastor Msuke with a confidence level of 99%.

"Sharara bara maka'mbamatara, kararapara maka'mba matara, mbarara twara matara kambale," the congregation exploded into speaking in tongues just as they had been pavloved by Pastor Msuke. After five minutes, though the "holy" chaos had faded away, giving room to Pastor Msuke to look at the angle where Omollo was lounging in wait for his turn.

"Child of God!" He called Omollo holily, "now march forward and testify to this congregation of how Jehovah Shamma cured your dumbness," he summoned Omollo in Linglish.

Upon hearing this, Omollo walked to the stage – wafting smiles on his way to the stage at a frequency even he himself was not comfortable with.

"Hallleluyaah!" He now bellowed with a distinctive Linglish-like twang.

"Ameeeeen!" Replied the congregation.

"Alleluyaah!"

"Ameeeeen!"

"Emmanueeel!" He shouted.

"Emmanueeel!" The crowd shouted together.

"When the pastor prayed for me last Sunday, I saw fire descending from Heaven like a lightning flash, and I started feeling dizzy. Halleluhiiaaa!" He burst into his well-rehearsed testimony that the church interpreter instantly interpreted to the audience into Kilayi.

"Ameeeeen," the audience said after the interpreter had come to a full stop.

"In fact, I went home like a drunkard, but miraculously, I started talking this good Linglish on the fourth day after your prayers," he said convincingly and the applause, which followed his utterance, literally shook the building.

"Did you say you saw water?" Pastor Msuke now started cross-examining him as per the protocol of the pre-planned fake testimony.

"No, I saw fire," Omollo opposed him.

"And how did you feel afterwards?"

"I felt dizzy and light," he answered.

"And would you tell this congregation what happened on the fourth day, son of God?" He asked cunningly.

"I started speaking this good Linglish you hear now," he said and Pastor Msuke now took the issue to a higher notch.

"Na na na na na na!" He bellowed, and triggered the congregation to start speaking in tongues, making ululations and acting as if Holy Spirit had filled them. It was therefore so chaotic that the doves who were living on the ceiling board of the *SPCH* went to a brief exile in the roofs of neighbouring buildings.

As the congregation was so mesmerized by his three-piece suit and his mastery of Linglish language, they believed Omollo's testimony almost in its entirety, which worked to the benefit of Pastor Msuke so well – evidence being that two men and seven women metamorphosed from goats into sheep soon after the testimony and, as usual, Pastor Msuke hurriedly baptized them at the swimming pool of a nearby hotel.

Put succinctly, Omollo's performance made Pastor Msuke

think of assigning Omollo a more challenging task, but also a more rewarding one. That is, he would make him his sole business partner in the *anointing water* dealings he was about to launch.

Anointing water was an innovation of the self-proclaimed Bishop Ndeli of *Unstoppable Devine Powers Church* (UDPC) in the neighbouring country of Nangali. According to the story, Bishop Ndeli woke up one day and proclaimed to his congregation that God had instructed him the previous night to pray for bottles of water and distribute them to people all over the world for healing sickness, exorcising evil spirits and solving personal challenges. Further, he fooled everybody that God had equally instructed him to charge faithful a small fee for the bottles and their distribution. Given the orchestrated promotional skills he was inherently born with, the bottles started selling among his faithful like hotcakes and soon became one of the most sought after commodities by the like-minded faithful abroad. This is when Pastor Msuke became the commission agent for the water in Kaya. He would, of course, get a handsome percent from the sales, but before long, he began to question why he could not get to keep the whole profit.

"Why can't I bottle the water myself, then sell it to these "sheep" and get all the money for myself?" He thought one day, "is Bishop Ndeli smarter than I am?"

Following this line of thought, he eventually struck a deal with a glass company in his town to confidentially manufacture for him replicas of Bishop Ndeli's bottles, which he would himself fill, "bless" and sell to the faithful as original Ndeli *anointing water*. Omollo thus teamed up with Pastor Msuke in filling up and selling fake *anointing water* to their loyal customers all over the town: luckily, not one single believer complained about the change of the product; on the contrary, they repeatedly testified how his anointing water helped them.

But in unforeseen circumstance, their business hit a snag only four months after its start. It happened that Omollo came face to face with a long experienced con artist – someone more experienced in connivance than himself and Pastor Msuke combined. This fraudster now deceived Omollo into believing he wanted to buy all the anointing waters in their storeroom at wholesale price. The following night, Omollo and Pastor Msuke filled up about 2000 bottles with well water and looked forward to harvesting a large amount of money from their wholesale buyer. Indeed the sale went well – save that two days after the transaction they discovered they had been given fake money for their fake water.

In the turn of events, Pastor Msuke now accused Omollo of conniving with the professional fraudster to swindle him of his worthy bottles and from that day on, he did not want to set his eyes on Omollo.

So, once again, the ill-fated son of Malaland found himself out of work and had to roam the whole town in search of any odd job that could put food on his table. After many days of such searching, he happened to come across a man by the road he was walking on whom he sensed having seen somewhere before. In his mental cross-examination, he realized this man was Abdul – a fellow fisherman who fifty years ago had organized his stowaway to Laurasia. With this knowledge, the two old friends embraced each other and later described what had transpired in their lives through the decades.

Abdul was currently running two lucrative businesses in his street. In the morning, he would work as a city sorcerer, distributing medicine and charms to the many clients in that street who believed in the occult. In the evening, he would sell old tires for burning muggers and pickpockets, who were so rampant in the same street, which was where Omollo met him that day. Helpful as ever, Abdul promptly offered Omollo the chance to team up with him in his primary job of city sorcery; Omollo's heart, however, was on a driving job.

"Finding a driving job is not a problem if you have 150,000 shillings for clearing a way for you through the crowd," Abdul told Omollo laughingly.

"Do you mean what you have just said, seaman?" Omollo wanted to ascertain.

"Aah, *the Peeper*, have you forgotten what I am?" Abdul replied.

A few days later, Omollo sold a golden ring he once picked in Laurasia for two hundred thousand shillings and gave Abdul one hundred and fifty thousand shillings, to be used for clearing the way to the employment of his choice.

"You will now be able to drive even the President of Kaya if you want;" Abdul guaranteed him on receipt of the money.

The first task for Abdul was to align Omollo's name to the President's name – finding him a birth certificate bearing a first name of the likes of the president's religion and a surname of the likes of his ethnicity. For this exercise, Abdul bribed 20,000/= on behalf of Omollo to the registrar of deaths, marriages and births, who, in turn, christened him Peter Tikisa.

"But what is the meaning of changing my name?" Omollo asked Abdul on the day he received his fake birth certificate.

"So as to present you in the competitive labor market as the brother to the President of the Republic," Abdul promptly replied.

"So what?" Omollo joked.

"Don't you know, *the Peeper*, that the brother to the President of this country is also president, his wife being the president of all women, and his dog the president of all the dogs," joked Abdul, and he and Omollo now laughed together.

"Every employer in this country would instantly take notice at hearing your name pronounced," Abdul added.

"Alleluhia!" Omollo joked.

"Every police officer will now slide his tail between his legs upon catching you red-handed raping a nun at the altar," Abdul added and two laughed even more.

A few days later, Abdul bribed 50,000/= and Omollo received his Master of VIP Driving certificate from Tavad University, qualifying him to drive any drivable royal item and walk any walkable royal pet. Further, he received a professionally written CV, showing that his last job was driving the Queen of Sangland and flying the omnipresent President of the Bundled States of Amandora.

What's more, his certificates showed that he was only 45 years old, of course, with a note to preempt anybody who discovered that he looked older than his stated age; *The candidate looks older than his age simply because he was very serious with his driving studies at Tavad University* – the note read.

With these excellent certificates obtained, Abdul bribed the remaining 80,000/= to the human resources officer of the Defence and Security Ministry so that he could create a vacancy for Omollo.

Soon after receiving the bribe, the man advertised the job tailored for Omollo in the government gazette as required by the law. Subsequently, 20,000 applicants applied for the job, out of whom seven applicants, including Omollo, were shortlisted for the interview.

During the interview, Omollo, of course, mismatched his crammed questions and answers: but the blame for this lay with the person who gave him the interview questions and their answers only a week before the interview. In any case, Omollo still beat every applicant in that interview to clinch the position of assistant driver to the Minister of Defence and Security of Kaya.

A few days after he reported for work, the minister now realized he was too old for the job, yet the fatty bribe he had received from the personnel officer prevented him from revoking Omollo's employment: he only left the lower cadre employees to murmur something about Omollo's age whenever they saw him passing by.

As Omollo had last driven a car fifty years ago, a few days before taking his new job, he contracted a taxi driver in his neighbourhood to update him on how to drive the new model cars an assignment the contracted party did quite successfully: Omollo thereafter managed to start the modern cars at the ministry and move them to the designated destinations, skillfully blaming every any shortcomings on the variances between driving in Laurasia and driving in Gondwana.

"Gears of Laurasian cars shift by themselves," he would say whenever he failed to transit from one gear to another on a hill.

As an assistant driver to the Minister of Defence and Security, Omollo was very busy on his working days. At around 8:00 a.m., he and the senior driver would drive their boss, for instance, to meet the chief of police, with whom the minister would discuss how to invent criminal charges against opposition leaders. At around 10.00 a.m., they would, for instance, drive him to meet chief drug dealers in the city center and discuss with them how to operate in complementary distribution with the police in the Bewitched Republic of Kaya. At 12:00 p.m., Omollo and his colleague would drive him to the state house to hand out Mr. President's share of the money harvested from the illegal dealings. At 2:00 p.m., Omollo and his colleague, for instance, would rush their boss to scold a gang of hitmen who would have failed to assassinate an activist within the two weeks' time they had promised. At around 3:00 p.m., they would, for example, drive their boss to a distant rural village to intimidate villagers who had refused to give a room to an investor who wanted to turn their village into a coffee plantation. Around 6:00 p.m., they would usually drive their boss to a five star hotel in the city center – the minister's dirty money collection point. At 9:30 p.m., they would, for instance, drive their boss to the national radio station, where he would address citizens on how their government was ready to go out of its way to see to it that every citizen was secure wherever he was in Kaya. At 11:00 p.m., they would usually drive their boss to a brothel to cheat on his witch-looking wife. At around 1:00 a.m., they would drive the red-eyed minister home to get some sleep before the whole cycle started all over again on the following day.

If a newspaper wrote something negative about the ruling party or the minister, the minister would have to meet the editor-in-chief in person for three options: scolding, bribing, or intimidating. While still at the media house, the minister would receive a phone call that national hospital employees were protesting over low pay and poor working conditions. Immediately, Professor Matiku would rush out to call a press conference to intimidate those workers with the ready-made phrases he always had at his disposal.

Saturdays and Sundays were nonetheless dedicated by the minister and his extended associates to what he referred to as 'living the life.' On these days, he would invite Omollo for a spree, mostly in a company of many other people who would introduce themselves as fans of the minister, but whom foreign journalists preferred referring to as sycophants. In Omollo's view, these other guys' only worth to the minister was their legendary ability to trigger claps and cheers of approval from the crowd at meetings which the minister would preside over – normally by initiating applause every time they realized the minister would welcome some support from the crowd. Alternatively, they were the minister's bodyguards-cum-attendants. Omollo was once quoted as humorously saying:

"If the minister, by chance, dropped his wallet on the ground, they would knock up their heads competing to pick it up for him; if the minister abused you, these guys would definitely beat you up. If he smiled at you, the guys would laugh at you as loud as feasting hyenas;

and if, by chance, the minister slapped you once, you would expect a minimum of four slaps from each of these guys."

Based on his own words, Omollo would never have associated with the guys - were it not for an Emolitche saying that 'a gardener cannot fire a cook.' Upon this realization, he eventually learnt to tolerate the guys' disgusting follies just to continue enjoying the minister's sprees.

In all honesty, the minister's sprees were no child's play. He would always foot all the bills for his troops 'from the cost of drinks to *adult entertainment*, if one wished to indulge in such,' as Omollo would latter narrate the story of his life under that man, especially if he was in jovial mood.

'The minister would order a grilled he-goat and a tray of *ugali* for each pair of us,' he would start his narration, and his face would always break into a grin upon remembering those golden days. 'So, we nicknamed the meal *eternity* – by virtue of the fact that we could never ever eat it all up, despite our frequent attempts to demolish it fully. I'm telling you for sure, our mouths would, at the outset, be so busy that none of us would risk choking by responding even to a question from a waiter, who would want to know if we needed more drinks to accompany our food,' he would say with a crackling chuckle, 'and we would surely raise mountains of bones and knock down a quarter of *ugali* within just the first twelve minutes of the exercise.'

He would laugh joyously before adding: 'But in the thirteenth minute, you would start seeing *the folks* backing off one by one from *the eternity* – and now one by one opening up for conversation. All our belly buttons would then be bulging as if we were pregnant women." By now, Omollo would be rolling with laughter.

Despite the hard work, money was no longer an issue to Omollo, (for his boss was in reality made of the stuff). As Omollo would later narrate, one of the backbreaking assignments his boss would assign them weekly was to count his uncountable bank notes. If he were not exaggerating, Omollo and his colleagues would often count their boss's money the whole night – and often fail to complete the assignment.

"We would sometimes slumber in the middle of the exercise, and sometimes our saliva would drip and soak the bundles of bank notes we were counting without our knowledge," he would say.

"The good thing, was only that the guard would allow us to carry home any amount of bank notes fitting in our trouser pockets the next morning – an act known as *blurring the eyes which have seen*," he would add amidst hearty laughter.

With his strong personal economy, Omollo moved into a two-room apartment in the rich and robust neighbourhood of Wayara and furnished his room to the brim. Enthusiastic about his achievements, he then invited Abdul to appreciate his self-contained apartment – but subsequently wished he had not: Abdul, instead of compliments, embarrassed him by stating that a self-contained apartment must also host a wife and children.

But even as subtle as Abdul's joke was, it remained with Omollo long after his friend had left: inwardly he now wanted to meet a prerequisite of a self-contained apartment as defined by Abdul. Accordingly, he unofficially started shopping around for wife material, but kept the plan to himself. Indeed, he was well on the way to finding 'Miss Right Wife' – until the day he bungled the exercise altogether.

According to the story, it occurred one day that Omollo was attending a disco at a nightclub in his vibrant neighbourhood of Wayara. Primarily, he just wanted to glory in his new mode of life that each of his old friends admired like a jewel. As usual, the nightclub was teeming with women in short shorts and T-shirts, reading on the front, *We say 'no' to a request* and on the back, *We take 'no' for a request.* By way of introduction, the women would always tell their customers something like:

'My name is so-and-so and I work here as an entertainer.' Upon hearing this ambiguous introduction, a new customer or rather *a mobile ATM up for grabs* – in those women's terminology – would quite often ask what *entertainer* meant, whereupon, the women, or *the taxis* – in their chronic customers' terminology – would often demonstrate practically the entertainment they were offering rather than just theoretically describing it.

To keep the story short, it was one such woman who that day grabbed Omollo's left palm at the club and started dragging him to the center of the poorly lit dance floor. Omollo, being shy, resisted the pull but actually to no avail and, of course, everybody would tell you that he was wasting his energy: the woman's T-shirt made it very clear that she answered 'no' to a request and reciprocally took 'no' to mean the same.

As was predetermined, Omollo eventually ceded ground and found himself in the center of the dance floor with the *taxi* in question. Once there, he stuck with the nostalgia dance styles – for those were, of course, what he had in his repertoire. On the other hand, his dance partner was already at a twerking age. Accordingly, she kept grinding her protruding butt on Omollo's groin until his manhood was bitterly protesting the exposure – as usual, by metamorphosing from a cartilaginous to iron bar state and vomiting a thick mucus on his pants.

After that twerk-intoxication, Omollo would claim that he unconsciously found himself inviting the woman to his table and subsequently waking up in the same bed as her the next morning – which, unfortunately, was Omollo's bed.

But the most interesting part of the story was that the woman did not show any signs of leaving Omollo's house, even after she had taken breakfast that morning. For the two following days, it was said she would dine and sleep the whole day long like a full cat in a sitting room. Pissed off to the brim, Omollo eventually chose on the third day to take the cow by its horns by blatantly asking her to leave his house. But alas, the response the woman gave him almost deprived him of his old breath: she swore to his face by God that even a bulldozer would not be strong enough to whisk her away from that house. More specifically, her defence was:

> 'that she had been fasting and praying to God to give her a husband for five consecutive years'
> 'that on the day before she met Omollo, God had personally assured her that Omollo was totally hers'
> 'and that there was no way she was going to let go his heavenly gift so easily.'

Upon hearing these words, Omollo was dumbstruck: firstly, because of the boldness of the woman in her wild claims of partnership in his rented house. Secondly, he wondered what had happened to the woman species as a whole in his Republic of Kaya.

"Before I stowed away," he reflected, "a Kayan woman was a docile 'domestic animal' whose duty was to jump as high as her man demanded. A proposal such as this woman is making was an unheard of phenomenon in the whole of Kaya, I bet. There were a lot of bureaucratic procedures before getting a woman to bed, but look at how this one got into my bed the other night."

He threw his hands asunder in the air – as if he was involved in small talk with some imaginary people, "the very few women of this character that did exist used to be called *low-hanging fruits* that even a cripple can pick," he contradicted himself and then fell silent for long time.

After recovering from his initial amazement, Omollo vehemently commanded the woman to leave his house before he counted to ten. Unfortunately, even his pepper-hot temper could not derail the *taxi* from a mission she considered worth dying for – and this made the incident so dramatic to witness. Omollo would rap a repelling expression like 'Nga, nga, nga, nga', after which the woman would come in with prefabricated Linglish expressions starting with "but:"

> 'But a bird can never fly with one wing,' she would assert,
> and then Omollo would explode again.
> 'Nga, nga, nga, nga!'
> 'But four eyes see well than two,' she would respond.
> 'Nga, nga, nga, nga!'
> 'But he who finds a wife finds something good.'
> 'Nga, nga, nga, nga... nga...nga......nga......nga!'
> 'But two heads are better than one.'

In the end, the Busy Malan was exhausted from quarreling, or rather realized that his partner was as clingy as a throat cancer and would not be shoved an inch away by his explosions. He thus wisely chose to let fate take its course, or rather realized that there was no human solution to his new problem.

All the same, the woman's expertise in babying furious men like Omollo was legendary. Omollo would sneeze and without fail, she would sprint to him at the speed of an ambulance, just to ask if he was okay. Omollo would later lament over her shameful background and she would gently urge him to stop judging a book by its cover. And when Omollo eventually took an interest in her excuses, she convincingly asserted that he had only found her in such a compromising situation because she had previously never met a serious man like him to hire her as a wife. And as if to prove Omollo's prejudices against her wrong, she conducted herself so decently at the onset of their forced union that Omollo soon started feeling guilty for having rebuked such an angel from Heaven. Probably to clear his feeling of guilt for so mistreating the angel, Omollo soon started ameliorating her nicknames from *sex worker* or *whore* to *quite understanding woman, blessing in disguise* and kindred expressions.

As if Omollo's wife had been waiting for such moment to come, one day she confronted him after a good breakfast with the Linglish slogan of *Love me, love my dog* – by which she was implying that Omollo adopt her two children who until then had been living with her mother in the village. Amazingly, Omollo endorsed the proposal more readily than even she herself had envisaged. Therefore, at the end of the day, she brought her children to constitute a united family living very happily in their self-contained apartment.

Two years later, Omollo went to his workplace to find his boss weeping at the entrance of their offices like a child whose umbrella is lost. Taken aback by the sight, he immediately asked what his boss was so upset about and received an instant answer from a cleaner who would always sweep around the main gate for a purpose.

"The President of Kaya has replaced him with his paramour, who is also the paramour of the President," she murmured in Omollo's left ear and resumed her work as if she had not just dropped a bombshell.

The spirit of sympathy now descended upon Omollo for his boss, although he had no solution to his problem, other than telling him 'sorry', wishing him well in his joblessness and promising to visit him at home from time to time. Deep in his mind though, Omollo did not worry about the security of his job in the absence of the sacked minister: he knew he was a government employee, not a personal assistant to the minister – as was the case with his first job at the Ministry of Natural Resources some fifty years ago. His heart nevertheless throbbed threateningly in premonition that his next boss might behave towards him like a goon.

"Will she be as good to me as Professor Matiku was?" He thought to himself but could not come up with an answer.

A few days later, the new minister appeared at the meeting hall to become acquainted with her staff and everything changed when Omollo's turn to introduce himself came:

"I am Peter Tikisa, an assistant driver to the Minister for Defence and Security," Omollo said and the minister's eyes rapidly became amplified before she began giggling childishly for a reason that Omollo only came to know later.

Following that encounter, the minister summoned Omollo to tell him that he should pack his things and leave the ministry before she counted to ten, allegedly, because she only wanted young handsome men to work under her; not someone as old as Omollo Orwa a.k.a Peter Tikisa. Omollo now begged her like God to retain him in the ministry: he even showed her his birth certificate proving that he was only 48, but in vain.

"I only look eighty because I was too serious with my driving studies at Tavad," Omollo defended himself as seriously as if he was telling the truth.

But talking with impunity like the Devil himself, the minister gave Omollo a good telling off. Eventually, on the fifth day after their conversation, she personally handed Omollo his termination letter, which contained the following curious passage:

> 'The ministry has chosen to terminate the appointment of Mr. Peter Tikisa as a precautionary measure to the safety of the Minister of Defence and Security. This follows the findings of an independent inquiry commission that the horny driver would concentrate unblinkingly on staring at the classic boobs of the minister, instead of concentrating on the steering wheel – even on highways'.

On the day he received the most poorly argued termination letter in the world, the world became darkish to the son of Orwa. He, of course, wanted to cry aloud, but his near-lethal past had made his heart shockproof and his eyes tearless. He rather turned and cast his eyes on the minister with all the hatred he could non-verbally emit but the minister was grinning widely like a kid at Christmas, blissfully unaware that Omollo was burning inside with anger and embarrassment.

"Big witch, hellfire is waiting to devour you," Omollo cursed her in protest and left with a heavy heart.

Upon straggling home that day, his wife, who did not expect him around that time, was clearly shocked and promptly asked him the reason for his early return in her usual comforting voice.

"My private website!" She called him romantically, "I wonder why you are home so soon today! Is something wrong with you?" She asked, but Omollo, who had lost his sense of judgment, did not immediately answer her – which kept her wondering about what had happened. Omollo rather walked to the sitting room and threw himself onto the couch like a log before breaking his sad news.

"Baby!" He addressed her and looked straight in her eyes before continuing: "I am sorry, she eventually fired me from the job," he said sadly.

Upon hearing this, a baleful look flashed across the face of Omollo's wife – a look that Omollo learnt five months later was an embodiment of the pain of losing a mobile ATM. Thereafter, she blatantly blamed Omollo for 'playing with a golden ring at the mouth of an anthill.'

"How can you leave me here just to go and stare at another woman's boobs? My God!" She bashed Omollo without giving him room to tell his side of the story.

"Now you come here and tell me with your ugly mouth: nyo, nyo, nyo! Nyo, nyo, nyo! nyo, nyo, nyo! Nzhzzzzzzzz!" She hissed, "of course, this is what happens when someone is a chronic idiot!" She scolded Omollo as if Omollo was an adopted kid.

From that day on, things were never the same in Omollo's house. He witnessed in disbelief how his home slowly but surely metamorphosed from a little paradise to a capital of disappointment. And the more the money harvested from Professor Matiku dwindled, the more the trouble in his house soared. Two months after his dismissal from work, the last coin in Omollo's household was spent on aspirin, which coincided with the onset of a literal encounter between the cursed man and the female angel of demons.

To make ends meet, Omollo then started peddling commissioned goods from house to house to lazy people who did not want to walk to the market. Nonetheless, the business did not fetch enough money to pay the bills. That is, he would sometimes traverse the entire city with an overload of invaluable goods stacked all over his body, without selling even a single pin. Worse still, he would, on some fateful days, be forced to flee from the city militiamen, who always wanted to confiscate such peddlers' goods in the name of executing the city's bylaws.

But to add insult to injury, his once 'quite understanding' wife metamorphosed radically into a 'quite misunderstanding one'. Quite demonstrably, she substituted her former professional kisses with deep-cutting insults and started spending more time in front of the mirror or at the hair salon than in the kitchen and started measuring sympathy to Omollo with a teaspoon. While Omollo would have peddled goods throughout the metropolis without selling so much as a nail cutter, she would pop up and ask him for 10,000/= for plaiting her hair in the latest style in town. When Omollo's head would be hurting with the stress caused by a lack of money to cover even the basic services – and he would probably be sleeping under a mango tree just to cool down, she would, like a cobra in deep grass, pop up and ask him for 50,000/= to contribute to her uncle's wedding expenses. Whereas, in the past she would address Omollo by names from the food industry, such as sugar, sweetie, or honey, she suddenly switched to names from the animal kingdom, such as baboon, dog or donkey.

Cornered like a tired boxer or rather attempting to avoid disadvantages, Omollo tried really hard to meet his wife's wild demands. All the same, she would always make a mountain out of a molehill, leaving Omollo tired and bitter like wild pepper. The case in point: it happened one day that Omollo was playing with his young stepdaughter in the sitting room. According to the story, Omollo then uttered something like, 'I will drink the milk of a cow paid for your dowry and grow stronger, my daughter.' Overhearing this, his wife cut in disgustedly:

"Stop it! You will get nothing from my daughter's dowry. What have you paid to my parents as a dowry yourself to guarantee your drinking from a cow paid as dowry to my daughter?"

"I do not care about your foolish rebuke, I will still drink milk from the cows," Omollo responded, thus infuriating his wife even more.

"You will not taste a single drop of it," his wife said and the verbal exchanges degenerated into a physical fight, after which Omollo's hand was twisted and hurt for more than a week, while his wife received a jackal-bite on her left cheek. Thereafter, there was a temporary ceasefire, simply because the two were either sick or too tired to fight. For the first time in three months, they found themselves making love again. But as Omollo was then starving for the act, he opened his legs so wide that he swept his young stepson, with whom they were sharing the bed, onto the floor. The boy subsequently cried madly, which obliged the duo to postpone their exercise in order to pacify the baby. A few minutes later, the boy went back to sleep and the two resumed the exercise; little did they know that their three years old daughter, usually sleeping on a couch in the bedroom, was awake and was closely following what they were doing in the darkness. As she feared her young brother being swept off for a second time, she now chose to shout him a warning.

"Ababu, ma brother! Watch out, they have resumed their fight!" She shouted and the two stopped all exercising for the rest of the night.

Even in the morning that followed, Omollo continued to be aggrieved at what his stepdaughter had done to them the previous night. To avoid foreseeable repeat of such a scenario, he now insisted that the little girl be shifted to the sitting room to allow them a total freedom in their bedroom. On the contrary, his wife maintained that her daughter was too young to sleep alone in the sitting room.

"I would not have adopted anyone's child if I had known the hidden costs of doing so," a disgusted Omollo now uttered in protest at his wife's position on the issue, which again launched a series of intermittent fights between the two of them.

One day, however, Omollo brought home a book entitled, *How to Deal with a Nagging Wife*. Contrary to his expectation, his wife was completely pissed off with the title of the book, and now ejected from Omollo's house for her own home like a rocket - leaving Omollo celebrating the divorce as if he had won the World Cup.

To clear the bad memories about the woman in his mind, Omollo soon moved streets but continued peddling his valueless goods. Now it happened that Omollo, one day, coincidentally ran into Abdul - same old friend he had been avoiding like a plague since he lost the job. Upon seeing Omollo, with his worthless goods stuck all over his body surface, Abdul laughed until his stomach was then hurting. After exhausting his delight, he genuinely pitied Omollo for choosing hard work over an easy option at such an evening age.

"I told you a long time ago to team up with me in the sorcery profession, but you blatantly refused, considering yourself cleverer than anyone else," Abdul scorned him, "but now look at yourself! With me, you would not be suffering like this, my friend."

"But I also told you that despite being a son of a famous diviner-priest, I am not a diviner-priest myself. It is like I fell out with my father long before I was fully initiated into the practice," Omollo defended himself.

"It does not matter at all *the Peeper*, you know very well that I am originally a fisherman, don't you?" Abdul asked Omollo and the two now laughed together.

"So, where did you learn sorcery, Abdul?" Omollo asked his old friend in a relatively composed tone.

"From my friend," Abdul said confidently.

"Your friend!" Exclaimed Omollo, "but sorcery is supposed to be inherited. Is it taught?" He genuinely wondered Abdul, however, laughed off this thought.

"Point of correction, we learn tricks here, not the real sorcery you have in mind," Abdul told his friend who continued to look shocked.

"Tricks?" Omollo asked.

"Of course, tricks, only how to trick the fools," Abdul said.

The following week, Omollo enrolled in a city sorcery-training course run by his old friend, Abdul - and was so good in absorbing the lessons that he was ripe enough to earn a degree in city sorcery in only three months.

In the fourth month, Omollo and Abdul unanimously agreed that Omollo should go and practice in a different location of the town.

In their wisdom, that would enable them to avoid competing between themselves for clients. Omollo would, however, surrender ten percent of his earnings to Abdul for two years, as a fee for the training – a commitment Omollo promised to honour. So, Omollo went out to a different street and started practicing city sorcery in a small medicine hut he had erected at his rented compound.

One of the key skills Omollo had learnt during his training was to research the contemporary needs of people and announce a solution for them. A few days after establishing his office therefore, he went into the streets and discovered that the salaries of the poor people in his new street would only last until the fifteenth day of the month. Similarly, he learnt that those people would have loved to see their salaries crossing from one 'bank' of the month to another. Armed with this knowledge, Omollo quickly went to a painter and had him produce a bold poster reading; *Professor Deep Waters from Songi – capable of stopping your salary from dying young.*

No sooner had he hung the poster on the electric pole by his medicine hut than clients started trickling in his compound one after another for the charm. As per the tradition of town sorcery, he prescribed each of those very hard terms and conditions as a buffer against being labeled a fake sorcerer.

"For this medicine to work for you, avoid stumbling Linglish like, 'Yous, I talk you talk, who hear who?' Sound like a native speaker and you will yourself call to give me feedback," he was heard instructing a Kilayi teacher – for whom, unfortunately, Linglish was the ultimate challenge.

"When you go to the toilet, ensure you defecate before you pee," he was again heard telling a dispensary cleaner who was seeking a promotion to a doctor of medicine.

But before long, clients were not as numerous as they had been at the start. As a result, Omollo was obliged to go out for researching what constituted burning problem to the majority of the street-dwellers at that particular time. Accordingly, he soon discovered that men were bullying their wives and the abused women would pay anything for a charm that could make their husbands so docile they could narrate them their exotic escapades with other men without any protest.

Armed with this knowledge, Omollo revisited his painter the following day and had him produce him another poster reading; The revered professional diviner-priest from Songi, with a charm that transforms your husband from a lion to a lamb in matter of seconds.

The next day, he erected the poster in the same place and again it did not disappoint: within three days, women from all walks of life were queuing in front of his medicine hut to get the metamorphosing medicine. Omollo as usual distributed the medicine with hard-to meet terms and conditions – actually as grounds for shifting gear whenever a ferocious client bounced back into the medicine hut to complain that the charm did not work.

Two months later, the women discovered that their husbands had resisted change, or rather that they did not meet the sorcerer's terms and conditions, going by the fact that they ceased flocking to Omollo's hospital. Discovering this fact, Omollo returned to the streets for more research and this time learnt that bandits wanted charms to enable them to steal without intervention of security officers or owners of properties. In this knowledge, Omollo returned to his painter and had him paint him a poster reading; *Prof. Deep Waters from Kagoma, with a charm that enables you to rob a central bank in broad daylight without anybody noticing.*

As was his custom, he mounted the new advertisement in the same location and a gang of robbers, popularly known as; *A Possessor of an Illegal Gun Need not Farm* (PIGNF), soon noticed it. The next morning the gang confronted him in his medicine hut and demanded that he recants his advertisement, which Omollo stupidly did not do. On the contrary, he quite irrationally insisted that his charm was indeed strong enough to make guards sleep on the job like logs when the robbers were majestically walking into a property for a kill. Now convinced by Omollo's advocacy of the powers of his juju, the robbers paid him handsomely – nonetheless with a stiff warning.

"Lying to us would have grave consequences," their boss said as they were leaving but Omollo thought they were joking.

That evening a group of seven robbers, under the auspices of Omollo's charm, marched proudly to the house of the richest man in the town. Most of the gang genuinely expected the guards would be asleep by the time they were walking in; only one junior robber appeared doubtful about the power of the charm but was savagely criticized by their leader.

'This house is fitted with a special device for deterring thieves,' the doubter read and, being concerned, swiftly tiptoed to his boss.

"Boss, let's be careful: the house is fitted with a thieves' detecting gadget," he murmured in the commander's ear but was instantly blasted:

"Move on, stupid pig! We are not thieves; we are bandits, remember?" Their boss reprimanded at the top of his voice – which alerted the guards of the mansion.

To cut a long story short, two robbers out of the seven were gunned down by the guards of the property that night; two escaped with mortal wounds; one was netted alive, whereas, two lucky bandits escaped without even a scratch on their shanks.

Unaware of what happened to his clients, Omollo continued with his practice: blissfully unaware that he had lighted a drum of petrol with a matchstick. Two weeks after the tragedy, the two survivors from

PIGNF stormed his medicine hut with the aim of reclaiming their extorted money and retaliating for the deaths of their loved ones due to Omollo's lies. Upon recognizing them, Omollo promptly threatened them with *jinni* – actually, as he had been trained at college – yet the daredevils did not give a damn about his hollow threats and continued encroaching on him.

"You failed yourself to follow the given conditions," Omollo changed tactics but the hotheads would take none of it.

As he continued spewing words like a radio, the two men restrained him on the ground and started skinning his nose with a razor blade. And because of the intensive pain, Omollo now emitted wild wails that might have attracted the neighbours' attention, but was soon viciously slapped with a frying pan to stop his racket.

"Shut up, stupid pig!" Screamed their commander, Mr. *There is No Hard Bread for Tea*, or *TNHBT*, in short.

"Where does all this come from?" He yelled at Omollo, "do you pretend that you did not know that this day would arrive with all the blunders you have been committing here?" Omollo, now lamb-calm amidst his surgery without anaesthesia, made no reply.

In summary, the evil men eventually dislocated his arm, sodomized him without lubrication and plucked out his two incisors, all without anesthesia. As if that was not enough, they took away everything he had garnered in those two years of his city sorcery practice.

"We are working hand in hand with the local police. So, any stupidity you try will be wired to us and we will promptly come back and nail you naked to one of those baobabs by the road. Get it, coffin dodger?" One of the men yelled at Omollo, while pressing his mouth wide open with his fingers in the form of tongs.

"Yes, sir!" A timid and shaken Omollo now replied in the loudest voice he could manage.

"Finally, get lost from this town before we pronounce 'knife,'" Mr. *TNHBT* ordered him and then the two men leisurely drove away.

<<<CHAPTER TWENTY-THREE>>>

On the following morning, Omollo set off on foot for his village of origin. His anus was aching so much he prayed to God to spare him the urge to defecate. At the same time, his skinned nose was attracting flies of all sorts, yet he had to march out of that city to in compliance with the order of the daredevils he encountered the previous day. As he had no fare on him, he would walk from one village to another until he reaches his ancestral village, some seven hundred kilometers north of Damasawa.

"I think I am haunted by spirits of my father," he reflected one evening as he wearily hitched along the tall-grassed path on his long walk to Malaland, "I have to go to my father's grave for a cleansing ritual."

As these reflections about his past continued, he at some point remembered the two golden bangles under the Sacred Rock that his grandmother once bequeathed him.

"I am going to dig bangles up and sell them," he thought, "subsequently; I can marry, have children and leave my mark on the Earth."

On the third day of Omollo's long trek to his village, the sun was scorching like Gehenna, the hill was so steep, the air completely still, and the atmosphere fully laden with dusty haze. In his entire body, sickness was taking its full toll on him, hunger bullying him severely and exhaustion successfully impeding his movement. Under the combined force of all these factors, Omollo eventually fell down like an old cactus, and could not raise himself up even after several attempts: his muscles were then too weak for him to raise even a finger, let alone his big head that was also infested with frustrations to the fullest. As if conceding defeat to these natural powers, Omollo now closed his eyes and gloomily felt that his cognizance was slowly but surely ebbing away from him. Four hours later, he woke up and was amazed to find himself in a small grass-thatched hut in the middle of nowhere. As he looked around, two bottles of medical drips were hanging over his bamboo bed and their catheters evidently connected to his veins through a needle. His inner voice now told him he was at a unique hospital, yet he was too weak to prove his supposition. Again, he closed his eyes and a sleep lying in wait for him instantly stole his sensitivity.

Of how Omollo reached there: a story was told that a Good Samaritan who was passing along the dusty road by which he had collapsed caught sight of him, and took him to a doctor, known throughout that region as Dr. Drip – a nickname derived from his frequency of using a synonymous medical practice on his patients.

Twenty years ago, Dr. Drip was a renowned thug in his village. It happened then that he was arrested and sent to prison for seven years. For four of the seven years he was behind bars, he was assigned the duty of cleaning the prison dispensary, which was when he learnt by observation to treat every disease.

When Omollo was admitted to his home hospital, Dr. Drip was the most revered doctor in the whole region north of Damasawa City, or rather the first flying doctor in the region. According to what I heard, an old man in village B would lament of his aching tooth and Dr. Drip would fly to him on his legendary Baatam bicycle, ready with hand-made pliers to uproot the man's aching tooth. But even before he had finished that dental assignment, his mobile would ring and the caller on the other end of the line would urge him to rush to village D to save a pregnant woman who had failed to deliver on her own.

As per his name, Dr. Drip heavily relied on an IV drip to resuscitate ill patients. Further, he would use chloroquine for malaria-like symptoms and Penicillin Procaine Fortified (PPF) injections for any other indefinite ailments. Fortunately, his three treatments often worked wonders for him – evidence being that Omollo's health stabilized on the eighth day of medical attention from Dr. Drip.

But in a twist of fate, Omollo failed to clear his medical bills, which changed his status from Dr. Drip's patient to Dr. Drip's prisoner. In an attempt to attain his freedom, I heard that he beseeched with Dr. Drip to let him go, saying that God would bless him. Unfortunately, the ex-thug did not subscribe to abstractions; worse still, he was not a believer in the existence of life after death. In other words, all he wanted was cash, not tales; otherwise, he threatened to inject Omollo with a potassium solution in a week's time to compensate for his time and medicine. Fortunately, a Baslim religious community in that village heard about Omollo's predicament, collected money among themselves and cleared his bills – God bless believers! Thus in the second week since his recovery Omollo resumed trekking in the direction of his original village. One evening of the fifty-fifth day of his long walk, he came across something that made all the hair on his body to stand on end – exactly, a skeleton of a lorry, posing as if on its knee beside a police post. From how his sensory organs reacted to the spectacle, he quickly observed the object and rapidly established it was the remains of Bishop Massawe's famous lorry – the one he had used to learn driving some sixty years ago. Although most parts of the lorry were blackened with age and rust, its number plate, which he knew by heart, was intact, and this confirmed it was exactly the same vehicle. With this realization, the hope of meeting Wankyo struck his soul, such he found himself involuntarily wobbling towards the dreaded police post without the normal fear of being accused of some crime, as it was the custom in all police stations in the Bewitched Republic.

"Would you tell me the whereabouts of the owner of that lorry over there?" He asked a police officer who had been dozing at the desk with a big leftover of *ugali* and fish beside him.

"Are you mad," the timid officer asked Omollo, reflecting that in his twenty years' experience he had never seen a man who could walk into a police post for such a silly question. And after his shock had worn off, he approached Omollo aggressively but Omollo calmly stood his ground and repeated his question about the owner of the lorry: whereupon the officer confessed he had no records about the owner of the lorry – and thus advised asking old men and women in the village.

"If at all that can cure your lunacy," he added insultingly.

On the very same evening, Omollo knocked at the door of a senior elder in Ingli village. Specifically, he wanted to know if the owner of the lorry near the police post lived in the village and especially if he lived together with his old lover, Wankyo the beautiful. Unfortunately, he was able to trace neither Bishop Massawe nor Wankyo. All he managed to discover was Bishop Massawe's grave, whose shining epitaph contained the weird inscription; *The man buried here is a very good example of a bad example to others.* Stunned by the strange epitaph, he questioned the reason why the villagers would have inscribed such a terrible sentence and he was given the mind-blowing account.

Bishop Massawe's appetite for a sausage pocket catapulted only a few days after his abandoning Omollo in the middle of nowhere and running away with his girlfriend. As a certified innovator of ideas, such as he was, Bishop Massawe came up with a plan he believed would enable him to be laid by as many women as possible. In this new plan, Bishop Massawe commissioned three mercenaries to go around Ingli Village proclaiming that God had rewarded the bishop with a magic seed that could make infertile women conceive just in one stab. The three mercenary women, with little babies in their arms, lied to everyone who cared to listen of how their husbands had divorced them after staying for so many years in a childless marriage – only for them to meet a man of God, gifted with the magic seed that had enabled them to become mothers.

Nonetheless, what Bishop Massawe did not know, or rather had underrated in his new plan, was the fact that love for babies in that part of the world exceeded love for careers – in fact, a joke went around in that land that 'a drunken head of an extended family does not need to walk the full way home after a drinking spree. He walks half the distance, pretends to have been blacked out by alcohol, and soon has a free ride on the shoulders of his people home.'

Accordingly, word quickly spread far and wide that there was a man of God in Ingli Village who could make infertile women pregnant with just one stab of his magic stick. Consequently, the second day after the mercenaries were dispatched witnessed the arrival in Ingli Village of women of all kinds from as far as the sixth village away. All these women took their positions in a queue in front of Bishop Massawe's tent for their share of the alleged magic seed – some on their own, but most of them in the company of their husbands or brothers.

Bishop Massawe happily used most of the first two days to distribute his proclaimed magic seed to the needy women as diligently as possible. On the third day though, he started sensing that he had involved himself in something that could possibly claim his life, if he was not careful, considering that the demand for the magic seed appeared higher than he could supply. At that juncture, the idea came to him that he should sneak away from the village, as he had been doing in past incidents. The problem was that women and their husbands were all over the place and even on that very day; at least two pairs of thin and fat women had wrestled twice to contest a position in the long queue leading to the man of God's tent. So, even when Bishop Massawe implicated *short call* and *long call* as excuses for escaping from his tent, the crafty women did not let him waste such precious time. Rather, they quickly gave him excretion pots they had incredibly brought with them. Now aware that his excuses about answering calls of nature were never respected by his 'devilish clients', the man of God next tried to fail his seed-distributing gadget to get some rest. All in vain though: each of the women, upon learning that the gadget had ceased working, would independently focus their mental manuals on ways to troubleshoot the gadget, after which, they would consult among themselves for a minute or so and eventually, as a group, settle on a solution that would instantly get it back to work even without the consent of its owner.

On the fifth day of the exercise therefore, the poor man of God died on the bosom of a woman people claimed was old enough to be his mother. Regarding this sudden death, the village nurse – who everybody believed was a physician – conducted a post-mortem examination on his body and cited a combination of fatigue and semen-dehydration as the causes. Unfortunately, Bishop Massawe died without writing a will on what to do with his many properties he left – which explained how his beloved lorry eventually made its way to the spot where Omollo saw its remains.

After four months of walking, Omollo eventually reached his second home, Dongruok Village. As he would later narrate, the village had retained its former name and was still at the exact location he left it, yet it looked as if it had just been heavily bombed by unmanned aircraft. Worse still, a few Dongruokans had deprived the masses of their properties, but interestingly their popularity had not dimmed, as would have been the case in the days when Omollo was still in the village.

On Lake Dongruok as well, students who used to sing while crossing it by boat were nowhere to be seen. Omollo was told they no longer traveled to distant schools on warrants, or rather that they attended clan secondary schools, better known for dating than teaching. Besides, all the local factories in Dongruok were dead, obliging Dongruokans to import even their brooms from the People's Republic of Zhang. Worse still, the white men, who had once been chased away from the country in jubilation and dance-processions during the independence of Kaya, were now all back on their former plantations around Dongruok Village – ironically, not as *the parasites* they used to be called back in the days Omollo first visited Dongruok Village, but rather as respected *the investors*.

In investigating what had brought about those radical changes at the village, an old man, who hosted Omollo, claimed that Dongruokans had become such fools because of a protein deficiency in their bodies.

"Dongruokans only eat fish bones now. All the fish fillets from Lake Dongruok are for export to Laurasia," he said.

Nevertheless, his wife persuasively argued that the white men had put something into their food that had eventually made them what they had become:

"My child," she addressed Omollo in a traditional style.

"Eeeeeee," Omollo replied in similar style.

"There occurred a famine in this country in the mid-80s following a three-year drought that people nicknamed *Humans' Wilter*," she said and fished out a snuff bottle from her dirty bra.

"People were so hungry then and our government, as you know it, was so hopeless in the face of that ruthless famine," she said in a tone distorted by the interference of snuff in her mouth.

"Ehehheheheeh," Omollo called for more.

"Then white men seized the opportunity to bring us philanthropic flour and oil, but which is stuffed with fool-turning substance to the brim," she said and dissolved into an infectious laughter.

"Eheheheheh!" The enthusiastic Omollo wanted to learn more.

"My child," she said and suspended her story as she was still stuffing the bottle of snuff back into her bra in a poorly lit room.

"As you can see now, every son of a woman who ate that flour instantly turned into a sheep or rather a duck," she stated amidst crackly laughter, "none of those who ate the flour has done anything right since then – worse still, it appears that the foodstuff went to their blood too. Believe me, their children are twice as senseless as their parents," she concluded and laughed even more.

"It is probably true, what this woman is saying!" Omollo now thought but did not say so audibly.

Since Omollo left the location forty-five years ago, the only new thing whose use had remained just as inspiring as when it first arrived in Dongruok Village, was the Zhangian cell phone. Even when Omollo reached the village, the story was still told that the first person to own the gadget in Dongruok Village was an old ugly rich woman known as Nyamira. According to the awesome story, Nyamira went to relieve herself in the bush with her cell phone in her hand – back in the days when such a gadget was as rare in the land as a hump on a goat. As she was in the process of relieving herself, an old stray pig who was spying on her from a respectable distance heard her phone ringing – and was said, it became so baffled with the realization that it prayed to God to take its soul.

> *'Papa, I thank you for keeping me alive all these years,'* it is
> claimed the pig broke out into prayer.
> *'..but now that I have lived to see a baboon talking on a*
> *phone here in the bush, may my soul rest in eternal peace.'*

When Omollo returned to the village though, even a mere beggar, scavenging the village dumpsite for food scraps, had a Zhangian cell phone in his hand.

As the village was a pale shadow of its former glory to Omollo, he left it for his home village after just six days. Five months later, he reached what he was made to believe was his home area. Destitute and homeless, he was wearing a faded T-shirt reading; *A young billionaire*, a pair of well-worn jeans and battered flip-flops: no wonder a kid from a well-to-do family pointed him out to his mother and asked which cartoon character he was.

Under the bridge where he now called home, Omollo reflected how what he had been told to be his homeland was a completely different animal from what he knew as a child. He had tried to look out for important landmarks of his village, like Ramar Valley and Rabar Hill, but they were nowhere to be seen – only a hill that looked like Gagamoya Hill, below which the shanty street of Majengo was sprawling zigzaggedly, contradicted his belief that the area was not his homeland at all. A good Samaritan, who found him puzzling sadly over the scenario, told him that Rabar Hill, the Sacred Rock and all other landmarks, had long been flattened by gigantic earthmovers of the Calodian Gold Mine. The same man also told him that the mine's headquarters, visible from the point they were standing, was standing on the same land as his former village, which Omollo found hard to believe. Three days later, he met Manduli, son of Opungo Danger – his age-mate and kin in the days the place was known as Rabar Village. Morphologically, Manduli was then quite different from the version he knew as a kid, yet his extra-large diastema remained intact between his heavily stained teeth – and it was from this that Omollo precisely remembered him.

As soon as they met for the first time, Omollo had a small problem on how to address Manduli: since Malan culture dictated that, given their age, he, Omollo, should have strictly addressed Manduli by his nickname rather than his real name; however, Manduli had never liked his nicknames as they were assigned to him on the grounds of his low IQ compared to his peers. As far as Omollo could remember that evening, in the days when they were young Manduli's nicknames kept on changing with the prevailing context. When an adult was in earshot, Omollo and his colleagues would address him as Mongoose – a nickname derived from the creature of the same name that often lives in sugarcane plantations, but is utterly unaware that sugarcane is sweet. Nevertheless, when no adult was listening, Omollo and his colleagues would address him as Clit – an organ of the same name that lives in the axe wound, but entirely unaware that the axe wound is sweet.

Amidst his perplexity, Omollo quickly euphemized Manduli's last nickname as Antenna – based on a small cartilaginous projection in the axe wound, which is equally wholly unaware that the axe wound is sweet. Luckily, Manduli did not object to this euphemized nickname – either because the underlying meaning was too well concealed for others to figure out, or rather that at his now advanced age, he had become a senior idiot. All the same, Manduli next led Omollo to a perimeter wall of Calodian Gold Mine and pointed him out a place in the middle of the gold mine.

"There is where our village used to stand," he said, indicating the same location the Samaritan had earlier on pointed out to him.

To Omollo's amazement, the landscape was an absolute mess: mounds of sands – or holes, if you like – implying that his wish of locating his father's grave for ritual purposes was nothing short of a dream. One engineer later told him that it would take a well-equipped researcher at least six months to determine the location of his father's grave in that successful mess his homeland had become. Strangely enough, not one old Malan apart from Manduli lived in Majengo slum then; there were only foreigners, popularly known as *watukuja* in the area. From what Manduli told Omollo, adult Malans either died fighting for their ancestral land or migrated to distant areas after losing the battle for their land to the Calodian Gold Mine.

Following Manduli's incredible revelations, memories of Omollo's joyous childhood at the destroyed village now flooded his mind like a raging storm. Overwhelmed by grief, he now looked at Clit, or rather Antenna, with moist eyes suggesting that he was greatly hurt for having been missing in action when his kin were fighting for their land.

"Maybe my people were overpowered in the war with these demons because I was not there to give them a hand," he thought but did not reveal it to Manduli.

As he departed with Manduli towards his temporary home under the bridge that evening, he felt very useless for failing to shield the

Sacred Rock from Calodian earthmovers; for missing in the battle to defend his beloved valley of Ramar from being choked by the Calodian Gold Mine and for missing in the national elections that could have removed the melon-headed man from the presidency.

Old, sick and depressed, the spirit of Omollo was absolutely dampened. To compound the problem, he had no close relative in that area to take care of him. In the absence of his relatives, the majority of the people in the slum were thieves, to whom humanity was a vice to be countered at every turn – one pastor claiming that their calling was to steal, to steal steadily and with steely determination. He would, of course, have done as the Romans did; only that his legs were then too tired to steal a pairs of sandals and run away with them without being caught and set ablaze. Above all, he was still a cursed man who could not succeed even in begging.

Now it happened that one solitary night Omollo dreamt about Günter Müller. The bad dream destroyed his mood even after he had woken up the following morning; but at least, it reminded him of what his friend Günter once told him about fighting for one's rights. Suddenly in combative mood, he vowed to honor his resting friend through fighting for his rights in a court of law – "... irrespective of how kangaroo they are," he said.

To the amazement of everybody, Omollo staggered to the district court one day and opened a case against the Calodian Mining Company, claiming that they had stolen two golden bangles his late grandmother Adongo Nyowino had bequeathed him from under the Sacred Rock. A case considered a fool's errand by the locals was nonetheless no laughing matter to the owners of Calodian Gold Mine. This is because the bangles he was talking about had indeed been dug out precisely from under the Sacred Rock Omollo and subsequently gifted to the Calodian queen on her eightieth birthday. Furthermore, to add extra value to the bangles, the company lied to their entire nation that the bangles were the only known naturally occurring bangles in the world, after which they were declared the coat-of-arms of Caloda. And because of the professional lies attached to the bangles, the Calodian Mining Company was thereafter exempted from paying a number of taxes by way of reward for a supposedly great contribution to their homeland's civilization and reputation.

The consequence of this was that Omollo's inconvenient allegations about the bangles were to be fought tooth and nail to keep the reputation of their company at home – the company even became more worried when some international journalists started poking their noses into the issue.

Due to the sensitivity of the issue to the company, which poor Omollo was completely unaware of, Omollo was summoned to attend a meeting of the company's board of directors and was pledged an offer that was too good to turn down: a modern house if he kept his mouth shut about the bangles: plus a handsome salary from the company, of course, the latter for a small service involving the distribution of drugs and alcohol to "the suspects", which is what the owners of the Calodian Gold Mine Company called the youths of Majengo slum.

To the company, the drug and alcohol supplies would keep the rascals permanently drunk, which effectively meant too disorganized to fight them. To Omollo, the drugs would prompt the rascals to make him their king, virtually guaranteeing his safety in that hotbed of crime. Further, he would be given money with which to finance all the burials and funerals of the suspects – allegedly, to encourage the goons to die without worrying about their funeral costs. As soon as Omollo accepted this offer, his life changed like a shot from rags to riches. To mask the source of his illicit riches, he told every bigmouth in the slum that his sudden wealth was inspired by a cult he had just joined – a rumour that added another layer of his protection in a slum teeming with hooligans. Before long, he migrated from his accommodation under the bridge to the most magnificent house in the street – all courtesy of the mining company. And following this resurrection, from that day on, he tirelessly served alcohol and drugs to the living rascals and burial gear to the dead ones. As envisaged by the company's mastermind, the supplies thereafter made the rascals love him to the extent they raised him to the status of *King of the Rascals*.

In a twist of fate though, Omollo soon developed a peculiar disease that no scientist has yet explained satisfactorily. He started claiming that some imaginary people were animatedly saying all sorts of nasty words in his ears – even when he was alone in his magnificent home. At first, he took this new development to be a sign of stress pertaining to his demanding job at that old age; nonetheless, the discomfort kept on soaring day after day until *the Busy Malan* was totally baffled. Fearing the loss of his sweet life, Omollo first visited the revered ear specialist in his town to find out what exactly was happening. From what I heard, the doctor diagnosed his problem as *tinnitus* – a condition whereby a patient hears ringing sounds, buzzes or other noises from within himself. Omollo, however, was unconvinced by the diagnosis because he did not hear buzzes or ringing sounds, but rather the clear voices of people he knew by name. These included his father scoffing at him for being a disgrace in Malaland; a game warden abusing him for misbehaving in the zoo; his abusive ex-wife nagging him; the bandits raping him in jubilation; Professor Girado rebuking him for abandoning Christianity, which he had told him not to abandon; or his grandmother despising him for the betrayal of his people. Omollo later tried other modern ear specialists in the town and was disappointed that all of them gave a detailed diagnosis that was not applicable to his case. Tired of the vagueness of the medical doctors, Omollo turned to diviner-priests, who were plenty in the suburbs of his town. But the diviner-priests, as usual, attributed his nightmares to evil spirits and prescribed him eating unpleasant things such as dry excreta and drinking menstrual leakage in order to frighten them. Nevertheless, even on that diet, the imaginary hecklers in his ears would not spare him for a minute. Tired of consuming nasty substances, Omollo switched to pastors for his sanity-threatening problem, but eventually wished he had not done so – for the men of God, in their usual roundabout-way of describing things, only hopped from one explanation to another for his problem – meanwhile, milking him dry of his money. And in what seems to have been a precautionary measure, the men of the cloth unanimously prescribed Omollo a series of fasting, likely to ensure that he was dead before realizing the rip-off and then bouncing back to reclaim the offerings he had been giving to their entrepreneurial churches.

Eventually, *the Busy Malan* could stand all the nonsense no more. Instead, he chose to end the series of problems he had been experiencing since his birth. That night, he went to his kitchen, took a kitchen knife, and bored his stomach with it while lying on his back on his bed. As per the local tradition, his history would normally have ended with his death; however, this hopeless man left an ambiguous suicide note that instead instigated sorrow to his remaining friends, well-wishers and relatives even more than his scary death.

Judging by his well-built body, sparkling skin, red eyes and a strong deep voice, Omollo looked tough and capable of tackling whatever the impediment which the world could throw in his way. But deep down, he was quite insecure and credulous. As a case in point, he is manipulated by an unscrupulous preacher to rebel against his lovely family and community – the act which turns him into a restless traveler through Africa to Europe. In this wandering life, he tries to settle down in several places but a flaw in his character always leads to his being rejected and pushed forward. When he reaches the point of envying the food of the pigs, he comes to his senses and chooses to return home and apologize to his kinsfolk. But upon his return after an absence of fifty years in the West, almost everything in his motherland has become a pale shadow of its former glory. And whereas, he had expected a relief at his home environment, fate renders an unforeseen consequence instead. His kindred consider him stranger than the foreigners in the land of his ramblings.

∞∞

"Ochieng's impressive first novel describes the dramatically fluctuating fortunes of a young African seeking to better himself in various cultural environments, both at home and abroad, only to end up as an old man fighting for survival on a daily basis. The author offers the reader a fast-moving narrative, skillfully combining scenes of slapstick comedy with witty dialogue and some genuinely poignant moments".

Andrew Tollet, University of West Bohemia, Czech Republic.

∞∞

"This is a book that should not gather dust on library shelves. Unless an African child inherits authentic stories from their circles, it will be difficult to prepare the next progeny for life-long success. Today, the negroid race lives in a mistaken identity. Omollo portrays it all!"

Milambo Mushani, the Open University of Tanzania.

∞∞

www.ingramcontent.com/pod-product-compliance
Lightning Source LLC
Chambersburg PA
CBHW061549170626
46811CB00001B/141